THE BEST AMERICAN HISTORY BOOK IN THE WORLD

Other Books by

Eric Burnett

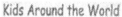

THE BEST AMERICAN HISTORY BOOK IN THE WORLD

ALL THE INFORMATION YOU NEED TO KNOW WITHOUT ALL THE STUFF THAT WILL PUT YOU TO SLEEP

Edited by
Eric Burnett

iUniverse, Inc.
New York Lincoln Shanghai

The Best American History Book in the World
ALL THE INFORMATION YOU NEED TO KNOW WITHOUT
ALL THE STUFF THAT WILL PUT YOU TO SLEEP

iUniverse, Inc.

For information address:
iUniverse, Inc.
2021 Pine Lake Road, Suite 100
Lincoln, NE 68512
www.iuniverse.com

ISBN: 0-595-28479-5 (pbk)
ISBN: 0-595-65816-4 (cloth)

Printed in the United States of America

ILLUSTRATION CREDITS

Sitting Bull—Kee Eun Shim

Ending the Trusts—Kee Eun Shim

Rebuilding Europe—Nina Rosche

A Web of Sorrow—Kee Eun Shim

Solving Unemployment—Kee Eun Shim

Hitler—Kee Eun Shim

The Holocaust—Kee Eun Shim

Bombing of Pearl Harbor—Mauricio Tsukuda

Taking of Iwo Jima—Eric Williams
Inspired by *Flag Raising on Iwo Jima*, Joe Rosenthal, 1945

Japanese Surrender—Kee Eun Shim

Berlin Air Lift—Mauricio Tsukuda

Passive Resistance—Kee Eun Shim

The King—Mauricio Tsukuda

The Battle of the Sexes—Eric Williams

Cool Inventions—Adam McCurley

Saddam's Fall—Luc Nutter
Inspired by AP Photo

For Justin Mickelson

C ONTENTS

▼

Student Authors

Caitlin Ameel	Kory Aldous
Anika Arya	Jake Emerson
Akshay Balsubramani	Doug Fagan
Deepti Dhir	Jessica Fries
Fred Glander	Junsuke Fukuda
Phil Haslett	Elizabeth Hunter
Yong Joo Kim	Jonathan Lee
Victoria Kitts	Adam McCurley
Christopher Lee	Mercedes Moore
Elise Nilsson	Jared Newton
Young Noh	Luc Nutter
Austin Radford	Nina Rosche
Aaron Rubin	Kee Eun Shim
Haileigh Sawhill	Kelly Waterman
Andrea Sullivan	Scott White
Dan Szeto	Eric Williams
Angela Tsai	Wei Wen Wong
Mauricio Tsukuda	
Sean Wiley	
Patrick Wong	

CHAPTER 1

▼

I'M A WANDERER: FIRST DISCOVERIES OF AMERICA

But…aren't Indians from India?

A long time ago, on a continent far, far away, a tribe of nomads wandered the land searching for a cure for the answer to life's deepest question—where's the food? These nomads were simple folk, hunter-gatherers. They hunted. They gathered. Oh, and they reproduced. And then they died.

Life wasn't fun in the Paleolithic Era (otherwise known as the Ice Age). Since they were always wandering around looking for food, kids died young, the traveling group stayed pretty small (under 100 people), and entertainment might have consisted of watching some smelly dude named Gunther run from a crabby pack of hungry tigers.

They hunted in groups for food, realizing ten guys with a spear had a better chance against a hairy beast than just one. Those who weren't hunting, were roaming through the land foraging for such yummy items as nuts, berries and mushrooms. You might be asking yourself, what in the world does this have to do with American history?

Ahhh…patience my child. We'll get to that. But before we get to talking about my friend and yours, Cristoforo Columbo, we have to first talk about the true first Americans. And since the Native Americans didn't just one day pop up out of a cactus plant in Lake Texcoco, we have to go back to the 12th of March, 36,204 B.C. (I might be off by a couple days. I've been having a bit of trouble with that whole carbon dating machine.)

Crossing the Bering Strait

The first Asiatic peoples crossed the Bering Land Bridge about 36,000 years ago.

During the tail end of the Paleolithic Era, a tribe of nomads just like the ones mentioned above, were on the run. Whether they were running from predators, other less-accommodating nomads, or that annoying little thing called starvation, these nomads were once again on the move. Well, they are nomads, so don't they have to pretty much always be on the move?

Anyway, as they kept heading east across Asia, they saw ahead of them an amazing sight—a long, chunk of flat land stretching as far as their eyes could see. They thought to themselves, "Hmmm...either we keep going east and risk the chance of dying in an unknown land, or we can turn around and die in a land we know all too well." They then turned to each other and took a vote. The vote was pretty close, but since super-tall Gunther stood almost 5'8", his vote outweighed the rest of the clan. They headed east.

As the rain beat down on their weary bodies and the sun refused to shine above the horizon, Gunther's son Cromagnon turned to his dad and asked with his best English accent, "Father, how is it that this land is elevated at this time? Shouldn't this be an ocean under our feet?"

"Ahhh...my curious little son. Over the past few millenniums, the global temperature has fluctuated dramatically and currently there's a huge glacier pack of ice up near the North Pole. And, as you know from your impressive knowledge of photosynthesis, water is a zero sum game. Since there is more water frozen up near the polar ice region, there is less water everywhere else, a process known as eustasis. Hence, we are currently walking on the Berengia land mass that is connecting Asia with America. In a few months, we'll be the first people to ever step foot in America."

"But...um...Nograt told me we were walking on an ice bridge?"

"Shhh...Cromagnon...go to sleep."

These first nomads set foot on America, and then, probably just kept walking. Because, as I said before, they're nomads. Gunther eventually died, and then his son Cromagnon took the tribe further down through the continent. Cromagnon then got in a fight with Leroybrown who decided to break the tribe apart and go his separate way. More clans then also decided to venture across the Bering Strait in their ceaseless quest for food. These tribes then ventured south, finding food, losing food, having babies, and generally staying out of each other's way. Ahhh...the life of a nomad. Eventually, through this pattern of wandering, dividing, and reproducing, the Native Americans spread across two continents over the course of tens of thousands of years.

By the time Columbus arrived in 1492, thousands of groups of Native Americans had set up shop around the Western Hemisphere. Some were small groups that stayed hunter-gatherers. Others created efficient empires that boasted highly evolved methods of agriculture, government, and warfare (evolved method of warfare…what does oxymoron mean?)

How many tribes do you think existed? Take a guess. Four? Twenty? 9,742? Well, not quite. But close. Here's just a few:

Abnaki Alabama Aleuts Algonquin Anasazi Apache Arapaho Arawak Arikara Assiniboin Aztec Beothuk Cabazon Caddo Catawba Cherokee Cheyenne Chickasaw Chinook Chippewa Choctaw Chumash Comanche Cree Creek Crow Delaware Erie Eskimo Flathead Haida Hidatsa Hohokam Hopi Hupa Huron Ioway Innu Inuit Iroquois Kaw Kickapoo Kiowa Klamath Kootenai Kwakiutl Mahican Makah Maliseet Mandan Mayan Melungeon Menominee Metis Mississauga Modoc Mohave Mohawk Mohegan Montagnais Mound Builders Narragansett Navajo Nez Perce Nootka Olmec Osage Ottawa Oto Papago Passamaquoddy Pawnee Pennacook Penobscot Peoria Pequot Pima Ponca Potawatomi Pueblo Quanah Parker Quapaw Sauk Seminole Seneca Shawnee Shoshone Shuswap Sioux Squanto Tlingit Toltec Tonkawa Ute Washo Wampanoag Wichita Winnebago Wovoka Wyandotte Yakima Yuchi Yurok Zapotec Zuni

As you can see, there was no one Native American nation, religion, language, or government. Not only were they not unified, but many of these tribes had conflicts with each other that the Europeans would later exploit to their advantage.

But that's another chapter.

A Bjarni, a Leif, and a Thorfinn

Up until recently, when a guy would come up to you on the street and ask, "Who discovered America?" you'd probably immediately respond "Christopher Columbus," and then walk away with a smug little smile on your face.

But, you shouldn't be so arrogant. What that guy really was asking was, "Who was the first European to accidentally bump into part of the American continent?" And since that was his question, your little Christopher Columbus guess was about 500 years wrong.

The first Europeans to set foot on the American continent weren't rugged Italians, but a few daring Norse explorers who kept taking their boats further and further west. For those of you not familiar with your Norse history, when you hear the word Norse—think Vikings. Think Iceland. Looking at a globe, it makes logical sense that the Vikings would first discover the Americas. They're already pretty close to the continent.

One of the Vikings, Bjarni Herjulfsson was blown off course on his way to Greenland and was the first to see North America. It is important to note here that being blown off course was responsible for 93.2% of all discoveries in the New World (However, remember 74.6% of all statistics are made up)

Unfortunately for the Herjulfsson family, because he never went ashore, the only Barney famous today is a purple dinosaur who has annoyingly enthusiastic friends. Luckily for the Erikssons of the world, Bjarni's adventure would not be soon forgotten.

Another explorer, Eric the Red, had a son who he named Leif Eriksson (get it…Eriksson…son of Eric…fascinating). Eric the Red is famous for discovering and naming Greenland around the year 982. Now, Leif grew up hearing his dad brag about Greenland and all the kids in town reliving Bjarni's travels, so he decided to wait until the right year to go on a journey to this mythical world. Whereas Columbus chose that awkward date, 1492, to bump into America, Leif decided to set sail in the year 1000. This choice makes all anniversary celebrations in his honor quite easy to remember. Tragically, his 1000th year anniversary was snubbed because everybody was afraid the world would come to an end once all computers got really confused about a date with a bunch of zeros.

Now, back to Leif. In the year 1000, Leif convinced 35 fellow Norsemen to board his good old, trusty knarr. A knarr's a ship, and the Vikings were famous for their boat building and their ability to wage lightning fast attacks (a Medieval Blitzkrieg if you like). Their boats usually had a single sail, a rudder and oars that could be extended when the wind was being finicky. Some of the lighter boats could even be picked up, carried across land, and then dropped back in the water. This allowed the Vikings to sneak up on people and attack. They turned out to be quite successful. Villagers and peasants weren't exactly expecting amphibious warfare in the late 800s.

Once aboard his ship, Leif and his men sailed west from Greenland toward Bjarni's new world. Here he saw, he landed, and he set foot on North America, or part of what today would be called eastern Canada. Over the next year and some change, he explored, claimed and named Helluland, Markland, and Vinland. To the Vikings these lands meant, "land of flat stone", "land of forest, and "land of vines." Today, they go by the names Baffin Island, Labrador, and Newfoundland.

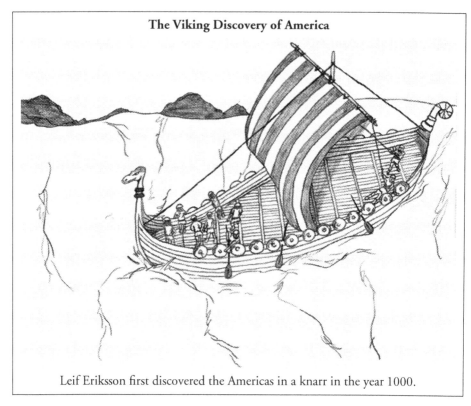

The Viking Discovery of America

Leif Eriksson first discovered the Americas in a knarr in the year 1000.

Whereas the voyages of Eric the Red, Bjarni Herjulfsson, and Leif Eriksson are based on fairly reliable historical evidence, the story of Thorfinn Karlsefni stands on a bit shakier foundation. According to Viking legend, in about 1010, Thorfinn set off with three boats and about 150 men to set up a colony in Eriksson's Vinland. After three years of near starvation and troubling attacks from the natives (nicknamed "dwarfs"), Thorfinn and his followers abandoned the outpost and returned to Greenland. Was this the first European settlement? Maybe. Maybe not.

From here the Norse explorations came to end. Why? We can only guess. Was it the deadly dwarfs of Canada? Did the Vikings run out of names that end with "land" to name the newly discovered regions? The world may never know. But the point is, this first wave of exploration died before it really got started.

The European world would just have to wait another 500 years until the son of an Italian weaver got up enough nerve to take his ludicrous shortcut idea to the Queen of Spain.

CHAPTER 2

▼

EUREKA, WE FOUND IT! COLUMBUS AND THE AGE OF EXPLORATION

Victoria Kitts
Yong Joo Kim

Christopher Columbus: Naughty or Nice

Being the man who discovered what would become one of the most powerful nations in the world is a pretty fantastic honor. Hopefully, by now you know that "In 1492, Christopher Columbus sailed the ocean blue." But what about the man who did the discovering? What was he like? What did he do? What did he actually discover? And, most importantly, was he naughty or nice?

Once upon a time, there was this man—Cristoforo Columbo, known to normal English speaking people as Christopher Columbus. He was born in 1451 but he doesn't do anything worth mentioning until later. He was actually the son of a wool weaver and grew up in Genoa, Italy. Oh yes, America's hero was the son of guy who spins wool, kind of like Rumpelstiltskin, but different. Like most people, he eventually grew up and got older. It was when he was older that he really had some exciting adventures.

In 1476 he went on an exciting boat ride to Portugal, England, and Iceland. Here he probably heard a bunch of guys bragging about how Leif Eriksson had discovered a new world. This probably got him all excited. Later, in 1479, he got back, got married, and he and his wife started having kids. She died in 1480 in childbirth, which was very sad and depressing for our friend Columbus so he decided to make himself rich and famous and go find the Indies. It wasn't that simple. The only problem was that Columbus didn't have any money to go on his journey so he went to the Italians and asked for some money. They thought his plan to find a short cut to the Indies would never work. They turned him away and in the true spirit of free agency, he looked for money any other place he could find it. He later went to Spain and asked Queen Isabella for some money.

After some years of persuasion from Columbus and her friend, Luis de Santangel, she agreed. There were some pretty good reasons for Isabella to agree. He promised her tons of wealth and power. And even if turned out to be an idiot, it was worth the risk? Isabella eventually agreed to give him three girl-named ships: the *Niña*, the *Piñta*, and the *Santa Maria*.

Columbus the Negotiator

Columbus tries to convince the leaders of Europe to finance his exploration.

On August 3rd, 1492, Columbus left Spain and headed to the Canary Islands in Africa. He believed that the wind would circle clockwise and take him exactly to where he wanted to go. His predictions came half true. The wind currents took him to a new land but not the Indies as he had hoped. Instead, it took him to a beautiful land filled with unique-looking people, bizarre foods, and rumors of gold.

On September 9th 1492, Columbus realized his predictions of distance were just a bit off. Instead of finding land, he found water, water, and more water. Being the clever navigator he was, he started writing two travel logs. One contained what he believed to be the correct distance and one with made up numbers. He wanted the crew to believe they had been traveling less than they really had been. Ironically, it turned out that the false numbers were closer to the actual ones than his so-called "accurate" calculations.

The men started getting antsy and wanted to get off of the boat but since they were in the middle of the ocean, they kind of couldn't. Some of the men talked about taking over the boat and turning around, a brilliant idea that almost assuredly would have killed the entire crew. To refocus his crew, Columbus set up a contest declaring whoever spotted land first would receive a cash bonus of 10,000 maravedis (maravedi was Spanish for "a lot of money"). Basically, you saw land first, you got the reward. Everyone now felt inspired and kept their eyes peeled on the horizon. Finally, after weeks of travel, one of his men, Rodrigo, spotted what he believed to be land. Now, how many of you thought Columbus would actually pay poor old Rodrigo? All of you that raised your hands, you're not paying attention. In a classic move, Columbus claimed that he in fact had seen the land the night before, but he was just waiting for the right moment to tell his crew.

The land that Rodrigo saw was an island the natives called Guanahani. Even though historians argue over which was the exact island first discovered, the consensus is that he landed in the Bahamas. The native people, called Arawaks (just think Ear a wax) were fascinating to Columbus because they were so different from him…their life styles, their food, their physical appearance. They were peace-loving people and had never seen swords or weapons before. In fact, when Columbus first greeted them and held up his sword, the Arawaks, fascinated by its beauty, reached out to touch the shiny stick and cut themselves on the sharp blade.

Once Columbus arrived, his true intentions became pretty clear. He wanted gold and he wanted it now. He refused to believe the minuscule amounts of gold his men and the locals found were all that existed. After finding nothing on Guanahani his quest for gold continued. His ships sailed to Hispaniola with newly acquired prisoners from Guananahi. So for those of you who are lost, he invades country, he "borrows" people, and he enslaves them for a while to find gold.

Along the way, he sets up a lovely method of motivation. This is a little gruesome so if you don't want to read about it, you may want skip down to the next paragraph. It all started, because Columbus had taken a little bit of gold back to Queen Isabella and told her there was much more of it to be found. He claimed the reason he didn't bring more back was because there was so much it wouldn't all fit into the boats (Lie #382). To get the gold he needed, he set up this rule that anyone over the age of fourteen had to find gold for him. Each month each person had to find a certain amount and anyone who reached their quota was awarded a copper token to wear on a necklace. Now, this could seem friendly enough but wait until you hear why Columbus did it. At the end of each month, anyone who didn't have a necklace around their neck had their hands cut off. Faced with this and many of Columbus's other types of torture, many of the Arawaks tried to run away. A lot of people committed suicide or even killed their children so that Columbus couldn't enslave them. In two years, Columbus erased half of Haiti's population.

However Columbus did have some good traits. Without his discovery, you can honestly say the world we know today would be a totally different place. His discovery introduced to Europe a variety of food. Before Columbus the diet of the Europeans was pretty pathetic. The foods discovered in the Americas helped balance the European diet, thus expanding their lifespan. Look at all of these foods that were nonexistent in Europe back in 1500: tomatoes, coffee, sugar, chocolate, turkey, avocadoes, pumpkin, and corn. Imagine Italian food without tomato sauce. How about a candy bar without chocolate? And you think your parents are grumpy now, imagine them with out their cup of coffee in the morning?

Aside from the food, Columbus opened up half of the globe because he was daring enough to try and find the Indies and Spice Islands. Sure, it was by chance he discovered the New World. And, yes, some other European would have found it eventually. However, he was the first, and for that he should be credited. Even though he was a flawed man with questionable morals, Christopher Columbus will forever be remembered and celebrated as the man who discovered America.

Was Columbus a Bad Guy?

Hero	Villain
• Discovery influential discovery in human history • Unlocked half the globe to the Eastern world • Advanced navigational technology and meteorology • Land eventually became home to democracy which later spread around world • Introduced foods Ended Middle Ages • Riches shared across Europe	• Abused natives • Brought slavery to the Americas • Set standard for destroying land and people for profit • Symbolized white man oppressing colored masses • Behavior can be considered genocide toward the native people

The United States of Columbus?

Even though Columbus discovered the New World, the new land was not named after him. In fact, he died not realizing what he had actually found. In 1501, Amerigo Vespucci, sailing for Portugal, realized this error and coined the phrase, "Mundus Novus"—New World. Later, when a German clergyman named Martin Waldseemuller created a map of the area, he wrote "America" across the southern continent. Here's a little song to help you remember. Sing it to the tune of "America the Beautiful."

> *About 500 years ago Waldseemuller made a map*
> *He plotted the land and shore and named it after a chap*
> *Amerigo! Amerigo! Our Country's Name for Thee*
> *If you didn't roam, we'd call our home the U.S. of C.C.*

Hey Buddy, Don't Be Putting Your Flag There!

Columbus's discovery of America set off a wave of exploration unparalleled in modern times, if ever. Every guy who had a boat that could make it across the

Atlantic and had dreams of finding gold, headed west. Though the Portuguese, Dutch, French, and British were all pretty active in the New World, the first to heavily settle the new land were the Spaniards. They basically came for God, for gold, and for glory. Just remember the three G's of exploration—God, Gold, Glory.

The Spanish flag flew over the Americas for nearly three centuries. Conquistadors demolished the civilizations of the Aztecs and the Incas and held territory from the Atlantic to the Pacific and from the tip of South America to almost modern-day Canada.

Exploration and Discovery

The 1500s saw the European nations competing for the riches of the newly found Americas.

How could the Spanish rule such a massive empire with so few men? First, they had gunpowder. Second, they had disease. These two killers combined to wipe out millions of the indigenous people. Some estimate that the Europeans wiped out over forty million Native Americans. Those who didn't die became enslaved through the encomienda system. Spanish for "entrust," the encomienda system legally forced whoever lived on Spanish-conquered land to work for their captor. Technically, the Indians were not slaves, but you'd have a difficult time convincing them of the difference. They had to pay tribute to the Spanish, either through crops or labor, and they were bound to the land—sounds like slavery to me. In addition to the encomienda system, Spain also sent their priests to convert the savages to Christianity. Set up by the "black robes," Spanish missions dotted the southwest of America, and can still be visited today. These missions became centers of religion, politics and economics for the surrounding Indians.

While the Spanish were settling America, the Portuguese were also pretty busy around South America. Because the Spanish and Portuguese were continually coming into conflict with each other regarding land claims, they agreed to the Treaty of Tordesillas in 1494. This treaty divided the New World at 50 degrees west latitude. Everything discovered east of this line would be Portuguese, everything west would be Spanish. That's why they speak Portuguese in Brazil, when the rest of the whole continent speaks Spanish. Look at a map someday, and see who got the better end of the deal. It's not a trick question. Spain got just a bit more land.

During this time of exploration, explorers acted like baseball's free agents, sailing for whichever country put out the highest bid. For example, Giovanni Cabot, born in Genoa, Italy, later sailed for England under the name John Cabot. Like many of the other gentlemen sailing around the Americas, he was looking for a water shortcut to the East. Because of this fascination with a western shortcut, the waterways of America were explored extensively. Cabot never found the shortcut, but he did sail around Newfoundland and set off a wave of British exploration in northeast America. Unfortunately, there is no magical east-west river that crisscrosses Canada.

Now these were just a few of the explorers. I had thought about mentioning more, but this really isn't a book about exploration, so let's get to the meat of American history. After a century of rampant exploration following Columbus' first steps in the Caribbean, the French, Dutch, English, Swedish, and Spanish all had their eyes on dividing up what we today call the United States of America. Now that the lands had been mapped and tenuously claimed, the race for colonization and permanent settlement was on.

CHAPTER 3

▼

HOW TO MAKE A COLONY IN JUST A FEW EASY STEPS: AMERICAN COLONIZATION

Akshay Balsubramani
Patrick Wong

Jolly Old England—1600ish

"It's over! Woohoo!" exclaimed Bob. "No more wars with the pesky Spaniards and the Scots!"

"Yeah," said Billy with a grin. "Well now that it's over, let's move to this New World, ok?"

"Boy, you're rather hasty, aren't you? Wouldn't you like to go to war with France for the 325th time?"

"Nah...Let's go! It'll be a hoot! You're always whining about how we never travel."

"But, I was just getting used to seeing my ribs through my skin and living in the sewage of our neighbors."

"Bob...you can be such a Separatist sometimes."

Bob and Billy argued whether to go to the New World or to stay, and by the end Bob was so weary that he finally gave in. Good thing for Bob, because if they didn't make it to Virginia by May 23, 1607, there were going to be a whole lot of textbooks to be rewritten. Since it was 1603, the wanna-be colonists chilled and relaxed for the next three years.

Elsewhere, at a business meeting, there was a loud commotion about the colonization of Virginia. One extremely loud voice belched, "We do not have enough money to colonize Virginia. I say we join two stock companies together! I think it was my old father who once told me, 'laddy, tis a fool who loses his money alone. Tis more fun to lose money with others."

Silence shut the mouths of people all around. Could this man have a point?

Finally a voice muttered, "Very well, Sir, how's this—the Virginia Company gets southern Virginia, and the Plymouth Company gets northern Virginia?"

"Excuse me," all heads turned to the mouse like whisper from the corner. "Why exactly do we want to colonize the New World?"

The room burst into laughter. Men pounded each other on the back and pointed at the ignorant chap in the corner.

Finally, the clamor died down and William stood to address the gathering, "I must say that is a ludicrous question. And of course, I know the answer," he stated, not exactly confidently. "However, for our pathetic comrade in the corner and any other ignorant chap, could someone explain our reasoning?"

The red-headed Edward pushed back his chair and stood before the group. "For God and Country I say. GOD AND COUNTRY!!!" Edward took a step back and admired the crowd. "And if we happen to make a pound or two, none of us will complain."

Leavin' on a Wooden Boat

Bob and Billy, along with 142 fellow men boarded three ships: *Godspeed*, *Discovery*, and *Susan Constant*. Bob and Billy boarded *Godspeed* because it was the fanciest of the three ships.

"I wonder which fool made up these names," Billy quipped.

The two men would have a lot of time to ponder the odd name choices, as their trip took nearly six months. It also took thirty-nine lives. Imagine spending six months on a ship. Where were you six months ago? Now imagine staying in one room with no TV, nothing to do, and only beef jerky and bug-infested oatmeal to eat. Oh, and imagine that one room is actually the bottom of a filthy boat that is rocking back and forth all day and night. You'd probably die too, and that is why only 105 of the original 144 ever made it to the New World.

You'll see in a minute how those who made it probably wished they had perished on the boat while they had the chance.

Anyway, on May 24, 1607, they arrived at Chesapeake Bay, and Bob and Billy frolicked in the green lands of Virginia, learned to sing the song "The Colors of the Wind" with Pocahontas and made friends with the Indians. And here we end the story of Bob and Billy. After all we must give them a 'happily ever after' ending! Don't worry, there's more to come, and that's where all the interesting 'stuff' happens. To appease the censorship board, the following information is rated PG-13. We will wait a bit until you ask your parents' permission to keep reading.

Mosquitoes, War, and Cannibalism: The Stuff of Legends

One of the first things the colonists had to do was name the settlement. And when in doubt, the English always named locations after their rulers, thus they named it Jamestown. On a similar note, Virginia was named after Elizabeth I, the "virgin queen." Now imagine for a moment if Elizabeth I had a different reputation. We'd be talking about how the colonists landed in Jamestown, Impuria. But I digress.

Actually they landed there without realizing the dangers that lurked in the area. John Smith recommended building their settlement on land that could be easily defended and might actually grow crops. However, his fellow settlers chose option B, sixty miles up the James River in a swamp infested land home to malaria-carrying mosquitoes and the Powhattan natives—not exactly the most welcoming of hosts.

Not only did they choose an undesirable locale, but many of the settlers were not used to manual labor. They were "gentlemen," accustomed to an aristocratic lifestyle. If you listen closely you can almost hear one of them saying, "I must sincerely apologize, dear sir, but I will not lay my pure hands on this brownish ectoplasmic entity, since I have no knowledge of what may transpire if I do. However, if by chance you come upon some aureate colored rocks, feel free to waken me from my slumber." To put it in simple words, "I won't work. I don't know how. Where's the gold?"

This type of work ethic is not exactly what you want when creating a settlement from scratch. Not only did these gentlemen not jump in and start building the defenses and securing food, they spent an abundance of time searching for gold. Many of these men came to America hoping to find their riches and then return to England with a load of cash in their pocket. This short-timer attitude doomed Jamestown from the start. By 1609, Jamestown's population had risen to almost 600. However, malaria, starvation and violence helped dwindle these numbers. Of the colonists that did survive, some actually ran away to join any native tribe that would take them. Others entered a charming part of American history known as the "starving time."

The Starving Time

During the "starving time," colonists resorted to some pretty nasty food options.

They ended up having to settle for a tasty meat that can only be found in simian creatures called Homo sapiens. In other words, cannibalism. Oooo-hhh…gross. Yes, they resorted to eating each other. But not at first. First they devoured all the living creatures in sight—rats, chickens, cows, horses—even grubs you'd have trouble passing off in a food challenge on *Survivor* or *Fear Factor*. Once they ran out of four-legged animals they survived on human flesh. This is where it gets gruesome. In one story passed down through the ages, a man ate his wife while she slept, though I have a feeling she woke up at some point. The not-so-reliable Sir Henry Spelman recounts this story:

And one amongst the rest did kill his wife, powdered her and had eaten part of her before it was known, for which he was executed, as he well deserved; now whether she was better roasted, boiled, or carbonated, I know not, but of such a dish as powdered wife I never heard of.

I have to agree with Henry. I've yet to try the powdered wife as a main course. Once they ran out of each other, they then started digging up graves of their fellow settlers and the local Indians. This last disgusting exploit added yet another reason to why the Powhattan's weren't too fond of these hairy intruders.

Things Start Looking Up

It would be an understatement to say life wasn't going to smoothly for our Jamestown founders. With no food, limited shelter, rampant disease and hostile neighbors, Jamestown appeared doomed. Between the winter of 1609 and 1610, nearly 90% of the 600 settlers died. Not a very high survival rate. However, this is the part in history where leadership saved the day. Humans make mistakes. Civilizations spin out of control. However, individuals always step forward and change history. For Jamestown, those individuals were Captain John Smith and John Rolfe.

Smith realized there was one way to bring order out of this chaos. Force. Brutal force. By gunpoint, he organized the settlers in the early years of Jamestown, and kept them focused on survival. He made allegiances with the Powhattan tribe that brought much needed food. When he was forced to return to England because of a gunpowder-induced injury, the colony plunged into the previously mentioned "starving time." However, because of his strong leadership, some survived. It was these survivors that laid the foundation for America.

Survival is a fun goal, but these new settlers didn't actually sign up for the New World experience thinking they were going to die in mass numbers. They had to find a way to prosper. John Rolfe found the solution—nicotine addiction. By importing a South American plant, Rolfe perfected the crop that would eventually be the staple of the South—tobacco. Great idea, you can't eat it and it causes lung cancer! But who cares? Because tobacco grew in abundance, it spurned a wave of immigration to Virginia. Finally, with an influx of new labor able to produce a heavily desired crop, Virginia's economy was off and smoking.

One side note, before we move on to the other twelve colonies, and no they won't be as long as the entry on Virginia. Nor will they involve cannibalism. The last important part about the early founding of Virginia was the House of Burgesses. When you hear Burgess, think Representative. Basically, on July 30, 1619, Virginians elected "burgesses" to meet with the governor. This set the precedent that the people would actually have a say in government, instead of just having one of the king's cronies calling all the shots. This House of Burgesses set the groundwork for the Constitution. Remember that!

Trick Question! Trick Question! Trick Question!

If ever a teacher asks you, what was the first permanent European settlement in America, do not answer Jamestown. Jamestown is the first ENGLISH settlement. Remember, though some might disagree, there are a few other countries in Europe that were actively colonizing the Americas—Spain, France, Portugal, and the Dutch. The first European settlement was at St. Augustine, Florida, twenty-two years before Jamestown. The Spanish win! The Spanish win! In fact, during the 1600s the Spanish were all over the Americas. You should be wondering right now, why don't we learn about St. Augustine's being the first settlement? Why don't we eat tortillas and guacamole for Thanksgiving? Let me ask you this, what language do Americans speak? English. Even though a bunch of Europeans were all over the Americas, the English eventually won and kicked the rest out, and the winner gets to write the textbooks. If the Spanish had won, you'd probably be hearing a different history. But let's not get ahead of ourselves. Just remember, St. Augustine was the first European settlement in 1585.

Our Religion's Better Than Your Religion

Now that you understand a bit of what was going on down south, you now need to know about the Plymouth Colony. This is the place that you think of when you celebrate Thanksgiving: Pilgrims, Indians, turkeys, pumpkin pie, cute little black hats that you made in third grade. This is their story.

Over in England, people were fighting over who had the best religion. If you weren't the same religion as the people in charge, you got persecuted. They'd insult you, damage your property, or even beat you up and torture you. Some people even died. The ironic thing is that they all worshipped the same God. They just wanted to worship him differently.

Things started changing in England around 1535 when Henry VIII was starting to get annoyed with his wife Catherine who wasn't making cute little royal babies. He realized he needed to have kids so he wanted to marry the young Anne Boleyn. Small problem. He was still married to Catherine, and the Catholic

Church didn't look to favorably on being married to more than one person. Henry VIII then asked the Pope if he could divorce Catherine due to a technicality, something about Catherine being the former wife of his brother. Unfortunately for Henry, Pope Clement VII stood up, and with an unseen animal force slapped his hand on the table, probably deafening everyone within a 25 ft. radius, and said "No."

To put it mildly, Henry VIII was a bit unpleased, and in the great tradition of men who have whined after losing a game and taking their ball home, he came up with a semi-great idea.

"No fret," Henry said, calming down, "I'll just establish a new church and I will rule it, and you know what? The Pope isn't going to do anything about it!" Henry named this new Christian branch the Anglican Church, also known as the Church of England. Now England had to start practicing a new religion. Henry sent out messengers all over the land to deliver the great news. Imagine being a farmer out in the middle of nowhere and a guy rides up on a horse and claims, "You will now believe in God differently!"

What does this have to do with America? Patience, we're getting there.

Why Is Everybody Always Picking on Me?

"We hate the Church of England! We hate the Church of England!" Not everyone was terribly fond of Henry's new Anglican Church. One group from the town of Scrooby (no, not the dog), really detested the formality of the church services. These Puritans saw no place for fancy clothes and ornaments in religious celebration. Other Englanders weren't too pleased with this complaining sect and gave them a first-hand lesson in persecution. Eventually, these Scrooby Puritans left England and settled in Holland in 1609. After awhile there, the Puritan parents wanted to leave because they didn't want their children growing up around the bad influences of Holland and away from their English roots.

They didn't like Holland. They weren't welcome in England. Now where is a wandering Puritan to go. The New World—America! Here they could be the persecutors instead of always being the persecuted. These Pilgrims (so named because they were religious wanderers) hopped on the *Mayflower* with a group of non-believers. These non-believers, known as "Strangers," were necessary because they actually had the skills to start a civilization. Unlike Jamestown where the people really didn't think about what it would take to establish a settlement, these colonists brought all the right type of people. Carpenters, hunters, farmers, blacksmiths. After sailing west for Virginia for 65 fun-filled days, they arrived just a bit north of Virginia in…Massachusetts on November 21, 1620.

Democracy Alert! Democracy Alert!

Remember how I told you to remember the House of Burgesses, well here comes another history nugget that laid the foundation for democracy in America. While floating off shore, the Puritans and Strangers got together and signed the Mayflower Compact in which they agreed to work together for the common good and follow the rules of an elected leader.

After signing this agreement, they then realized that it was December, and winter was coming. A good question you might want to consider is why do these colonists arrive in a foreign land during winter time? Wouldn't it make sense to arrive in springtime, so you could possibly plant some crops and kill some animals before they run away and hibernate? Well, for whatever reason, the Puritans didn't consider this tidbit of logic and subsequently half of them froze to death the first winter.

Luckily, the next year they were taught techniques in surviving in this environment by the local Wampanoag Indians, especially Squanto and Samoset. After being kidnapped and brought to England under false pretenses by an English explorer years before, Squanto had picked up the English language and used this to help relations between the Indians and the Pilgrims. Squanto was then rewarded, along with his tribe, since they ensured the Pilgrims' survival. They invited Chief Massasoit and his family, and over ninety of his closest relatives for dinner. And what is this day called? No need to crack your heads for that one. We'll give you a hint, you eat turkey and those orange yams with marshmallows on top. Here's the answer: Githvankings (unscramble to figure out).

The Pilgrims eventually survived these first early years and later other Puritans joined them in Massachusetts. However, these Pilgrims kept to themselves and didn't become incorporated into the larger Massachusetts Bay Colony until 1691. However, their settling set the precedent for later America. One after the other, Puritans started settling this area that would go on to become New England. However, once in America they still argued over religion. Now though, instead of arguing over which type of Christianity was the best, they now debated over which type of Puritanism was the best. Those who agreed with the majority were allowed to stay. Those who disagreed were banished and a few started new colonies. Which brings us now to…

Boston: A City on a Hill…Or At Least a City on a Harbor

Other Puritans got kicked out by King Charles I and went to Boston. In 1629 the charter, a contract, was set up for Massachusetts Bay Colony. In Boston, John Winthrop and his fellow leaders established this system of government where the church and state ruled together, called theocracy. These Puritans believed that they should be looked up to as the supreme city, the role model, the "city on a hill". Winthrop took on a very important role in founding America. He knew how to rule justly combined with kindness, and his governing of Boston was top notch. He had a deep faith for God, and even advocated that the Native Americans be treated with respect so that they, in turn can do the same and be delivered to the hands of God when they die. Without Winthrop, Massachusetts might not exist. Many people were losing faith in Massachusetts, but Winthrop took his own money and bought more provisions, and eventually the colony survived and grew strong. With Winthrop at the lead and a Puritan work ethic motivating the citizens, Boston thrived and became the center of New England.

The Making of New England: Kicked Out of the Cool Club

Ever noticed how people who get picked on a ton when they are younger go on to pick on others when they get older? Think of Doofus Perwinkle, that freshman kid who always got beat up by the seniors. You'd think he would have learned the lesson about how it's not nice to pick on others and wouldn't it be great if everyone just got along? Tragically, when Doofus got a little older and he became the senior, he ended up picking on the incoming freshmen. This phenomenon has been termed by leading psychologists Getevenism, and it has been prevalent throughout history. The majority in any society likes to pick on the minority. Once the minority becomes the majority, then they pick on the new minority. Make sense? If not, go back three sentences and read them again until it does.

I digress. The Puritans that arrived in Massachusetts had their brand of Puritanism and if you didn't like it you could feel free to leave. Thus the remaining Puritan colonies were founded. Each a bit different than the original Boston version, but having a majority of similarities. Here is the Cliff's Notes version of their founding.

Connecticut

The founder of this colony, Thomas Hooker, believed in a form of democracy not very noticeable in early Massachusetts. Whereas John Winthrop believed in government by a few, Hooker believed more people should have a say in the administration of the colonies. He also thought women should have a vote. Imagine! How progressive. He finally took his congregation out into the wilderness in 1636. Eventually, they settled and signed the Fundamental Orders, which said your religion shouldn't be a criteria for citizenship and you can't be a governor for two successive terms. These Orders also helped establish the democratic tradition of the early colonies. On a side note, if you want to remember Hooker founded Connecticut, just remember that you can get "Cut" by a "Hook". Try to create mnemonic devices for all these and you can impress your relatives and win friends with your incredible knowledge.

Rhode Island

Roger Williams was kicked out of Massachusetts in 1636 due to his 'odd' beliefs. He believed such horrible things such as 1) individuals were more important than priests, 2) theocracy was bad, and 3) Indians should be paid for their land. After leaving Massachusetts he headed South and bought land from the Narragansett Indians. He must have not been that wealthy because if you've ever seen Rhode Island on a map, it's pretty tiny. Rhode Island became a sort of refuge for those wanting to rebel from the structure of Puritan New England. Think of it as the San Francisco hippie refuge of the 17th century.

New Hampshire

Like Hooker and Williams before, John Wheelright was booted out of Massachusetts in 1638 and set up New Hampshire, though it stayed a part of Massachusetts until split by the king in 1679. He was a follower of his sister-in-law Anne Hutchinson, a lady who used to have weekly Bible meetings where she criticized the church elders. Not a good idea. Anne was banished too.

Five Down, Eight to Go: The Middle Colonies

Pennsylvania

Pennsylvania was founded by William Penn in 1681 as a home for Quakers, a religious group established by George Fox. They were also known as the "Society of Friends." This group of people believed in ideas like non-violence and racial and gender equality. Their state motto was "Mercy, Justice, Truth, Peace, Plenty". They even signed treaties with Indians pledging friendship and abolished prison for debtors. These radical thoughts brought Pennsylvanians into great conflict with their neighbors. Regardless, Pennsylvania would go on to be home to the largest city in colonial times, Philadelphia, the city of Brotherly Love.

Delaware

Delaware is more than just a joke in the great cinematic classic, "Wayne's World." Back in the 1600s, it was one of the most desired pieces of land in America. First settled by the Dutch in the early 1630s, the Swedes then owned it and named it appropriately New Sweden. Though they didn't win any points for name originality, it remained Swedish until 1664 when those Brits conquered New Amsterdam and Delaware. Then in 1682, it was sold to William Penn. Yes, the same Penn as above. As far as the founder and date, it depends again on who's writing the history. Feel free to take your pick from one of the options above.

New York

You've probably heard of the story of how New York was founded. The Indians sold Manhattan Island for $24. It looks like the Indians really got the short end of a scam. Actually, the payment was in trinkets: a few hatchets and few pots, and the price was sixty guilders. But that's not the point. You have to look at the Indians concept of land ownership. Indians looked at land like we look at air. If you offer to give me $100 for all the air in the world, I'll take your money in a heartbeat. Now, who got the better end of the deal? The Indians essentially thought they were getting paid for something they couldn't even sell.

The Dutch ended up taking over this land, known as New Netherlands, and set up the main city of New Amsterdam. New Amsterdam became a sailor's town with all the perks of living with single men with questionable morals and an abundance of alcohol. The leadership of the island was not quite impressive. One lovely chap, Governor William Kieft, went to war against the local Raritan Indians. After promising them sanctuary, he then had his Dutch soldiers massacre them and bring their heads back to the city for a friendly game of football. This lunatic was sent back to the Netherlands and was replaced by Peter Stuyvesant who built a defensive wall, aka Wall Street, to keep out defenders. In 1664, the British fleet strolled up to New Amsterdam's doorstep and after an amazing battle that lasted nearly seventeen seconds, the Dutch citizens who really didn't care surrendered and the land became known as New York.

New Jersey

New Jersey is another colony that bounced back and forth between countries. First the Dutch owned it, then the British, then the Dutch, then it was sold to William Penn and a bunch of other guys at an auction. In the early years, it followed a similar path as New York, so you can look above for more information.

Maryland

In 1634, Lord Baltimore was kicked out of Virginia for being Roman Catholic. Maryland was then set up as a refuge for Catholics, and Lord Baltimore became the first proprietor, a man given almost full control over the colony. Even though it became a haven for Catholics running from persecution, Protestants mainly lived there. To guarantee the rights of the Catholics, Maryland passed the Act of Toleration, which ensured that different religions could all live in peace. Of course, they had to be one of the mainstream Christian denominations to qualify. However, the spirit of this act would again be seen in the Bill of Rights which granted freedom of religion across the new nation.

Almost Done, Here's the Rest of the South

The Carolinas

King Charles II wanted to extend his empire south, so he granted this land to a few of his political supporters, his "Eight Noble Lords." In return, they named it after the Latin word for Charles, Carolina. Like Maryland to the north, Protestants soon populated this colony and made tobacco and rice its staple crops. Founded as a big chunk of land in 1670, it eventually split into North and South Carolina in 1719.

Georgia

Georgia finishes off our stroll through the original thirteen colonies. Not founded until 1732, Georgia was the philanthropic (fancy word for helping others) experiment of James Oglethorpe. Basically, Oglethorpe saw the great numbers of vagrants, debtors and criminals in England and believed that if he gave them a fresh start they could prosper. All they needed was land and opportunity. What better place to go for land and opportunity than America? Oglethorpe had little trouble getting a land grant from the king. King George III was already a bit anxious about the Spanish colony of Florida to the south, and what better way to protect the prize colonies than throw a bunch of debtors onto some useless land. Oglethorpe wanted to improve humanity. George wanted a buffer zone. Oglethorpe and his group of financiers had great intentions. They established rules that forbade rum and slaves and that prevented the purchase of huge tracts of land. Unfortunately, as normally happens, human nature took over and it took about fourteen seconds for these rules to be broken. Georgia went on to resemble closely its northern neighbors.

Eeesh! And we're finally done. All thirteen colonies. Now if you count them up, you'll only get twelve, so just remember, one of them split into North and South. These colonies all became independent little worlds, though similarities could be seen within the three regions: the North, the South, and the Middle Colonies. Before we start talking about what it was like to live in these colonies, here's a helpful little chart to help you remember the key points. Because the concept of "founding" can vary based on who's writing the history, the dates might contradict what you've seen elsewhere. Does it really matter? You'll forget the dates in four days anyway.

Name of Colony	Date	Fascinating Facts
Virginia	1607	• House of Burgesses—1619 • John Rolfe discovers tobacco grows splendidly
Massachusetts	1620	• Pilgrims sign Mayflower Compact—later Thanksgiving • Puritans believe they are creating "City on a Hill"
New Hampshire	1623	• Wheelwright banished from Massachusetts Bay Colony
New Jersey	1623	• Owned at one point by British, Dutch, William Penn

New York	1624	• Land "purchased" for 24 guilders worth of stuff/things • English took control from Dutch without a fight
Maryland	1634	• Founded as refuge for Catholics • Passed Act of Toleration to ensure freedom of religion
Connecticut	1634	• Thomas Hooker wanted to expand democracy • Fundamental Orders next step in democratic government
Rhode Island	1634	• Roger Williams and Anne Hutchinson kicked out • Very liberal colony
Delaware	1638	• Went back and forth between Swedes, Dutch and British
Carolinas	1660	• Eight Noble Lords given land by King Charles II
Pennsylvania	1683	• Philadelphia—"City of Brotherly Love" • Quakers championed non-violence and equality
Georgia	1733	• Buffer zone between British and Spanish colonies • James Oglethorpe had noble ideas for debtor relief

CHAPTER 4

▼

SURVIVAL AND STRUGGLE: LIFE IN THE COLONIES

Life Ain't A Bed of Roses

Living in the 17th and 18th century was not exactly what we would call fun. You got up in the morning, worked all day, and hoped you didn't catch some deadly disease. To understand life in the colonies you have to try to imagine a life where you're starting with nothing. In the year 1648, there were 14,367,287,542 trees in America, most of which happened to be right in the way of where people wanted to live. So the people had to cut down the tree, dig up the roots, haul the tree off, cut up the tree for wood, and then start the process all over again with the next tree. Not exactly fun.

However, life did eventually get better. By March 4, 1987, people actually started enjoying their lives. Before that, life was a pain in the neck.

Remember how in the last chapter, we listed all the colonies and how they were founded? Well, we could use that format when describing life in the colonies. I could start with Massachusetts and then work my way south. But, unfortunately, now don't be too sad, I'm going to make some huge generalizations and just group all the colonies into three basic regions.

North. Middle. South.

Repeat after me.

North. Middle. South.

Each of these regions developed differently due to their geography and the type of people that settled the area. Because of these differences, if you traveled across the colonies in the 18th century, you wouldn't see a united nation, but many little communities all trying to survive in their own unique way.

Life in the North

Sometimes the Northern Colonies are called the New England Colonies. There are four colonies: Massachusetts, Connecticut, Rhode Island, New Hampshire. These were the religious colonies that all branched off from the original Puritans.

The development of this area was molded by its geography. What is geography? It's the way the land looks. In figuring out geography, ask yourself these questions: What kind of water is available? Rivers, lakes, or oceans? How about the land? Is it flat, rocky, or hilly? And the weather? Does it snow, rain? How hot does it get? What's the vegetation like? Are you living in swamp weeds or surrounded by gigantic trees?

For the North, their climate and land pretty much resembled that of England. The winters were long and freezing, the land was rocky and the vegetation consisted of a ton of trees. Not exactly prime farming land.

Because the prospects for farming were pretty much garbage, the economy of the North revolved around the waterways. There were lots of deep harbors, but very shallow, tiny rivers. These deep harbors were great for docking big boats. Salem, Boston, and Plymouth became major ports where supplies came in from all over the world. Fishing also became a main industry in this region. Seafood was dried and salted then shipped to other parts of the world. The whaling industry also took off as men started hunting these huge mammals to use their fat for lamp oil. Lovely. Nothing like a little whale fat to lighten up your life.

At first, England liked this idea of New England being a big fishing area because they were using English ships for all the transportation. However, when the New England colonists started building their own fishing ships, the King of England got a bit nervous. This would lead to problems later for American/British relations.

Now not all of these shippers were being nice. Some were just a bit too naughty. Through the end of the 17th century and into the 18th, England had enacted a series of Navigation Acts. These told the Americans who they could sell their products to. England. Who they could buy their products from. England. Whose ships they could use. English. And what type of sailors they could choose from. English. Do you see a pattern here?

Not all Americans liked this idea, so many just ignored the laws. What were the English going to do, find them on the ocean and blow them up? That would have been possible if England wasn't busy fighting yet another series of wars with all those other annoying European countries. This period became known as the years of "salutary neglect." Otherwise known as, "We made a bunch of laws. We have no way of enforcing them. So please be a good chap and try to follow them for us." America was essentially left to govern itself.

So what were they doing at home? Working, working, and working some more. Women really loved life back then. They got to be the nurse, cook, seamstress, maid, farmer, gardener, and teacher. This was true throughout the colonies. Women did it all, and on top of that they were mothers. Sometimes they had give birth to ten or eleven kids, and with the healthcare industry being fairly primitive back then, a lot of women died during childbirth.

Though women did a great deal of the teaching from their home, many of the Northern colonies began offering local education. In Massachusetts, once your town got large enough you had to go to school. Yippee! They also started setting up colleges. You might have heard of a few. Harvard, Yale, Princeton.

Children started working at an early age, and because these colonies were very strict religiously, they had little time to play. When they did, they had to make all of their toys, because Toys 'R Us just wasn't big back then. Luckily, because you had so many brothers and sisters, you already had a ton of playmates.

Colonial Games

Yo-Yo	Pick-up Sticks
Jump Rope	Rocking Horse
Tennis	Marbles
London Bridge	Hopscotch
Flying Kites	See Saw
Cricket	Leap Frog

Life Down South

Down South, they did things a little different. Again, like the North, this region developed differently due in large part to its geography. Land was flat, summers were hot and moist, and the winters were chilly (but not too chilly). They were great for growing crops. Rivers were deep and went pretty far inland so ships could bring supplies right to the doorstep of plantations.

Also, the people that founded this area were a little more focused on the joys of making money than were their neighbors to the North. The life of New England was a bit more centered around religion and each little town grew up around a priest and a church. Because of this, oftentimes the church leaders and the town leaders worked together to run the city. But we're not talking about the North any more, now are we?

Down South, life started a bit differently than that beautiful little Mayflower story up North. These people weren't anti-God, but religion wasn't as much of a focus in creating the individual societies. Instead of God as the focus, many came to the South in an attempt to replicate life back in England. Even though it was the Northern colonies that were called New England, in reality, it was the Southern colonies that really started to look like England. They created a nice little wanna-be English gentry population, that created the whole Southern hospitality image. Think *Gone With the Wind*. Scarlet O'Hara and her family were the perfect examples of the recreated English world. Instead of nobles that worked on fiefs and ruled over peasants, masters controlled plantations and used slaves as their labor force. Because land equaled power, the larger landowners became the most important and trusted members of society.

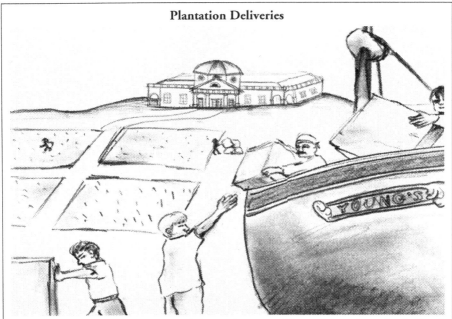

Plantation Deliveries

Because of the deep waterways, English supplies were delivered directly to the docks of the plantations.

Unlike up in the North, schooling wasn't compulsory, yet. Students learned out of their homes, and if they were rich they could even go to England to study abroad. Kids played the same games as up North, and women still had a ton of kids. Life was extremely different though because of the issue of slavery. After a century of slave labor, the South began to see the racial discrimination as normal and an unquestioned right of their society. Even though only a small percentage actually owned slaves, this reality would be difficult to change.

The Middle Colonies

The Middle Colonies were between the North and the South, and had a little in common with both areas. OK…moving on.

The Great Awakening

America faced a religious problem in the 18th century. People were starting to get bored with the four hour long sermons on why they were going to hell. Church attendance started to drop and churches subsequently had to start looking for ways to make it easier to be a membership.

A battle began for the minds of Americans. There was the conservative, your "naughty and your damned for all eternity" view. And then there was the liberal, "you control your own destiny so why don't you start actually being nice to people" view. By the 1730s something had to be done.

Enter Jonathan Edwards and his Great Awakening. Edwards liked scaring the heck out of people and telling them that if they didn't shape up and start believing that they should put their lives into God's hands, they were going to be in big, big trouble.

Excerpt from "Sinners in the Hands of an Angry God" Jonathan Edwards

The God that holds you over the pit of Hell, much as one holds a spider, or some loathsome insect, over the fire, abhors you, and is dreadfully provoked; his wrath towards you burns like fire; he looks upon you as worthy of nothing else but to be cast into the fire; he is of purer eyes than to bear to have you in his sight; you are ten thousand times more abominable in his eyes than the most hateful venomous serpent is in ours....

O sinner! Consider the fearful danger you are in: 'tis a great furnace of wrath, a wide and bottomless pit, full of the fire of wrath, that you are held over in the hand of that God, whose wrath is provoked and incensed as much against you as against many of the damned in Hell: you hang by a slender thread, with the flames of divine wrath flashing about it, and ready every moment to singe it, and burn it asunder; and you have no interest in any mediator, and nothing to lay hold of to save yourself, nothing to keep off the flames of wrath, nothing of your own, nothing that you ever have done, nothing that you can do, to induce God to spare you one moment....

Now, isn't that nice. Other priests soon followed. Eventually, a whole bunch of ministers were touring the colonies warning the colonists that they better mend their ways. Many of the more conservative members of the clergy believed this "fire and brimstone" style was inappropriate, yet many clergy believed it was revealing the true power of God to America.

This argument divided the church. Many stayed with the "old lights," the conservatives who held absolute power over their congregation not by their speaking ability, but by their education and presence. Others joined the other denominations, like the Baptists, where passionate speaking was encouraged. Churches started to compete for members and this made religion truly democratic.

Other than increasing church competition, many people were inspired to go out and convert the nearby Indians. Others formed colleges that encouraged these new religions.

And for the first time Americans were involved in a movement that was purely their own. Whether you lived in Georgia or Connecticut, the Great Awakening affected you. This touched off the sentiment of oneness in being American.

Doesn't Anybody Have an Original Thought

Life in America was all about survival in the early years. However, as the decades past, people gradually had more time to spend on leisure activities. In other civilizations around the world, free time usually meant that people would experiment with music, art, architecture, literature and dance. But not America. No sirree.

In America, if you had free time, you needed to go out and find more ways to make money. Because of this, no real American culture developed in the colonies. Everything we had, we borrowed from Europe. Our architecture was borrowed from England and Rome. Even the cute little log cabin idea was stolen from Sweden. Artwork wasn't too exciting. Name a famous colonial artist. Yeah right. And as for literature, Americans pretty much just read books sent over from England. Sure, America had its share of authors and poets, but they never really took off. I can't understand why. Here's a fun little diddy from a lady who liked to write about such hot topics as her husband leaving, her husband returning, her children being born, and even her house burning down.

Here followes some verses upon the burning of our house, July 10th, 1666.
By Anne Bradstreet

In silent night when rest I took,

For sorrow neer I did not look,

I waken'd was with thundring nois

And Piteous shreiks of dreadfull voice.

That fearfull sound of fire and fire,

Let no man know is my Desire.

I, starting up, the light did spye,

And to my God my heart did cry

To strengthen me in my Distresse

And not to leave me succourlesse.

Then coming out beheld a space,

The flame consume my dwelling place.

Now, wasn't that poem just beautiful. It kind of makes you want to go outside and bang your head against a tree.

Finally, by the middle of the 18th century, America started to create its own personality. The first true American was Benjamin Franklin. In his articles in *Poor Richard's Almanack,* he combined sarcasm with stuff that was truly Americana. Famous for flying a kite with a key and inventing a stove, Franklin also wrote a ton of witty little sayings that stay with us still today.

Witty Little Sayings by Benjamin Franklin

"A penny saved is a penny earned."

"Any fool can criticize, condemn and complain and most fools do."

"Early to bed, early to rise makes a man healthy, wealthy, and wise."

"Fish and visitors smell in three days."

"Haste makes waste."

"Little strokes fell great oaks."

"Never confuse motion with action."

"Never leave that till to-morrow which you can do to-day."

"Read much, but not many books."

"Three may keep a secret, if two of them are dead."

"To find out a girl's faults, praise her to her girl friends."

"Well done is better than well said."

Life Sucks and Then You Die

If you've ever seen a movie about the colonial era, it looks like it would be a lot of fun. The men wear cute black pants that look like something you'd find on a baseball player and instead of hair they have snazzy white wigs. Women have those adorable little dresses and they always seem to be making butter.

But life wasn't really that exciting. You pretty much worked, worked, and then when you were done you worked a little more. The big excitement around town would be an election, a wedding or a funeral. Then, people finally had a reason to gather. Other than that, gathering usually took place while doing work—putting up a barn, making a quilt or cutting apples. Even Christmas was outlawed in New England, because it was just too much fun. Acting was still seen as a sin, whereas today the most respected human beings in the world are actors.

So, life basically sucked. You had little to no water, boring food, and you only bathed whenever you fell into a river. And after you were done with that, you would then go to church and learn about how bad you were and how you were going to hell.

What is the moral of the story? If ever you get a time machine and have to decide where you want to live, you might think twice about clicking the little button that says "Colonial Era."

But We Were Here First

In recent years, nobody has tried to hide America's annihilation of the Indians who already lived on the continent before the European colonists arrival. But just for a moment, walk a bit in the Indians' moccasins. Imagine this scenario. I'll put it in modern day terms.

You're at home, sitting with your family, watching *The Simpsons* and some guys ram through your door holding a huge, shiny weapon that can incinerate your entire family with a push of a button. They then push you off the couch, raid your fridge and start sleeping in your bed. The whole time, they're looking at you like you haven't showered in a century, like you're some sort of freak from Mars. Then, they start trying to teach you some new religion about how tacos and rocks are actually the true rulers of the world. Next, they kick you out and force you to live under the tree in the backyard. Once in awhile, they don't know how to operate the stove or the microwave, so they bring you into the house and ask for your advice. You tell them, and then they kick you out again. After a few months, they decide to renovate the house, so they point a gun to your head and suggest that you move. You think this isn't exactly fair so you slap one of the soldiers on the cheek. He then slays your family. Realizing there's no hope for you, you finally leave.

That, ladies and gentlemen, was what we call an "extended metaphor." See if you can make connections to what really happened to the Indians.

Anyway, the Indians realized they were getting a bum deal, and at times they decided to fight back. For the hundred and fifty years of settlement leading up to the Revolutionary War, there were sporadic fights throughout the wilderness.

At times, these fights even turned into wars against the colonies.

All Hail King Philip

On June 11, 1675, an Indian went up to a farmer and started to steal some of his cows. The farmer killed the Indian. His fellow Indians didn't feel this punishment was fair and asked for some sort of punishment for the trigger happy farmer.

The leader of this group of Indians, the Wampanoag tribe, was Metacomet. Ironically, Metacomet's dad, Massasoit, helped the first Pilgrims years back. However, this initial friendship soon dissolved as the New Englanders spread over the Massachusetts area. When Metacomet went to the local authorities asking for retribution, they chuckled and sent him on his way.

Metacomet would make them pay. He took a small group of Indians to the farmer's house, and then killed the farmer and six other settlers. The colonists were getting worried. They named Metacomet, "King Philip." Over the next two years, King Philip waged war on the colonists. He burned towns, killed settlers and raged havoc. Initially, the colonists could do nothing because they were so unorganized. Eventually, they realized the only way they could survive was to join together and fight this force. Like other times in American history, having a common enemy actually increased community bonds.

Eventually, King Philip was defeated, but the damage was done. New England lay in ruins and the colonists knew they would always have to fear the Indians existence.

Do You Guys Ever Feel Like Pawns?

The European powers were quick to take advantage of the Indian dislike for the colonists. Not only did the Indians not like the colonists, they also feuded against each other. Remember, there was no united nation called "Indian," but instead hundreds of tribes that survived independently of each other. Like any other peoples, these Indians got into conflicts with their neighbors.

The European nations took advantage of these disputes. Oftentimes, wars that started in Europe were carried to North America. France would fight England, then they would get Indians to fight English settlers. After that, the English settlers would get Indians to fight other Indians. Pretty soon, Indians were fighting Indians for the same Europeans who would kick them off their lands once the battles ended.

But the Indians had little choice. They were fighting for their survival and they would ally themselves with whoever gave them a better chance of keeping their land. One after another, European wars landed on American soil. King William's War, Queen Anne's War, King George's War, and finally the French and Indian War.

Indian Guerilla War Tactics

The Native American's usage of terrain and unconventional battle strategies helped them defeat the technologically advanced colonists.

In each scenario, the outnumbered and outgunned Indians used guerilla war tactics of hide and fight to attack their enemy. When all was said and done, the Indians would eventually lose and the colonists would punish them for their alliances. The conflict from 1756 to 1764, known as the French and Indian War, took the highest toll on the Indian population. France enlisted the help of Indians and took the battle to the wilderness. War waged on year after year, as Britain and its colonists tried to fight off the cunning and resilient Indian foes.

Eventually the British won, and the Indians lost more land, and more lives. Over the next century, tribes were extinguished and those that survived had to move far away to unfamiliar lands where they were forced to live on reservations.

This was not a shining moment in American history.

CHAPTER 5

▼

TICK-TOCK: COUNTDOWN TO REVOLUTION

Christopher Lee
Angela Tsai

Somebody's Going to Have to Pay For This

The Proclamation of 1763 brought an end to the French and Indian War. To avoid future conflicts, the British told their colonists they weren't allowed to cross west of the Appalachian Mountains. The west was Indian land. The British realized the colonies were totally unable to unite and defend themselves against the Indians, so they figured the best solution was to keep the two enemies away from each other.

A year after the end of the French and Indian War, the British treasurer George Grenville came up with a brilliant idea to pay for the debt accumulated over the 120 years of the war (especially since the last war was fought on American soil). Being a talented policy maker, Grenville used the colonists' heavy reliance on the British troops for protection as a valid excuse for the Parliament to impose the Sugar Act in 1964. The Sugar Act, which charged a tax of three cents for a gallon of sugar, was actually cheaper than its predecessor, the Molasses Act which taxed six cents a gallon. However, colonists were outraged that they had to pay any tax whatsoever.

Even though the earlier Molasses Act looked like it was more oppressive, the truth was that the British never enforced it. The Sugar Act would be different.

The years of Salutary Neglect were over. From now on, the British were going to start enforcing their laws. It was this enforcement that truly enraged the colonists. For nearly a century, they'd been able to do as they pleased and many a man had grown rich while the British mother country was off fighting innumerable wars. Now, the British wanted to dip their hands into the pie of American prosperity. Tyranny!!!

While Parliament tried to enforce the Sugar Act, they passed an additional law, the Currency Act, which gave only Parliament the sole right to produce currency. This was a result of the high inflation of colonial currency. Money was becoming worthless. The Currency Act did not help improve the economy, instead it evoked further anger among the colonists.

However, these two acts were just the beginning. To further please the King and fill the empty British treasury, Grenville came up with the Stamp Act in 1765. Unlike the Sugar Act that was external, the Stamp Act was an internal tax. No longer were the colonists simply being taxed on goods coming in and out of the country. The Stamp Act affected a majority of the population. Even though Stamp Act sounds like it has something do with mail, in reality it taxed papers used in the daily lives of the colonists—newspapers, posters, pamphlets, contracts, playing cards, licenses and ship's papers. Just imagine having to pay a tax for your daily newspaper, something that you probably just read and threw away that same day.

Now the colonists were even angrier. Parliament underestimated the power of the colonies. The colonists coined the phrase "taxation without representation," believing it was unreasonable for them to pay taxes if they were not represented in the Parliament. If they were going to be taxed, they deserved to have their voice heard in a public forum. To protest, the dissatisfied colonists boycotted British goods, which led to the drastic drop of merchant's trade by 14%. To further express their discontent, Samuel Adams organized the Sons of Liberty, a secret society that threatened the stamp collectors. These hooligans would harass the stamp collectors and even tar and feather them. Because across the ocean the British merchants were suffering great losses from the boycott, Parliament finally repealed the Stamp Act on March 18, 1766.

The Psychology of Making a Nation

Before we move on, there is something that needs to be noted. For the first time since the Great Awakening, colonists started to feel part of something larger than their town, their colony, their region. Up until this point, the colonists felt extremely isolated from each other. The idea of a United States of America would have seemed ridiculous.

However, one of the best ways to unite a group of people is to create a common enemy, someone people can unite against. Before you can even imagine defeating another nation, you must demonize your enemy. You can see this strategy work in your own house. Sometimes you feel closest to your brother or sister when you're uniting against your parents.

It worked the same for the colonists against England. The evil King George and the corrupt Parliament wanted to destroy their livelihood. With a little help from propaganda, men who never would have united under other conditions now felt a kinship with their colonial neighbors. This bond would only grow stronger.

And a Few More Acts

It was difficult for a powerful nation like England to admit when they had made an error. To remind the colonists of their sovereignty and power, the Parliament established the Declaratory Act in 1766, right after the Stamp Act was repealed. Basically, this Declaratory Act said, "Don't forget, we're still in charge!"

Not only did Grenville fail to please the King by paying off the war debt, he stirred up even more trouble in the colonies, so he was fired and replaced by Charles Townshend. Although this Townshend guy made it big by having the Townshend Act named after him, he didn't seem to have learned the lesson from Grenville and once again the British got into trouble with the colonists.

In 1767, the Townshend Act imposed duties on several imported items, forced the New York legislature to provide supplies to British troops and reorganized the custom agents. Immediately after the implementation of the new act, in an attempt to unite the colonies, master of propaganda Samuel Adams circulated letters opposing the new system. Members from the colonial assemblies reacted sternly.

Remember how well the boycott worked the first time the colonists wanted to reject a colonial act? Well guess what? The colonists used this strategy again to achieve their goal. This time, the colonists dropped British exports over 40%. Now who said the colonists couldn't unite? Similar to the fate of the Stamp Act, British merchants forced Parliament to repeal the Townshend Act.

Recognizing a pattern of growing intrusion in America's economy, the Virginia House of Burgesses met in May 1769 and composed the Virginia Resolves.

Led by George Washington and George Mason, these resolutions outlined the American disdain for interference from Parliament.

You Call This a Massacre?

The British were losing patience. Weren't they the Mother Country? How dare those ungrateful colonists refuse to follow British mandates? Trying to calm a tense situation, the British sent troops to unruly Boston to closely monitor the colonists before they lost control. While in Boston, these troops were not exactly treated fondly by their American hosts.

Tensions kept building between the local Bostonians and the British troops. Then on March 5,1770, the townspeople pushed the redcoats too far. It all started when a young boy shouted an insult at a few of the soldiers, and the soldier then thumped the boy on his head with a rifle. Then the boy did what any courageous, enraged boy would do in the same circumstances—he went whining for help. He had little trouble finding a mob filled with the unemployed drunkards ready to search out trouble.

This mob then got right in front of the faces of the soldiers and dared them to fire. They cursed and threw snowballs at the redcoats. They might have even made comments about one of the soldier's mothers. Finally, the order was heard, "Don't fire!" To which, a soldier fired. The smoke cleared and the damage was done.

Now, this was a "Massacre". This was one of the main catalysts for the Revolutionary War. Obviously, the death toll had to be horrific for it be labeled a massacre. How many do you think died? 50? 200? 10,000?

Close. Five. Yep, only five. No offense to the families of the slain, but five deaths isn't exactly a massacre. However, this is where America saw one of its first examples of "spin doctoring." Samuel Adams was the master of propaganda, and definitely not a fan of the British. Thanks to his story and Paul Revere's famous engraving, the "Boston Massacre" radicalized a large group of colonists. Blood had been shed, and more blood would follow.

A Wacky Night Out with the Boys

Soon after the Boston Massacre, Britain removed soldiers from Boston and the colonies prospered for the next two years. This peace and prosperity wouldn't last long.

In 1773, the British East India Company, who had a ton of tea rotting in British harbors, wasn't doing to well financially. To help out the British East Indian Company, Parliament allowed the company to sell the tea to America without paying export tax. This allowed the British tea to be sold in America at a much cheaper price than that of the local American merchants. The price was so low that the American merchants could not compete with the British merchants. Rich men were losing money. Must be time for a revolt!

To express their resentment of the unfair enforcement of taxation laws, Samuel Adams had an idea. On the night of December 16, 1773, a few colonists dressed up like Mohawk Indians boarded the British tea ship and dumped the tea into the sea. Some even watched while these feisty young men did their work. The story of these men dumping tea while dressed in their finest Halloween costumes spread through the colonies. Tea was being dumped all over the place.

The Boston Tea Party

To protest unfair advantages given to the British East Indian Company, a few guys got together and took out their frustration on some chests of tea.

Extremely angered by the Boston Tea Party, in 1774, the British passed the Coercive Acts, which would be labeled the Intolerable Acts by the colonists.

These acts closed all ports in Boston, prohibited the organization of private meetings, gave British soldiers the right to live in private homes, tried certain crimes in England and expanded boundaries of Quebec. This last act, the Quebec Act, was the lone act not meant to punish Boston, but many of the colonists saw the Quebec Act as symbolic of how the British planned on extending their power.

It Looks Like War

The colonies decided to come together for a meeting called the Continental Congress on September 5, 1774 in Philadelphia. At this meeting, twelve of the thirteen colonies (Georgia couldn't make it) decided how to respond to the latest British threat. The main result from the meeting was that the colonists formed the Association. This Association decided to "boycott British goods and pass resolutions asserting colonial rights" until the British repealed the Intolerable Acts.

In the following months, the British had General Gage make sure all the New England colonists were following the Intolerable Acts. By April, the colonists had begun preparing for conflict. The Association also organized the collection of military supplies. And where would they look for these? In the British armory at Concord. The British, worried that Massachusetts would become more organized and dangerous if they took over any British garrisons, decided to stop the pillaging.

Gage set off for Concord. On the way he stopped in a town called Lexington. The British were not alone. All through the night, Paul Revere, William Dawes and Dr. Samuel Prescott rode from house to house trying to alert the colonists that the British regulars were coming. Not only were they trying to prepare the minutemen (name given to farmers who could be ready to fight in a minute) for battle, they wanted to warn John Hancock and Samuel Adams that the British were coming for their arrest.

So, when Gage and his Redcoats reached the nearby town of Lexington, they were greeted by about fifty minutemen who began shouting insults at the British soldiers. Back and forth, they shouted and yelled and chaos took over. By the end of the morning, the revolution had begun.

If we had the ability to travel back in time and interview members of both sides, the recounting of events might go something like this:

> *Minuteman: "Oh it was terrible. We were just gathering with our fellow Church members discussing the week's sermon when out of nowhere, without any provocation from us, I promise, the British started firing. They killed eight of my best friends, and not a single one of them did anything wrong."*

Redcoat: "We marched up to a bunch of hoodlum Americans to ask what they were doing and they started shooting at us! Can you imagine our shock and surprise? They then proceeded to scalp and cut of the ears of our wounded comrades. Barbaric!"

Who fired the first "shot heard around the world" wasn't clear, but the militia and the British soldiers had their first real engagement. As the British continued on to Concord they were eventually defeated and pushed back to Boston. Along the way, the militia showed off their new strategy of guerilla warfare by hiding behind homes and trees and firing at the retreating soldiers.

The next big thing that happened was the Second Continental Congress, which was held in May 1775 in Philadelphia. Now, guess which colony out of the thirteen came late? If you guessed Georgia, good job. This time they appointed George Washington to be commander in chief of the Continental Army and decided that they would need American privateers to gather supplies from British boats. They met, and met, and met, and met…and finally after a year of meeting, they decided to write a Declaration of Independence. Written by Thomas Jefferson, John Adams, and Benjamin Franklin, with Jefferson having the greatest impact, this document would go on to be the model for democratic revolutions around the world.

A big date to remember is July 2, 1776. That was when the colonists announced their separation from Britain. Jefferson's Declaration of Independence was broken into two parts. It started off with the preamble. This portion describes the rights of man and borrows directly from books and declaration the British themselves had written. Then the Declaration itemizes how King George III acted as a tyrant and broke his own laws and therefore the colonists had the right to start their own government. On July 4, 1776, a more important date to remember, the Declaration of Independence was approved by the Second Continental Congress. It was first signed by John Hancock, the president of the Congress, a man who got a little carried away with his signature and took up a big chunk of the bottom of the document. It was later signed by a total of 56 delegates. Knowing that if they lost the war, they'd be tried for treason, Benjamin Franklin noted, "We must all hang together, or we shall all hang separately."

During the year of deliberation before the signing of the Declaration of Independence, colonists started slowly believing in the cause of the radicals. On January 15, 1776, *Common Sense* written by Thomas Paine was published. It was a pamphlet that stated it was "common sense" to rebel against Britain because of their tyranny and the obvious flaws of monarchy. Thousands of copies were sold and public opinion began to shift. They would need it, because, as John Adams once calculated, one-third of the colonists were for revolution, one-third were against it, and one-third really didn't care.

The Revolutionary War

The Revolutionary War lasted from 1775 to 1783 and it was full of important battles, but here are just a few of the biggies.

We already have the battles of Concord and Lexington. Next came the Battle of Bunker Hill. What's weird is that the hill where the British and Americans fought on was Breed's Hill. They call it the Battle of Bunker Hill because the battle was supposed to be on Bunker Hill. They just fought on the wrong hill. Smart huh? Anyway, the British charged twice up the hill but were pushed back by the Americans. Only on the third try did the British break through the American defenses and that was because the Americans had run out of ammunition. Though technically the Americans had lost, they had won a great moral victory. The British had lost 1/8 of their officers and 1000 men while the Americans lost less than half that number. More importantly, a band of farmers stood up to and fought gallantly against the most well-trained, successful army in the world. Bravo!

Perhaps a bit of background knowledge of how the British and American soldiers fought might be helpful. The British back then were very big on neat, orderly wars. They would only fight if the weather was just right. When that perfect day came along, the soldiers would line up in a horizontal line, fire once at the enemy, stop, and wait until the next command to fire had been given. The Americans on the other hand used a rather different tactic to fight. They made use of terrain to hide and defend themselves. They also didn't fight at predictable times, which you'll see a bit later.

Anyway, after Bunker Hill, the Continental Congress sent the Olive Branch Petition to King George asking for peace. King George turned it down believing that his great military force would be able to take out the rebellious colonies.

Washington did a great job in March 1776 by ending the long siege of Boston by taking Dorchester Heights. Once he took this spot, he pointed a cannon at the British fleet in the harbor and the British general, William Howe, smartly decided to sail away. I guessed he might have known that ships with holes don't really sail very well.

What the Americans needed most was the aid of France. To get this aid, they opened all American ports to everyone in the world except the British. They also sent Silias Deanne of Connecticut to ask France for more men and money. Luckily for the Americans, France was already planning to destroy the British Empire so they willingly gave the Americans loads of gunpowder. Ships and soldiers would follow once the French were certain the Americans had a chance of winning.

After the British left Boston, they continued to attack Washington's Continental Army. First they met in New York City and the British gave Washington's army a big whipping. The British pressed on and attacked Manhattan Island and eventually pushed the Continental Army to Pennsylvania. It was the lowest point of the war for Washington but he felt he had to attack while he still had some soldiers. So, on the night of December 25, Washington and 2,400 soldiers were brought across the Delaware River in the middle of a sleet storm. Notice the date? December 25th. After a night of celebrating and merriment, the redcoats were awoken in their pajamas to face Washington's force. The Americans lost only four men, but took 900 prisoners.

Washington Crosses the Delaware

Washington and his troops chose Christmas Eve to cross the Delaware River to launch a sneak attack.

Following that victory, Washington again took the British by surprise in Princeton and forced the British to give back New Jersey and retreat to New York. Washington did this all in a span of ten days. Awesome feat!

Almost Over

The British then thought of a comeback. They wanted to send three armies moving from different directions to invade New York and meet up at Albany. What the British did not know was that they were walking right into the American militia's trap. One army was defeated before it even reached Albany. Another sailed off in the wrong direction and captured Philadelphia instead. The third army had to move through forest which was terrain that was favorable to the American militia. The militia also outnumbered the third army and so on October 17, 1777, the third army led by Burgoyne surrendered at Saratoga, New York. This was the turning point in the war, and the defining moment the French awaited. Also on February 7, 1778, the French decided to openly declare their involvement with the war and signed a treaty of alliance with America.

The British then began to move south and Washington's army began to advance their attacks. There was a battle at Monmouth, New Jersey on June 28, 1778 which was the last major battle of the war north of Virginia.

The British were not without a few victories of their own, claiming Savannah, Georgia and Charleston. But on October 7, 1780 several regiments of militia attacked a British force at King's Mountain, South Carolina resulting in the bloodiest battle since Bunker Hill. The British then planned to move to Virginia but were outmaneuvered by the American army lead by the Marquis de Lafayette and had to move to Yorktown, Virginia. Washington thought of a brilliant plan then and put it into play. He strengthened the number of his troops by joining up with a French force under General Rochambeau. They then surrounded the British troops led by Cornwallis at Yorktown. Outnumbered two to one, Cornwallis tried to escape by sea, but the French navy was already there to prevent that from happening. Seeing no way out, Cornwallis surrendered his entire army of 7750 men, 850 sailors, 224 cannons, and all his weapons on October 19, 1781.

The Surrender at Yorktown

Cornwallis surrenders at Yorktown while the French ships block their escape.

Can't We All Just Get Along

In April 1782, peace negotiations began in Paris and a final treaty was signed on September 3, 1783, by Britain, America, France, and Spain. The treaty stated that England recognized America's independence, would allow them to fish in England's Newfoundland fisheries, and that Britain would help out the Loyalists with money and land in Canada. Loyalists by the way were Americans who wanted to remain British citizens and were forced to leave America. Some returned to England. Some moved to Canada.

Now you may be wondering how the best army in the world could be beaten by a bunch of farmers, and there are actually a number of reasons why. One reason was that an ocean separated the British from home. Sending messages back and forth or getting help took a long time. The British also underestimated the strength of the Americans and relied too much on the Loyalists for help, which never came. Having able men such as George Washington lead the army was another big reason why the British could not conquer America.

America's fight for independence was a long and hard one and was eventually attained in the end. And so ends the countdown to the revolution. Now came the hard part—making a nation.

CHAPTER 6

▼

WHAT A FINE MESS WE GOT OURSELVES INTO: THE ARTICLES OF CONFEDERATION

Deepti Dhir
Dan Szeto

There's Nothing United About These States

The post revolution period began after the Declaration of Independence on July 4, 1776, when the thirteen colonies formed the United States of America. But could these thirteen states, after years of fighting, come together as one? America would now have to face its biggest task—surviving as one nation. The country would have to establish a system of governing itself, and prove to the world that it was capable of standing on its own feet. The war was over, but the nation would now have to face the challenges that became part of shaping and forming a successful America.

You would probably imagine that once a united nation, the states would communicate readily and accomplish urgent tasks with ease. But that was not so. The thirteen states that were supposed to form America had no desire to unite as one. You might think of the thirteen colonies as thirteen siblings living in one house. They all wanted to have their own space and freedom to run their own lives.

They did not want to be pestered by their annoying little brothers and sisters. Each state wanted to be independent and wanted to have their own way of running things.

Back in 1776 there were no phones, no telegraph, and obviously no Internet. The only way to communicate was to put your message on a horse or on a boat and wait for it to get to your desired location. Since mailing took a long time and was highly priced, one hardly heard of the welfare of other states. They pretty much lived isolated from the other states and continued to identify themselves with their local community rather than the USA. They might have been united during war time, but things are always different after war. During the Revolutionary War, the states had a common enemy, England. They united to defeat this enemy for the common cause of independence. Once that goal was accomplished, it was back to daily living and they had no reason to come together.

Rules, Rules, Rules

In May 1776, before Independence was declared, the Second Continental Congress asked states to establish their own constitutions. Massachusetts set a precedent in how they drafted their state constitution. The steps they took would be later followed, both by other states and later by the entire country. A committee was formed with John Adams as their leader. A draft of the constitution was sent out to town meetings where the people criticized and tried to improve sections of it. When a two-thirds majority was reached, then the document was approved, making it the law of the state of Massachusetts. This procedure of having each community partake in the creation of a legal document illustrates democracy at its finest. Other states also formed committees to create constitutions, while a few still relied on the moneyed elite to make these decisions.

So you might be asking yourself, what exactly do these state constitutions say? Most of them included a declaration of independence and a bill of rights, which the people felt helped secure their own privileges. After all, America's whole goal was to break away from the rule of a king. It was to become a nation for the people. The state constitutions differed from Britain's because they specified what the government could do and not do.

The governor's powers were also greatly reduced in state governments. In the years of colonial rule, the governor's power was modeled after that of the king. The states feared that if the new position of governor was given too much authority, things would revert back to the way they used to be. Only in two states did the governor have the power to veto, but his decision could still be overridden.

The state legislatures were granted most of the power instead. No longer could a governor be the law. They would have to answer to the law. The colonists had fought for and secured autonomy. Why would they give that up now?

Learning Things The Hard Way

Even though there were state governments, a central power was necessary to run the country, taking the needs and opinions of all the thirteen states into account. The Continental Congress formed a committee that would create what was known as "The Articles of Confederation and Perpetual Union." It's kind of a long name so people normally cut out the last bit and just call it the Articles of Confederation. A man called John Dickinson from Pennsylvania was its main author. The Articles bestowed the power to control western lands on the central government. The states, despite their population, were given one vote each. You can only imagine how large states reacted to such proposals. Just think, Virginia and Massachusetts, the economic and political centers of the new nation, both having the same power as miniscule Rhode Island? The large states still feared the idea of a central power and therefore edited down Dickinson's original Articles till only one-eighth of them were left! Congress adopted the edited Articles in 1777, but it was not until 1781 that all the states had approved the document.

The main reason why it took the states so long to sign the Articles of Confederation was because of a dispute over land between the states. It was mainly a battle between the smaller and larger states. Maryland and New Jersey, who did not have any land in the west, were afraid of larger states like Virginia and Massachusetts claiming boundless tracts of land as far west as had been explored. With the amount of land they could acquire, Virginia and Massachusetts could sell it all and pay off their debts from the war. This would also reduce the state's taxes. Now the smaller states thought that if this happened, all their citizens would move to the states where taxes were lower. So the decision was finally made that all the western land would go to federal government, and in 1781, Virginia, the last state, gave up its land to the country.

The Articles of Confederation were not perfect; in fact, they were actually far from it. Under the Articles, states were given most of the power, as people feared a strong federal government. The biggest problem with this was that Congress could not force states to give money. This was a problem. As the country was in great debt, money was urgently needed. America owed money to its own soldiers, army officers and other countries (France, Spain and Netherlands). Congress had no power to tax any of the states and therefore could not pay off any debts. This created an uprising in 1783, when soldiers marched up to the State House in Philadelphia and demanded that Congress pay them back. The soldiers said that if they didn't get paid, they would start taking members of Congress into their custody. Congress had no way of meeting their demands and resorted to escaping to Princeton, New Jersey.

There were also many disputes between states because they all wanted to get the maximum benefits from trading with each other. Farmers from New Jersey needed to get their products to New York City via the Hudson River. You can only guess what New York did—they taxed New Jersey. In retaliation, the small state laid a tax of 1,800 dollars on New York, for the right to keep a lighthouse on the New Jersey Coast. And Congress did nothing. They had no power.

It was also extremely hard to get anything done or change any policy in the Articles of Confederation. Nine out of the thirteen states had to agree to pass anything through Congress. This meant that if only nine states came to a Congress session, which did happen in those days, all nine states would have to approve a measure before it got passed. This created problems for the young nation. What worsened the situation was the fact that the central government was hardly given any importance, and sometimes the states did not even bother to appoint representatives into Congress.

There were also various boundary disputes that Congress could not prevent. While Vermont was wanted by both New York and New Hampshire, the use of the Potomac River was disputed over by Virginia and Maryland. There was one land policy, however, that Congress was able to control, and that concerned the territory in the Northwest.

Congress, like any protective and nurturing guardian, felt a strong obligation to look out for its young territories. Thus, they devised an Add-a-State Plan. Even now, people in the states that were created by this plan call Thomas Jefferson, founder of the plan, their second mother. This plan was made out of three simple steps for statehood. When you had a few people in an area, Congress would selectively choose one governor, one secretary, and three judges. But once you could count up to 5000 adult free men, then you would have a legislature— the people would make their own state's laws. You could finally apply to be a state once 60,000 people occupy the territory. This was the Northwest Ordinance of 1787.

There was a considerable amount of land in the west, but nobody knew how many states would be added to the nation using this plan. Originally, they predicted three to five in the Ohio Valley. Little did they know that in a few decades, America would stretch to the Pacific Ocean. The Northwest Ordinance is extremely important because it granted religious freedom and outlawed slavery. Slavery in the territories would become a huge issue by the middle of the nineteenth century, but until then, the law curbed the expansion of slavery. In addition, the precedent was set that future colonies would be equal to the original thirteen.

There comes the time in everyone's life when they have to face depression. America, like any adolescent, hit its great depression after just a few short years. The people had their fun and celebrated victory in the war, but they also had to deal with a HUGE financial predicament. They had money problems. For one thing, each state used a different currency. Imagine paying off debts with money that had an unknown value. That would be like paying off your credit card with Monopoly money.

Another problem was tariffs on goods. You could bring your shirts from England into Boston harbor and pay a $2 tax, and bring them into New York and pay a $4 tax. Who would you go to? Boston, of course. This inequity of tariffs started causing competition between states, and competition doesn't usually lead to unity.

Crabby Farmers with Pitchforks

Another problem was that people didn't have enough money. They owed money to the bank for land, tools, food, and other necessities of life. The banks wanted to collect their money, but the farmers didn't have any money to repay their debt. Courts were putting people in jail for defaulting (not paying) their loans. Now, a person named Daniel Shays decided he didn't want to starve or go to jail, so he organized a protest that blocked the court steps in 1786. His philosophy—if they can't get in the courthouse, they can't put any of us in jail.

After they protested, Daniel Shays and his little group of farmers decide to raid the armory. They couldn't simply throw their corn at their enemies. They needed guns. So in January 1787, Shays and his well trained farmers got guns and ammunition. They raided courts in, Northampton, Barrington, Worcester, and Concord. Shays and his men struggled for about a month, but were eventually captured in February 1787. This little farmer's revolt ended up being a huge catalyst for change.

How? Well, rich people were getting scared. Nobody especially the rich and powerful wanted angry farmers running around the countryside causing a ruckus. Something had to change.

In January 1786, Virginia took the initiative to form a meeting with all the other states. Well, we had thirteen states, and how many accepted the invitation? Nine. Well, that's not so bad. But how many showed up? Just five. Only twelve men. Now, this angered the men who showed up. It was like having no one show up at your birthday party. So Alexander Hamilton, decided that they needed a stronger union. At this Maryland Convention he proposed a new meeting, one that would fix the Articles of Confederation. Where would they meet? Philadelphia.

And what would they call this meeting?

The Constitutional Convention.

America would get one more chance to see if they could make this self-government idea work.

CHAPTER 7

▼

OUR NATION'S RULEBOOK: THE CONSTITUTION

Phil Haslett

Nothing Beats America's Rule Book

In order to avoid total chaos, the leaders of America wrote one of the world's most influential documents: the Constitution. However, there are parts that might be a little confusing for you. Hopefully this chapter will enlighten you and put you on the path to full understanding. It is my attempt to make the Constitution as simple as pie.

For starters, let's take a look at what led to the writing of the Constitution. Our founding fathers wrote the Constitution for many reasons. The biggest reason related to how the Articles of Confederation did not bring success to the country. Basically, the Articles gave way too much power to the states. The states couldn't be forced to pay any money, which can be quite a big problem when you owe 70 million dollars to Spain, France and the Netherlands. Other problems included: a lack of a judicial branch (the branch with all the judges, in case you didn't know), conflict between the states, and no clear method for enforcing laws.

Knowing that the colonies were in deep trouble, the nation's leading politicians held the Philadelphia Convention at Independence Hall in 1787. Their mission: make a replacement for the Articles of Confederation. The convention leader, George Washington, along with Benjamin Franklin and John Adams, spurred the convention into action. After many heated debates and numerous sleepless nights, the convention members signed the Constitution on September 17, 1787. But that was only the beginning. Once it was signed it still had to go through a long process of ratification, where America would have to wait to see if each individual state agreed to the rules.

The Constitution officially went into effect once New Hampshire signed it on June 21, 1788. However, the two states which were most important to the success of the young country signed the Constitution after the ratification. Virginia signed on June 25 and New York signed on July 26. Without the signatures of the delegates of these colonies, the Constitution would still be valid, yet much less powerful. These states were the wealthiest and the most powerful, for Virginia was the center of agricultural activity and New York was the center of industrial activity. To give an example of Virginia's influence on America in the 1700's, four of the first five Presidents of the US were Virginians (called the Virginia Dynasty).

And now for our feature presentation: The Constitution in plain-ole' English, for your reading and intellectual pleasure.

Preamble:

The Constitution was written to: make a better union, create fair courts, keep peace within America, give America independence, support a good army, and make America a cooler and more successful place than it used to be.

The Federal Government

Article	Branch	Common Name	Job	Workplace
I	Legislative	Congress	Makes and passes laws	Capitol Hill
II	Executive	President	Enforces laws	White House
III	Judicial	Supreme Court	Checks if laws are legal	Supreme Court

Article 1: Congress

Article 1, Section 1:

Congress can make laws through its two parts: the House of Representatives and the Senate.

Article 1, Section 2:

To be in the House of Representatives, the candidate must be 25 or older, have been a U.S. citizen for 7 or more years, and come from the state he or she is running for. Terms last for two years, and the number of Representatives per state is based on the amount of people. Every 30,000 people count for one Representative. This has since been changed, and now there are 435 Representatives and each state receives a proportionate amount. If they kept this same 30,000 to 1 ratio, the Capitol Building would need to seat 9,333 people. Our Founding Fathers didn't do too good of a job estimating the future size of the country.

At the time, slaves only counted for 3/5 of a person. This was taken away once slavery became illegal. Slavery was abolished in 1865 through the 13th Amendment.

Also, the House can bring impeachment charges on someone. Just what is this "impeachment"? Well, to the average Joe, it is accusing a member of political office of a crime. Not just any crimes, but treason or "high crimes and misdemeanors."

Two guys named Andrew Johnson and Bill Clinton will allow us to later discuss the concept of impeachment in a bit more detail.

Article 1, Section 3:

There are two Senators per state, regardless of the population, and their terms last six years. To run for a Senator, one must be 30 or older, a citizen for 9 years, and a permanent resident of the United States. The Vice President gets to be the President of the Senate, and only votes if he needs to break a tie (if 50 Senators say "yes" to something, and 50 Senators say "no" to something). The Senate can elect their own "President Pro Tempore", which is a fancy name for the Senate Majority leader. If the Vice President is not around, this lucky man or woman gets the privilege of running the Senate. And…because the Vice-President is pretty much never around, this President Pro Tempore pretty much runs the show.

The Senate also tries impeachments. This means that once the House of Representatives has brought impeachment charges, the Senate gets to be the jury. The most they can do to the impeached person is take him or her out of office. For instance, you may not have heard of him, but this president named Bill Clinton was impeached for not being totally honest when asked how well he knew Monica Lewinsky.

Article 1, Section 4:

States will determine where Senate and House elections are held, how the voting will occur (for instance, what the ballots look like), and when it will take place. Also, Congress has to meet at least once a year (this date is now January 3 of every year). This law really isn't of much concern anymore, considering that Congress meets many days out of the year.

Article 1, Section 5:

The Senate and House get to watch over their own elections, and make sure that no one is cheating (by failing to have the requirements, such as age or citizenship). Either of the two houses can kick out a member with a two thirds vote, so long as there is a good reason. Records of Congress must be made, and Congress can only meet at Capitol Hill, which is the building in D.C. that looks like a white block with a giant Hershey's kiss on top.

These laws were important in the beginning because people could lie about their age or citizenship. Also, they didn't want any meetings to be secret or held without the public's knowledge. Today, I pretty much doubt that someone would lie about their age or that Congress would decide to just randomly meet at the local KFC.

Article 1, Section 6

Though this might be a surprise to you, Senators and Representatives get paid for working! Can you believe it? Amazing. And to think I always thought they did it in their free time, out of the kindness of their heart. Also, if you are a Senator or Representative, you cannot hold any other government job at the same time.

Article 1, Section 7

Only the House of Representatives can propose a law that concerns revenue or taxes. In the beginning, the only congressmen people directly elected were Representatives. By only allowing the House to propose tax laws, the people could have say in how much money the government steals from them on April 15 of every year.

A majority vote in Congress can bring a bill to power. However, it must be approved by the President first. If he doesn't like it, he has ten days to "veto," or cancel the bill. If he just accidentally "forgets" about the bill and it stays on his desk past the ten days, it automatically becomes a law. If he does veto the bill, it goes back to Congress and they can override him with a 2/3 vote.

Article 1, Section 8

Section 8 concerns the powers of Congress. They can:

- Create taxes.

- Borrow money from US credit.

- Regulate business with the states and other nations.

- Have equal citizenship in all states.

- Have one currency. If you try to make counterfeits, you'll be in deep, deep trouble.

- Make roads.

- Promote science and arts.

- Issue patents (something that protects your invention so that nobody else may use it).

- Declare US Supreme Court as the most powerful court in all of the land.

- Defend US people and ships

- Take over property during war if US wins—what a useful idea!

- Raise and support army and navy.

- Make rules for the government.

- Have a National Guard.

- Pay for militia.

- Declare Federal property (for instance, state property would be a school or a playground. However, post offices and military bases count as Federal property.)

Last but not least, this section talks about the "ELASTIC CLAUSE". The elastic clause is extremely important, maybe even the most important legal wording ever written in the history of America. It says that Congress has the power to do anything necessary to make sure the other parts of the Constitution work. For example, think about feeding soldiers. No, it doesn't say in the Constitution, "Congress has the right to purchase groceries from the local supermarket and cook three yummy meals a day for all the soldiers." However, it does say that Congress has the right to support an army and it is "implied" that this means they can feed them.

Now, this has been a huge debate through the years. Who gets to define if something is "implied" or not? For a prime example, wait a bit and we'll talk about Thomas Jefferson and how he decided to buy a bit of land.

Article 1, Section 9

Okay, Section 8 told us what Congress can do. Now Section 9 states what Congress cannot do.

- The Writ of Habeas Corpus (don't be intimidated by the Latin) says that somebody must have a document explaining why someone is going to be arrested. In high-school terms, it's an arrest warrant.

- The Ex Post Facto law says that you cannot be charged for breaking a law that hadn't existed at the time of the action. For instance, let's say that I ate a spoonful of glue in 2002 (hey that rhymes). Well, if a law is passed in 2008 which clearly states that eating glue out of a spoon is not allowed, I can't be charged for breaking the law back in 2002. Yippee...I'm free.

- Goods traded between different states can't be taxed.

- Boats don't have to pay any tax or duty for going into the port of another state.

- Money can't be taken out of the national treasury without Congress' permission.

- Noble titles (such as highness, king, queen, etc.) cannot be given to people of Congress, only to people who play professional sports or sing on MTV.

Article 1, Section 10

Alright, so the Congress can and cannot do a whole bunch of things. But what can't state governments do? Section 10 prohibits them from:

• Making treaties.

• Taxing imports and exports.

• Declaring war or running their own militaries.

Article 2: The President

Article 2, Section 1

The President of the United States has all the power of the Executive Branch. He has a cabinet around him that helps him make tough decisions and do the research, but he's the guy that makes the final choice. He gets to work for four years and he has a vice-president that is elected with him, though the vice-president usually doesn't do anything except smile. Unless of course the President dies, and then the VP becomes very important.

Here's where it gets confusing. You don't elect the president. Regular old people don't elect the president. Just look at the results from the 2000 election.

2000 Election

Candidate	Popular Votes	Electoral Votes
Al Gore	50,996,116	267
George Bush	50,456,169	271

Who got more votes? Gore. Who's president of the United States right now? Bush. To figure out why, you have to go to the last column, "Electoral Votes."

Every state has a certain number of electors. It's all based on how big your state is. Everybody gets a minimum of three, one for each Senator, and one for population. Here are the electoral votes for the 2004 election.

2004 Electoral Vote Allotment

State	Population	Electoral Votes
California	33,871,648	55
New York	18,976,457	31
Indiana	6,080,485	11
Alabama	4,447,100	9
Wyoming	493,782	3

As you can see, California has a ton of electoral votes. You want to win the popular vote in California. Let's say for instance, Bob has 13,764,323 votes in California and Timmy has 13,764,322 votes. Even though Bob only wins by one vote, he gets ALL 55 votes for California. ALL of them. Now, you need ½ of 538 votes to win. They get the 538 votes by adding together the total number of Senators and members of the House of Representatives: 100+435+3 (Washington D.C)=538. If you zoned out through the mathematical explanation, that's okay! Basically, once you get 270 electoral votes, you win the election.

Now, these electors are actually people, and they then go to Washington D.C. and deliver their votes. They're supposed to deliver their votes according to whichever candidate won, but they are still humans and they can actually change the vote at the last minute if they want to. However, if ever they did that, they could pretty much bet that the whole political world would be less than happy. I'm not sure if this has ever happened before. Why don't you look it up for extra credit and let me know?

So that's how the president is elected. Here's what it takes to be elected. You have to be 35 years old, born in the United States, and a resident of the United States for 14 years. It also helps if you're tall. In the 20th century, the tallest of the two final candidates always won. Pretty scary.

Lastly, the President gets paid. Again, I know this is a surprise, but he does receive a salary. In fact, as of 1999, the President of the United States makes $400,000 a year. Granted he doesn't pay for too many meals and his landlord rarely collects rent, but still, a lousy second baseman for the New York Mets makes millions of dollars a year. Then again, which job is more important?

Article 2, Section 2

The President is in charge of the Armed Forces. That means he is more powerful than all the generals of the Army, Navy, Air Force, and Marines. He makes the decisions as to who does the attacking, when and where. However, he needs permission from Congress to declare war and he takes a TON of advice from the generals of these services.

Here's some other things he can do:

• Appoints judges, but the Senate approves

• Appoint ambassadors

• Appoint other public ministers

Article 2, Section 3

At least once a year, he needs to give a State of the Union address in which he tells Congress how the country is doing. If you've ever seen this speech, it's where the president talks and whenever he says something like, "And America is the best country of all time," everyone stands up and gives him a standing ovation. The current record is 743 standing ovations in 45 minutes (again...remember...75.4% of all statistics are made up).

He also has to agree to talk to Ambassadors from other countries. He needs to make sure laws are followed by the nation. If any state or person decides to not follow a law, he can enforce it. How does he enforce it, you ask? Well, if you're really bugging him, he can always call in the Armed Forces, put them at your doorstep and then ask again nicely if you'd like to follow the rules. Having a tank pointed at you is usually fairly persuasive.

Article 2, Section 4

Presidents, Vice Presidents and other public leaders can be impeached for "Treason, Bribery or other High Crimes and Misdemeanors." Clinton was impeached for lying under oath. Impeached doesn't always mean the guy is fired, it just means that he's publicly told that he's naughty.

Article 3: The Supreme Court

Article 3, Section 1

All final decisions go to the Supreme Court. Whatever they say goes. They are the bosses. If they think a law that Congress or one of the states passes is illegal, they have a right to overturn it. They're like your parents, but older. The qualification for being a Supreme Court Justice is you must have "good behavior," which disqualifies about 87% of the nation. You serve until you die or retire, which can be for a long time. This prevents them from being fired, or having Presidents simply get rid of them simply because they weren't going with the flow.

That's not to say Presidents haven't tried. Franklin Delano Roosevelt tried to solve the problem of the Supreme Court rejecting his ideas by simply adding a few more judges to help swing votes in his favor. Even the great Thomas Jefferson tried to axe Justice Samuel chase because he was saying mean things about the Republicans. Luckily, in both cases the Senate solved that problem and kept the president from getting to power greedy.

Current Supreme Court Justices

Justice	Began Term
William H. Rehnquist—Chief Justice	1972
John Paul Stevens	1975
Sandra Day O'Connor	1981
Antonin Scalia	1986
Anthony M. Kennedy	1988
David Hackett Souter	1990
Clarence Thomas	1991
Ruth Bader Ginsburg	1993
Stephen C. Breyer	1994

Article 3, Section 2

This section just lists every single little case that the courts will listen to. Basically, it's just about everything. However, sometimes courts can throw out cases if they think they're stupid. Watch Ally McBeal to see what I mean. Man, that show comes up with some dumb cases, and luckily judges will sometimes throw them out.

It also says that trials need to be done wherever the crime was committed. If you rob a bank in Florida, you have to be tried in Florida. They can't take you to another part of the country. This can work in your favor if everyone in the town you rob from is your buddy. The jury might just let you go free.

Article 3, Section 3

Treason means that you are trying to do something to hurt the United States of America. Either you can actively hurt America or you can help out America's enemies. To be convicted of treason, two people have to witness you doing the treasonable act. So, feel free to go into your bathroom and repeat a thousand times, "I'm going to burn down the White House. I'm going to burn down the White House. I'm going to…" As long as your mirror can't talk, and there's not someone hiding in one of the stalls, you're in good shape.

Article 4: Stuff About States

Hang in there. We're almost done. Section 1 and 2 say that even though all the states are independent, we're still one country. You have to follow the laws in each state. Just because you can go 100 miles per hour in Montana doesn't mean you can speed in California. Also, if you commit a crime in Georgia, you can't escape to Wisconsin and hope to evade being punished. However, if you make it to Canada, that's a whole different story. Also, contracts you entered into in one state are valid in other states. You don't have to get married all over again every time you go to a new state, and you don't have to take a new test for your driver's license just because you left Oregon for Idaho.

Section 3 talked about how new states would be added. Each new state automatically receives all the rights and privileges of the other states. No one is more powerful than another, and no one can make another state a colony. For example, even though Texas and California think they own America, in reality they are just as important as Wyoming.

Section 4 says that all states have to have a Republican form of government. Utah can't go and decide to have a king, and Vermont can't decide to try out communism for a few years. Nope. They all have to be democracies. Subsequently, the federal government will protect all states. Japan found this out in a hurry during World War II. You attack Hawaii, you mess with the USA.

Article 5: In Case We Left Something Out

The creators of the Constitution knew they hadn't thought of everything so they allowed for amendments to be made. Congress could propose a new amendment if 2/3 of Congress approve. Then the amendment gets sent out to all the states. The states then hold meetings and decide if they are in favor of or opposed to the amendment. If ¾ of the states agree to the amendment, it gets passed. If not, it dies. As of the year 2000, there were 27 amendments added on, with the first ten being called the Bill of Rights. This is a list of basic human rights given to all citizens.

Article 6: You All Have to Follow the Rules

The Constitution is the supreme law of the land. If you don't like it, tough. This is it. In fact, if you want to hold an official office, you have to take an oath saying you'll support the Constitution. If you don't say that, you can't be an elected leader.

Article 7: How Do We Get This Thing Approved?

Once nine states approved the Constitution, it became official. In some states, it wasn't difficult to get the vote to pass. In others, there was a bitter dispute. Some were afraid it made the government too powerful, others thought it didn't go far enough. The two most important states were Virginia and New York. Even though the Constitution was officially legal after New Hampshire's approval, if the Constitution wanted any substance, it needed the support of the two most powerful states. Finally, after the *Federalist Papers* (a Federalist newsletter) circulated, stating all the benefits of the Constitution, it was passed in both states, but by a narrow margin.

Ratification of United States Constitution

State	Ratification Date	Vote
Delaware	1787	30-0
Pennsylvania	1787	46-23
New Jersey	1787	36-0
Georgia	1788	26-0
Connecticut	1788	128-40
Massachusetts	1788	187-168
Maryland	1788	63-11
South Carolina	1788	149-73
New Hampshire	1788	57-47
Virginia	1788	89-79
New York	1788	30-27
North Carolina	1789	194-77
Rhode Island	1790	34-32

And with that, it became law. Finally those pesky Rhode Islanders agreed to the Constitution making it a perfect baker's dozen (13) in favor. However, the story of the Constitution wasn't over just yet.

The Amendments

I'd thought about giving a lengthy description of each amendment, the issues that caused its creation, and its effect on society as a whole. Then I thought about the second option. Just give you a short, basic version in the form of a chart. It was a tough call, but this chapter's getting long, so here they are:

Amendments to the Constitution

Amend-ment	Ratified	Super Brief Definition
1	1791	Freedom of speech, religion, press, and you can have meetings
2	1791	You can have a gun
3	1791	Soldiers can't stay in your house
4	1791	Can't search people or property without a warrant
5	1791	No double jeopardy, don't have to be witness against self
6	1791	Fast trial in front of person who accused you
7	1791	You're allowed a jury of your peers depending on cost of lawsuit
8	1791	Reasonable bail and no cruel and unusual punishment
9	1791	People have rights not mentioned here
10	1791	If a state or federal government doesn't' have right, people have it
11	1795	People can't sue states they don't live in
12	1804	Vote for Vice-President and President on two different ballots
13	1865	Freed the slaves
14	1868	Gave slaves citizenship
15	1870	Gave slaves right to vote
16	1913	Congress can collect income tax
17	1913	People elect senators directly
18	1919	Can't make, sell, or transport alcohol
19	1920	Women can vote

Amendments to the Constitution (Continued)

20	1933	President takes office on January 20, not March 4—less Lame Duck
21	1933	Prohibition is repealed—alcohol is legal again
22	1951	Only can be president for two terms
23	1961	People living in Washington D.C. can vote for President
24	1964	No poll tax to vote
25	1967	If the President is sick, VP takes over
26	1971	You can vote when you're 18
27	1992	Can't raise Senate and Representatives salaries until after election

CHAPTER 8

▼

THIS TIME WE'LL GET
IT RIGHT:
THE FIRST DECADE

Why Isn't He on the Dollar Bill?

Who's the first president of the United States?

George Washington?

Wrong.

Think about it. When did America declare independence? 1776. Washington is elected president in 1789. Now, using your incredible subtraction skills, this means that we're missing about 14 years in American history. Who was running the show?

As we discussed earlier, this period of time America ran under the Articles of Confederation, not exactly the best country's rule book ever invented. The colonies weren't exactly united, and things didn't run too smoothly. Because of this confusion, the presidents of this time are usually not mentioned, and America prefers to count its history starting from George Washington.

However, if you want to know who was the first president after Independence, the correct answer is John Hanson. The Articles of Confederation was our first constitution, and it said that there would be a President of the Congress that would serve a one year term. Therefore, when Hanson was elected in 1781, he became the first president of the United States. Washington was the ninth.

We give this knowledge to you for the sole purpose of winning bets with your friends and family. Feel free to try it. Walk up to someone close to you and dare them, "I'll bet you five dollars you don't know the first president of the United States."

Of course, your buddy will accept the bet. He'll say George Washington. And you'll collect your winnings.

Presidents Under the Articles of Confederation

First Presidents	Years of Office
John Hanson	1781-1782
Elias Boudinot	1782-1783
Thomas Mifflin	1783-1784
Richard Henry Lee	1784-1785
Nathaniel Gorham	1785-1786
Arthur St. Clair	1786-1787
Cyrus Griffin	1787-1788

Call Me Mr. Cherry Tree

Now, the whole John Hanson business is fascinating, but the truth is he really couldn't do too much because the Articles of Confederation made the presidential position extremely weak.

George Washington was the first president with any real power. He set the precedent for every president that followed. Washington found the perfect middle ground. Everything he did was watched by the world. It is an amazingly difficult job to be the first at anything, but Washington was the man for the challenge. He was the true father of our country.

Not only does his name now shine over one state, a capital city, nine colleges, 33 counties, and seven mountains, his legacy fills our federal government in countless ways.

When Washington took his oath of office on April 30, 1789 on the portico of Federal Hall, located on Wall Street, New York, America looked to him for guidance. He was the obvious choice to be America's "first" president. He was unanimously chosen by the electors and he gave a power and honor to the role of president that was lacking under the Articles of Confederation.

He wasn't the smartest man of his time. Or the best looking. Or the best political thinker. Or even the best speaker. But he was the perfect leader. With his victories on the battlefield and his unquestioned aura of authority, Washington showed that the President of the United States is not always the most talented man in America, but he has to be a leader.

When George Washington finally retired to his home at Mount Vernon, he was already a national icon. Since that time, his legend has grown to the point that he now is looked at as almost superhuman. This perception has been helped by stories and myths that focused on his strength of character and prowess on the battlefield. One such fable, the one where he tells his father he cut down a tree, has over the years become inseparable with the truth.

Legend of the Cherry Tree

"When George," said she, "was about six years old, he was made the wealthy master of a *hatchet!* of which, like most little boys, he was immoderately fond, and was constantly going about chopping every thing that came in his way. One day, in the garden, where he often amused himself hacking his mother's pea-sticks, he unluckily tried the edge of his hatchet on the body of a beautiful young English cherry-tree, which he barked so terribly, that I don't believe the tree ever got the better of it. The next morning the old gentleman finding out what had befallen his tree, which, by the by, was a great favourite, came into the house, and with much warmth asked for the mischievous author, declaring at the same time, that he would not have taken five guineas for his tree. Nobody could tell him any thing about it. Presently George and his hatchet made their appearance. *George,* said his father, *do you know who killed that beautiful little cherry-tree yonder in the garden?* This was a *tough question*; and George staggered under it for a moment; but quickly recovered himself: and looking at his father, with the sweet face of youth brightened with the inexpressible charm of all-conquering truth, he bravely cried out, *"I can't tell a lie, Pa; you know I can't tell a lie. I did cut it with my hatchet."—Run to my arms, you dearest boy,* cried his father in transports, *run to my arms; glad am I, George, that you killed my tree; for you have paid me for*

> *it a thousand fold. Such an act of heroism in my son, is more worth than a thousand trees, though blossomed with silver, and their fruits of purest gold.*
>
> From *The Life of Washington*, by Mason Locke Weems, 1809

Getting Started

Once in office, Washington immediately got to work. Though not outlined in the Constitution, Washington set the precedent that the president would surround himself with great minds that would specialize in particular areas and report to him on both domestic and foreign issues. This group of men became known as the president's Cabinet, and most of the leaders of each Department were addressed as Secretary—not the kind of secretary that takes notes and tells people who call that you are busy, but the kind of secretary that runs the show.

Originally, his cabinet was made up of five men—Secretary of State Thomas Jefferson, Secretary of War Henry Knox, Secretary of Treasury Alexander Hamilton, Attorney General Edmund Randolph and Postmaster General Benjamin Franklin. Basically, these guys dealt with foreign affairs, war, money, law, and the mail respectively. You might wonder why the head mailman would have a position equal to the leader of the entire military, but at the time the mail was the only form of communication aside from yelling out your window, so the mail was fairly important.

George Washington also had to sort out how he would be addressed. Some people were willing to call him king. Others brought up ideas like "His Mightiness," "His Excellency," "His Highness," or even "His Elected Highness." Washington thought all these were pretty silly so he went by the pretty ordinary, "Mr. President." This is another trait that made Washington so unique. He was humble. Whereas other revolutionaries who took power from kings wanted to merely become supreme rulers themselves (think short, little dude with hand in his jacket over in a place known for Freedom Fries), Washington had no desire to be an absolute ruler. A few years later he would shock the world, when he stepped down as president after two terms and retired to his home.

Once he had finished completing two very important tasks—surrounding himself with smart people and figuring out his name—he then needed to accomplish a task a bit more difficult—prove to his citizens and the world that America was a country that could survive in an orderly, well-governed fashion. Basically, he needed to prove that democracy could work in the modern world.

His first step would be defining the role of the executive branch. The Constitution said that Congress made laws, but was that really going to be the case? One time Washington went to Congress to hear the Senators debate the pros and cons of a treaty. While he was there, all the Senators pretty much just shut up and refused to talk openly in front of their awesome leader. Imagine what would happen if your parents went on dates with you. How comfortable would you feel talking to little Miss Mary Jane, when your Dad was across the table listening to every word?

Washington got the hint, and he stopped going to Congress meetings. This gave the executive and legislative branches a chance to be truly separate. He then organized the legal system by appointing judges through the Judiciary Act of 1789, set up the Supreme Court system, and pushed through the Bill of Rights.

However, the power of the executive branch had yet to be truly tested. How would the president enforce laws broken by people or states? Did he really have any power, or would the states just fall back into the disorder common during the era of the Articles of Confederation? He was finally tested with some guys who had a problem with whiskey.

Alexander Hamilton had a great idea to make some extra money for the government. Tax whiskey. However, whiskey makers didn't share his enthusiasm for the idea and started rebelling by abusing the tax collectors with mature little antics like putting tar on their bodies and then clothing them with feathers. By the way, whatever happened to good old tarring and feathering? These days, people just don't seem to have as much fun humiliating others in public.

Washington had a problem. What was he going to do about the rebellion? A few years before, during Shay's Rebellion, the federal government did too little, too late, and it proved that the government was totally weak. Would this executive department also be powerless to control its population?

Not even close. Washington put on his military uniform and took 12,000 troops into Pennsylvania to bring these rowdy men under control. Considering there were only a few hundred men involved in the rebellion, Washington made his point. No one better dare mess with the federal government. Like the cute little bunny rabbit that thinks twice about attacking a pack of hungry wolves, the Whiskey Rebels surrendered and faced the consequences. Washington showed compassion and eventually let all of the men go free.

While Washington was improving the stature of the federal government, he also had to deal with Europe, where France and England were starting to feel frisky again. France wanted to take over Europe and of course England wasn't exactly thrilled about the idea. France's ambassador, Citizen Genet, came over to

America asking for help. Washington wanted to stay neutral and give America a chance to survive on its own. Citizen Genet had a bit of difficulty understanding Washington's position and decided to go all over the east coast trying to convince Americans to help out the French. Nothing annoys a country more than an ambassador ignoring the President, so they told Genet to hop on a boat and head back to France.

But this conflict between France and Britain would carry into the next century. The British started harassing American boats, taking their supplies, and even forcing the sailors into joining the British forces against France, otherwise known as impressment. Washington was pretty powerless to fight back because America's navy wasn't exactly intimidating. Washington began to solve this problem by commissioning the building of a strong navy that would play a strong role in the coming decades.

When his term finally ended, Washington had succeeded in building America. Throughout his entire presidency, he clearly realized his role. "I walk on untrodden ground. There is scarcely any part of my conduct which may not hereafter be drawn into precedent." He took this reality through until the end, when he stepped down after two terms, thus ensuring that future presidents (excluding Roosevelt and his four terms) would likewise only seek a maximum of two terms in office.

The Feisty Man from Boston

Replacing Washington would be difficult; however, the task went to John Adams, one of the men most responsible for the Revolution and the creation of America. Boston was the center of conflict during the Revolution, and Adams had his hand in every aspect of the revolting colonies. He had been in politics all his life, and the presidency seemed like the natural next step.

From his election, it was obvious Adams' presidency would be difficult. He ran against Thomas Jefferson who finished just a few electoral votes behind. Adams and Jefferson respected each other, but they had different views of how the government should be run. Adams was a Federalist. Jefferson was a Democratic-Republican. This difference caused a problem because according to the Constitution, whoever finished second became the Vice-President. This was essentially like being forced to be best friends with the guy that just stole your girlfriend. It was a bit tense.

Differences in First Political Parties

Democratic-Republicans	Federalists
• Philosophies:	• Philosophies:
• Spread power	• Concentrate power with elite few
• Feared tyranny	• Feared anarchy
• Championed liberty	• Championed order
• Held hope for human spirit	• Held humans as inherently flawed
• Believed with education, humans could be trusted	• Believed humans make poor choices
• Supported agriculture	• Supported shipping and manufacture
• American Vision:	• American Vision:
• Farming community	• Success founded on commerce and wealth
• Mild laws	• Strict laws
• Equal opportunity	• Society of rich and poor based on English model
• Asylum for oppressed	• Make America a new Europe
• Preserve simplicity and equality	• Advance into new technological age

However, Adams did win and he dealt with a few of the problems left behind from Washington's presidency. The British and French were still annoying American boats, and people out in Pennsylvania started complaining about taxes again. Adams' reactions to these issues would make him a temporary hero, but eventually destroyed his political party.

The ABCs of XYZ

Here's where things get a bit confusing so follow me.

America had to deal with both Britain and France capturing its ships. America was losing between 200 and 400 ships a year, and American businessmen were not pleased about it. With the British, Washington had tried to solve the problem by having John Jay work out a treaty. Named after himself, Jay's Treaty helped ease tension between Britain and France.

Of course, France didn't like this treaty, because it looked like America and Britain were getting too chummy. What to do? What to do? The French stepped up their efforts to annoy the Americans by capturing 316 ships in just one year.

America immediately sent out Charles Pinckney to Paris to try to work out a treaty between France and America. However, there would be no Pinckney's Treaty, because those darn French didn't want anything to do with America's ambassador, and he was forced to head for the Netherlands.

America was totally insulted that France wouldn't even talk to Pinckney, let alone that he had to spend the winter in the Netherlands. No offense to the Netherlands intended. Adams then tried again. This time he sent Pinckney with two other guys, John Marshall and Elbridge Gerry to France to try to work things out. They were met by a Frenchman named Talleyrand and three mysterious agents. I could tell you their names, but you already are getting confused. Anyway, let's just call these mystery guys "Secret Agents X, Y, and Z." Anyway, these agents said they'd sign a treaty if America paid a $250,000 bribe, promised to give a huge loan to France, and had Adams publicly apology.

I'm not sure if France failed the lesson on making a bargain, but this idea didn't go over too well. The three Americans were insulted by Monsieurs X, Y, and Z, and they returned to America to tell everyone how naughty those French can be. Adams won a lot of points from Americans for being anti-French, but eventually he softened his stance and sent another guy over there to work out a treaty.

But the Federalists were angry.

That Annoying Little First Amendment

Adams' next step was the beginning of the end. Backed by his Federalist allies, Adams signed off on the Alien and Sedition Acts. These acts were an attempt to strengthen the Federalist Party, by punishing anyone who might oppose them.

The Alien Acts sought to keep Federalist control of politics by keeping immigrants out of America. Immigrants liked that wacky little idea called equality, and were more apt to favor the Democratic-Republicans. Very few poor, starving, desperate immigrants hopped off the boat and said, "Hey, do you guys have a political party that just favors rich people and thinks that the rest of us are a bunch of ignorant hoodlums?" No, most went with the party of Jefferson. The Federalists attempted to control this rise in their enemy's numbers by simply kicking out or not allowing in those immigrants that would eventually favor Democratic-Republicans.

But it didn't just end there. They also wanted to silence criticism. The Federalists believed that people in politics should not be made fun of, and anyone who insulted them should be punished severely, or even kicked out of the country. Now try to imagine a country where you couldn't make fun of your political leaders? That's almost not fair. If we can't make fun of our leaders, what are Jay Leno and David Letterman going to talk about for the first fifteen minutes of their shows?

Now the states had a problem. When many Americans thought of the whole democracy idea, they didn't exactly envision a place where you can get kicked out of the country for being an immigrant or thrown in jail for making jokes. Thomas Jefferson and James Madison rebelled by secretly writing the Kentucky and Virginia Resolutions, which declared that states wouldn't have to follow laws they thought were illegal.

A few things came of these Acts and the subsequent resolutions. First, the battle lines had been drawn. For the next seventy years, states and the federal government would fight over who truly had the power in American politics. Second, the Federalist Party was on the path to death. In the next election, Americans chose Thomas Jefferson, the man who wanted to take government out of the hands of just a few rich guys and spread the power around.

▼

CHAPTER 9

A New Path:
Thomas Jefferson

Elise Nilsson
Andrea Sullivan

The Man, The Myth, The Legend

Unlike Millard Fillmore or Warren Harding, most people have heard of Thomas Jefferson. There's a reason for that. His presidency was one of the most successful in American history. He also changed the course of American politics by being a different kind of president. Washington and Adams had been stuffy aristocrats who modeled themselves after the fancy-shmancy nobles of England.

Jefferson was different. Nicknamed "red fox," he was not only cool, calm, and collected, but he was a pretty good-looking man at 6 feet tall with a thin, sharp body and light colored hair. Most men of his time wore a wig, but he proudly flaunted his own light hair, which was "tinged with red". He was a casual dresser and was often seen wearing sloppy clothing. But don't be mistaken, although he wasn't a snappy dresser, he still enjoyed a life of Virginian luxury. Early on, he developed a passion for elegant French cooking. Because of his obsession with French wine, his wine bill once totaled $2800 in one year! Jefferson was what we today would call a jack of all trades, a Renaissance man. He was pretty well-rounded. He was a philosopher, scientist, inventor, avid reader, and a star-gazer. He was fluent in many languages such as French, Italian, Spanish, Latin, and English, which allowed him to communicate with the well-known thinkers of the world, a definite plus when you're Secretary of State.

Jefferson did not like public appearances, so he avoided crowds, but when needed, he was a charming conversationalist. Supposedly, he did not speak to Congress in person because he did not want to seem like a king addressing Parliament. This was probably just an excuse to avoid these public appearances that he disliked so much. Regardless of his speaking abilities, he was a fabulous architect and designed his own home that he named Monticello (which means "little mountain" in Italian). He also designed and started the University of Virginia. Jefferson said he did not support slavery, but ironically, along with a grand house, he owned a large plantation with 150 slaves. One of which, Sally Hemmings, he got to know pretty well. He shared his home with his wife Martha Wayles Skelton. Unfortunately, Martha died 10 years after their marriage, and Jefferson was naturally devastated. It has been said that he actively entered public life after her death, to ease his overwhelming sorrow.

On March 4, 1801, he became the first President to be sworn in at the new capitol. Washington D.C. was located by the Potomac River, between his home state and Maryland. At the time, the "presidential palace" had not yet received the common name we use today. It was given the name White House only after the British torched it during the War of 1812. The scorch marks that the British caused were painted over with white paint, hence the name.

Back to Jefferson. He was admired by many types of people because of his strong belief in equal rights to all men of every political or religious opinion. He believed in friendship with all nations but no alliances, and the rights of states. Also, he supported agriculture and commerce, as well as freedom of speech, press, and elections. He wished to reduce the army and navy and use public revenue to pay of public debt. The majority of these traits were not shared by his predecessors, and definitely not shared by his political enemies, the Federalists.

Let's Get to Work

Jefferson called his election the "Revolution of 1800" as he thought it had turned the country away from militarism and monarchy. This was probably an exaggeration on his part, in an effort to make his election sound like a big deal. But was it really a revolution? Were Washington and Adams really kings? On top of that, he barely won the election. The electoral votes were 73 to 65, in his favor. Not exactly a revolution.

One of the first things Jefferson did as a President was to make sure that the Alien and Sedition Acts were not renewed. This wasn't a huge surprise, considering the whole purpose of the act was to shut up Jefferson's party and make his Democratic-Republicans less powerful. Instead, a new Naturalization Act was passed, bringing back the five year waiting period for those who sought citizenship. Jefferson believed America should welcome the immigrants, because they would in turn become farmers and populate this great land of ours. And Jefferson just loved farmers.

From the start, Jefferson had international problems. On the north coast of Africa, or the Barbary Coast, annoying little pirates were seizing American ships in the Mediterranean Sea. To avoid a war, European countries had gotten into the habit of simply paying a tribute to these Barbary pirates. For this very reason, America gave offerings worth of $2 million from 1790 to 1800.

Jefferson protested. It wasn't nice, and he wasn't going to stand for America being bullied. Washington and Adams would have loved to have been as direct as Jefferson, but they lacked something, a navy. However, Washington was a smart man and during his office started the nation building a ton of ships. By 1800, America actually had the semblance of a navy. Since Jefferson had these fun toys, he decided to send them out to Africa to try to put an end to the situation through a bit more forceful means. Unfortunately, sending the navy was extremely costly and forced Congress to set a 2.5% tax on imports. In the end the taxing was worth it because peace was finally reached in January 1805 and the bribes ended.

I Won't Give You My Wallet, But Do You Want to Have My House?

The next issue Jefferson had to deal with was the West. More people were settling between the Appalachian Mountains and the Mississippi River, and the rivers were used to transport crops. The rivers ran into the Mississippi River, which was also known as the "father of waters." They flowed down to the Gulf of Mexico, and out to the ocean, leading to the rest of the world. Because of this, the Mississippi River was extremely important and if anyone took control of the entrance, westerners would be shut off, and trade would be ruined.

Jefferson understood this and worried over how to keep this highway open to the world. He wished all people would move west and start new farms, but this would not likely happen without the control of the key gateway. Great! That meant he would have to deal with Spain, because they controlled land on both sides of the mouth of the river. However, the Spanish issue quickly changed because of a short little man you've all heard of, Napoleon Bonaparte. He had plans on expanding the French Empire once again into America. The land west of the river that *used* to be French property was named Louisiana after King Louis XIV. However, the Spanish now controlled this land because of a compromise during the wars of the 18th century.

Using his persuasion skills, Napoleon got Louisiana back from Spain through the Treaty of San Ildefonso, which involved some land for a Duke in exchange for half a continent.

It was one thing to have the land ruled by those weak Spaniards, but to have the powerful Napoleon in control of the region worried the Americans. These French smarty pants really knew how to make the most out of their control of New Orleans. They used the city as a tollgate, and extracted whatever price they wanted from the Americans, making it tough for them to pass through to the open seas. Jefferson got extremely frustrated over their tactics and sent James Monroe and Robert Livingston to France to have a little chit-chat. He told Livingston and Monroe to buy the mouth of the Mississippi River. He said if they did not succeed, then they would have to do whatever they could to make it possible for Americans to pass the river. Congress sent them off with $2 million but said that they could pay up to $10 million if needed.

While all this was going on, France was having some problems with a Caribbean island called Haiti. Back then it was called the West Indies, not the Caribbean. Before Napoleon could make his new French empire he had to take over Haiti, because of the large amount of money he would get from controlling this little sugar land. Also, he needed the island as a base to control any possible empire in the Americas. But too bad! The 500,000 slaves in Haiti revolted and killed the white people during the French Revolution. Soon, slavery was abolished and this genius named Pierre Dominique Toussaint L'Ouverture was appointed as commander in chief of the armies on Haiti. This, of course, ticked off Napoleon, who wanted to rule the island himself!

Not one to lose easily, Napoleon sent a bunch of troops to the island in hopes of defeating this L'Ouverture fellow. Unfortunately, by 1802, Napoleon had not re-conquered Haiti, and the war still went on with hundreds of his troops dieing from disease and warfare. What was Napoleon going to do now? Once he realized his dream of an expansive empire was not possible, he shifted gears, and just abandon his plans for an empire in America.

Napoleon decided to sell Louisiana in another effort to get money and rid France of the burden of caring for a foreign colony. This was the set-up to the meeting between Livingston, Monroe and the French dignitaries. When they asked if the mouth of the New Orleans was up for sale, the French answered with an emphatic, "No!"

Monroe and Livingston thought they were in a bind until France countered with, "How would you like to just go ahead and buy the whole darn chunk for the nice round sum of $15 million?"

They didn't know if Jefferson would approve, because he had given no permission for such a purchase, nor had they been granted that sum of money with which to bargain. Remember, they were just supposed to buy the mouth of a river, not half a continent. However, common sense told them that when someone offers to double the size of your land for a mere four cents an acre, you better accept. They couldn't risk Napoleon changing his mind in the time it would take to get the message back and forth across the ocean. So, they bought the Louisiana Territory.

Back in America, the purchase was received with mixed feelings. Many saw the land as "worthless wilderness." The entire purchase was a great test of Jefferson's political skills since he had always been a firm believer in a strict view of the Constitution, yet nowhere in the Constitution was there anything about the President's power to buy land.

Regardless of the complaints, the purchase was accepted by Congress in October 1803. This wise decision made it possible for Americans to move even further west, doubling the size of the nation. From this land, eventually, thirteen new states were added, and America became a transcontinental nation, from sea to shining sea. One of the few countries able to claim that distinction.

Hey Guys, Are You Interested in Doing Some Sightseeing?

The addition of western land made Jefferson and many others curious and eager to learn more about the land beyond the Mississippi River. For this reason, Congress gave Meriwether Lewis and William Clarke $2500 and sent them on an adventure into the uncharted territory. They were to look for a water route to the Pacific Ocean and study Indian tribes as well as rocks, plants, and animals. Jefferson appointed Lewis as the leader of the expedition, and Clarke as the Lieutenant. With forty men accompanying them they headed out into the wild. They ended up spending the winter at Fort Mandan in North Dakota, at the Mandan-Hidatsa villages on the Missouri River. Because the Indians living there were so kind, they made up their mind to stay for the winter. William made a fascinating entry on November 3 that same winter. Brace yourself! It said…"We commence building our cabins." Exciting news.

They then met Sacajawea, a Shoshone Indian, who, with her brilliant guiding abilities, helped them cross the Great Divide and reach the Pacific Ocean. In a historic moment, William Clarke took out his gargantuan knife and carved "William Clarke, Dec 3rd 1805 by land from the United States in 1804 and 1805," into a tall yellow pine tree. This momentous occasion signified the U.S. ownership of the Oregon region.

Western Migration

Lewis and Clarke's exploration of the Louisiana Territory opened up decades of Western migration.

Somebody Take This Guy's Measurements for a Strait Jacket

Because of the Louis and Clarke expedition, Jefferson increased his popularity with the Anti-Federalists. Economic fears of western settlers were put at ease. With the Louisiana Purchase, there then was a seemingly endless supply of land. Federalists, on the other hand, feared that settlers of the new land would support Jefferson, thus draining the power from the East. Timothy Pickering of Massachusetts and his New England Federalist followers went so far as to threaten breaking up the union and setting up a "Northern Confederation." This plot to secede and create a new nation needed a leader. Aaron Burr, a pretty smart guy (admitted to Princeton University when he was a wee lad of thirteen) was promised the presidency of this new confederacy if he just accomplished one simple task.

All Aaron Burr had to do was win the governorship of New York, and then grant its allegiance to this new outlaw nation. Unfortunately, another man named Alexander Hamilton turned out to be the thorn in Burr's side (get it thorn=burr). Hamilton went around town criticizing Burr and when Burr eventually lost the election for governor, he blamed his poor showing on Hamilton and challenged him to a duel. Hamilton never planned on firing a shot, and was subsequently killed by Burr. From there Burr's life approached the absurd as he headed down South and tried to convince Spain and England to help him break apart the Louisiana Territory, and form yet another country. This ridiculous plan was foiled and Burr was later tried for treason. Nice try Aaron. He finally decided to stop trying to create a new country.

This Is How We Are Going to Start Doing Things Around Here

During his first term, Jefferson tried to please Federalists by being moderate in his approach to various problems. For instance, by attacking the Barbary pirates, he had helped the New England merchants. Apparently, this wasn't enough to satisfy the Federalists. After the Federalists lost the Presidency in the election of 1800, they tried to keep control of federal courts and as many offices as possible. In 1801, Adams passed the Judiciary Act which increased the number of judges and added minor judicial offices. John Adams meant to bring as many Federalists into these positions as possible before Jefferson was inaugurated. Remember, judges are judges for life, so if he could fill the seats with Federalists, the Federalists would have a say in government for years to come. Subsequently, Adams appointed a ton of Federalists for these new positions the night before he was going to leave, March 4th. This event came to be called the appointment of "the midnight judges."

But Jefferson wasn't going to put up with this silliness, so he ignored the appointments and repealed the Judiciary Act. He thought he would fix the problem by just not delivering the appointment notices that were sitting on his desk the next morning. William Marbury was a bit upset, because he kept waiting for his job offer to be delivered. But it never came. What happened next forever defined the power of the Supreme Court.

The Chief Justice of the Supreme Court was Jefferson's cousin John Marshall, a guy who actually acted and dressed a lot like Jefferson. Before Marshall's appointment it did not seem like the Supreme Court would be important in shaping the nation, but this whole "midnight judges" issue would change that prediction. William Marbury asked the Supreme Court for a writ that commanded James Madison to bring him his commission. When the case came before him, John Marshall used this case to declare key powers of the Supreme Court. He said Marbury deserved the commission, but declared that irrelevant because one section of the Judiciary Act of 1789 was unconstitutional. No where in the Constitution did it say anything about the Supreme Court issuing writs in cases like Marbury's. Basically, because it wasn't in the Constitution that they had to deal with annoying things like writs, the Judiciary Act was unconstitutional. The Supreme Court shot down the case. This started a process known as "judicial review," a precedent that allowed the Supreme Court to determine if a law was constitutional.

Jefferson and Republicans were afraid of the power of judges. Seeing as most of them had Federalist tendencies, because Washington and Adams appointed them, Jefferson believed the judges were a handicap to his policies. One of the most important trials of that time period was the dramatic one of Samuel Chase in 1805. For his anti-Republican comments, he was tried for impeachment. The trial was presided over by Vice-President Aaron Burr (yes…the guy that would later try to form a new country). Ultimately, the Senate decided that Chase's behavior did not deserve impeachment. If he had been convicted, the government would not be what it is today and every political party would be tempted to use the impeachment process to get rid of any politician who challenged their views.

Don't These Guys Ever Get Along?

In the spring of 1803, a war between France and England was renewed, and they attempted to damage each other by shutting off trade with other countries. The British issued "Orders in Council" which forbade neutral ships to trade with ports under Napoleon's control. The French, on the other hand, issued "imperial decrees" authorizing French seizure of all ships trading with British Isles or allowing British cruisers to search them. "Orders of Council" were more damaging to America because the British controlled the seas. Yet, both were damaging as they lost cargoes and ships. American businesses were in danger.

America was having another problem with former British sailors. The American merchant marines were growing at such a fast rate that 4200 more sailors were hired in 1805 alone. The sailors' wages increased, leading to British sailors leaving jolly old England for America. This caused even more problems for America! The American ship *Chesapeake* was sent to the Mediterranean, but the British messed with it by letting their warship Leopard overtake her. Remember all those Brits who ditched the British navy for the American? Well, the British were not too happy about losing their sailors, so they demanded to search the *Chesapeake* to find out if any of these deserters were hiding on the ship. The *Chesapeake* captain refused, so the British simply did not have any other option but to kill 3 men and wound 18. Uh…oh. American ship sunk! American ship sunk! Could be a catalyst for war.

In another attempt to get soldiers back, the British started the policy of impressments, where they basically stole any sailors that look like they were once British and forced them to join the British military. Jefferson did not want a war, even though many hawks in Congress were begging for it. Instead, he ordered James Monroe in London to ask the British for an apology for what they did to the *Chesapeake*, and put an end to impressments. The British smirked and refused to put an end to impressments, but they did apologize. Aww, wasn't that sweet of them? The British would not yield.

On December 17, 1807, Jefferson asked Congress for an Embargo Act, which would bring an end to trade with all European nations in an attempt to pressure France and England to stop being mean to American sailors and ships. What was he thinking? Cut off all trade with Europe? How would merchants make money? This was definitely not the smartest idea Jefferson ever created, as foreign trade shrank to one third of its value from the previous year.

The following year, 1808, was an election year and Jefferson wanted James Madison to take over. Madison lost all New England states except Vermont, but the south and west saved him, enabling him to defeat Pinckney by 122/47 electoral votes. Three days before Jefferson left Congress on March 1st 1809, the Embargo Act was repealed, and replaced with the Non-Intercourse Act, which prohibited trade solely with England and France, instead of all of Europe. America promised to start trade again, but only after the unfair treatment stopped.

Despite the failure of the Embargo Act, Jefferson was proud of his hard work and accomplishments during his presidency, and as he walked out of the White House, he could feel confident knowing he left America a better place than when he entered the Presidency eight years before.

▼

WHY DID WE
FIGHT AGAIN?
THE WAR OF 1812

Aaron Rubin

What Were These Guys Thinking?

Back when President Thomas Jefferson was in office, Great Britain and France (under Napoleon) were mauling at each other once again. The whole world must have thought that the British and French got some sort of bizarre joy from fighting each other. Anyways, that is beside the point. France and England were hating each other once again as well as stealing American seamen, ships, and supplies. The British were even doing this naughty thing called impressments. Even though this sounds like some sort of cruel Medieval torture, it actually had to do with the British boarding American ships and forcing the sailors into military service for Britain. Because of these nagging naval issues, in 1807 Jefferson passed the Embargo Act. He figured the one way to stop the French and British from stealing American stuff on the high seas was to forbid trade with everyone. Yeah! That'll show them.

Economically speaking, this didn't make a lot of sense. Imagine if McDonald's one day said, "We don't like the fact that you guys are buying food at Burger King, so we're going to close down all of our restaurants around the world. That'll show you."

Well, American merchants were less than thrilled with this idea so Jefferson replaced it with the Nonintercourse Act. Though this catchy little title might make you chuckle when your teacher says it in class, it isn't nearly as intriguing as it sounds. Basically, unlike the Embargo Act that forbade trade with the world, the Nonintercourse Act solely stopped trade with France and Britain. This act also didn't work because France and Britain continued to pirate the seas.

After Jefferson's second term as the United States President came to an end, the Oval Office was handed over to James Madison. When Madison got into office, the Nonintercourse Act was coming upon its date of expiration. Madison was looking for ideas here and there and everywhere for a solution to this problem of not having intercourse with England and France.

Then a guy who had the job of the chairman of the Senate foreign relations committee came up with a bill. His name was Macon. Macon, not bacon, not break-him. Macon. They called his bill Macon's Bill Number Two. Not number one, not number seventy-seven and three thirds. ¡Numero dos! Macon's Bill Number Two said that the first country to stop being a big fat bully to America would get a prize. And that prize. America would agree to only cut off trade with the *other* nation. Macon's Bill really turned out to be number two, if you know what I mean. Napoleon then, like a cat, a small cat, a small cat with his paw in his jacket, knew he had an opportunity to manipulate the situation. He said that France would stop being mean to American ships, and so, America subsequently cut off all trade with England and its colonies. Amazingly, in some strange, totally unpredictable twist of fate, the honorable and trustworthy Napoleon Bonaparte broke his promise and his country continued to raid American ships on the seas.

Exactly Why Were We Fighting?

Around this same time, the indigenous people of America were getting really mad at the white American settlers who were trampling on the natives' land. The people moving west felt claustrophobic at the millions of acres available to them, so they wanted to keep pushing west. This insatiable lust for land ended up infringing on the land of the local Indian tribes, and eventually led a very influential guy called Tecumseh to make a large confederation of many Native American tribes to defend their holy land, Mother Earth, from being desecrated by the Euro-Americans. Eventually, the natives struck first against an American army, led by General William Harrison (remember this name…he became president later on when the only criteria was being in the military). This was the Battle of

Tippecanoe. No canoes were tipped, but if some had been that would've been the icing on the cake. The natives were defeated, and this marked the first un-official battle of the War of 1812.

Some American people wanted to go to war against Britain more and more after finding out that the English had been supplying the natives with weapons and supplies. These "war hawks" pushed Congress to declare war and stirred up propaganda in the papers. It's kind of hard to explain. I can't think of anytime in American history when a group of politicians pushed Congress toward war regardless of the desires of the people. Hmmm. I'm thinking. I'm thinking.

Anyway, meanwhile back in Europe, the American embargo on England, as well as Napoleon's systematic boycott on the UK, convinced the British they needed to modify some of their foreign policies dealing with America. However, the Prime Minister who had planned on implementing these changes was assassinated. Once the new Prime Minister settled into the position, America was already on the path to war. Ironically, this means that one of the primary reasons America went to war, the whole trade issue, no longer actually existed by the time the war started. Unfortunately, communication back in 1812 was a bit slow and word didn't reach the proper authorities in time.

Subsequently, America was on a conquest north, towards Canada, which at the time was controlled by the British. The Americans sent militia and soldiers north to fight the British and invade Canada. American General Hull crossed a river into Canada, but was defeated and forced to surrender the town of Detroit. So much for America's plan for a quick and tidy invasion of Canada.

The Americans and the British both had many glorious victories and defeats throughout the course of the war, but perhaps one of the most impressive victories (for the Americans) was on august 19th, 1812. This battle occurred on the ocean, and signaled to the world that America had a naval force to be feared. In this battle, The *U.S.S. Constitution* defeated the English ships *H.M.S. Gurriere* and the *H.M.S. Java*, as cannon balls bounced off the *Constitution*'s hull. Because the nickname "Cannon Balls Bounce Off You" was too long to put on the souvenirs, the *U.S.S. Constitution* became known as "Old Ironsides".

The Americans also successfully defeated the British at the Battle of Lake Erie, forcing the English troops to retreat back to Canada. General Harrison followed the British, who were in retreat along with Tecumseh, and defeated them at the Thames River in the Battle of the Thames. Tecumseh was killed in this battle, his second defeat by Harrison. The Battle of Lake Champlain was a major moral victory for America. America had seemed to have lost more than they were willing to fight for, however this battle changed that. American naval officer MacDonough led a small weak fleet against a sturdy and powerful English fleet, and using all his naval prowess managed to prevail through the battle. This gave the Americans control of Lake Champlain, a good stronghold for defending the American-Canadian border.

Burning Down the House While a Lawyer Gets Poetic

Later on March 27th, 1814 General Andrew Jackson, a future U.S. President, successfully defeated a tribe of Creek Indians at the Battle of Horseshoe Bend. William Weatherford, the chief of the Creek tribe, later became personal friends with Jackson because Jackson admired Weatherford's courage at Horseshoe Bend. A few months later on August 24th, English General Robert Ross defeated the American troops defending Washington D.C. and invaded the nation's capital. They burnt the Presidential House. However the president escaped. Dolly

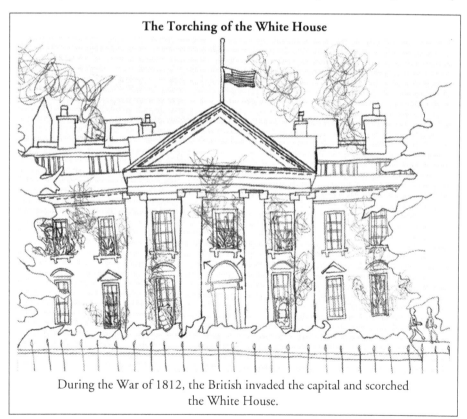

The Torching of the White House

During the War of 1812, the British invaded the capital and scorched the White House.

Madison, the president's wife, managed to save many historical items from the house before it was burned. One of these was a famous and unique original painting of George Washington still in the White House today. While the Presidential House was being torched, President Madison was rushed away in a wagon of hay. Hidden inside the hay, besides Madison, was a large bell. Madison did not want the British to get the bell and melt it down for bullets, so that is why he hid it along with himself. Later, the smoke-stained presidential home was painted white and thus today we say that the president lives in the White House.

After the Red Coats sacked Washington D.C., they sailed on to Baltimore. The people of Baltimore were prepared for the British and were able to easily defeat them. The English general was killed, and their fleet went on retreat (hee hee, that rhymes!). Later, on September 13, 1814, the British fleet attacked Fort McHenry, but the Americans would not be defeated. It was that night that Francis Scott key wrote the "Star Spangled Banner." Francis Scott Key was a lawyer who was thrown in jail by the British. Held in the brig on an English ship in retreat, he started to get *really* patriotic. Key started singing lyrics that glorified America to the melody of a traditional English drinking song. Wow! The American national anthem is based off a British drinking song! Maybe this is why soo many people that try to sing the song end up being "off *key.*"

The Star Spangled Banner
Francis Scott Key

Oh, say, can you see, by the dawn's early light,
What so proudly we hailed at the twilight's last gleaming?
Whose broad stripes and bright stars, thro' the perilous fight'
O'er the ramparts we watched, were so gallantly streaming.
And the rockets red glare, the bombs bursting in air,
Gave proof through the night that our flag was still there.
Oh, say, does that star-spangled banner yet wave
O'er the land of the free and the home of the brave?

By this stage of the war, it was pretty much over. The reason for fighting was long gone, and few people wanted to keep the war spirit alive, even the war hawks. Leaders from both sides were looking for the war's end, and a treaty was the way to do this.

Did Someone Forget to Tell Us We Weren't Fighting Anymore?

After two years of fighting both sides decided to end the hostilities. The two sides met in Ghent, Belgium, in August of 1814. The British came into the talks demanding land but after they saw that they were already losing the war they decided to just live with *status quo ante bellum*. This meant that relations between the United States and Britain were to return to exactly what they were before the war. The treaty also called for complete universal peace between Britain and America and set up boundary lines between the United States and Canada. But just because both sides said the war was over didn't actually mean that the war had come to an end. So now both sides of the war, who had already decided to stop fighting, were going to have their most incredible battle yet.

Six months after the meeting in Ghent, British troops were still advancing on the Louisiana territory and had set their sights on taking New Orleans. For years, New Orleans had been seen as the gateway to the rest of the Mississippi River, and the jewel of the South. Unfortunately for the British, the Americans saw this too. So on January 19, 1815 British troops landed in the area and were met by the friendly greetings of Andrew Jackson's men (Blacks, Creoles, Pirates, militia, and professional soldiers).

Friendly greetings? Not exactly. Andrew Jackson came down on them like a ton of bricks and inflicted a final blow to the devastated British army. The English were crushed, and their commanding officer Major General Sir Edward Pakenham was slaughtered in Jackson's onslaught. There's a funny story about Major General Sir Edward Pakenham. During the battle, a band of pirates fighting for Jackson killed Pakenham by severing his head. Then they sent his body back to his ship in two barrels: one for his body and one for his head. During the battle his wife had been on the ship, and on their voyage back to England her servants brought her to the cargo hold of the ship and pulled her dead husband's severed head out of the barrel. She totally freaked out, and they had to put her in a straight jacket for the remainder of the journey home.

Anyway, in February of 1815 Congress passed the treaty and the war was *really* over. But what did America gain out of all this? Well nothing really…besides a great deal of patriotism and a new American hero, Andrew Jackson, who later by the way (as I mumbled a tad bit earlier) became President. It really was a sort of disappointing end! Well what can you expect from a war that should have never taken place because the reason for fighting had been fixed before the war was declared? With the end of this soon to be Forgotten War and the return to the way things were before the war (*status quo ante bellum*), America was on its way to greatness!

CHAPTER 11

▼

THE NEW KING: JACKSONIAN DEMOCRACY

Let's Speed Things Up a Bit

Well, we've covered the terms of four presidents in about thirty pages. At this rate, you'll be reading this book until 2037, which was not exactly our goal. What do you say we speed things up a bit? Here's your choice: Study about the next forty years in one simplified, easy to read chapter, or become totally bored reading every single little detail until you hate American history and want to study the history of Luxembourg.

Well, if you chose the second option, please put this book down, go pick up your thirty pound textbook, curl up on the couch and have a blast. However, if you want the shortened version, here we go.

What Happened to the Other Political Parties

The Federalists died. Remember Washington's and Hamilton's and Adams' party that started off this country. Well, they were a bunch of snobby aristocrats and their party died. Jefferson started the killing by becoming the champion of the farmer, but the War of 1812 sealed their fate. The Federalists came out and totally criticized the war. When America eventually won and everyone was feeling patriotic, they weren't too excited about the crabby Federalists who didn't want the war in the first place.

Now that the Federalists were dead, it was time for a new series of presidents. Because there was only one political party, people believed this new era in American history would be the "Era of Good Feelings." Ahhh…now doesn't that sound nice and happy?

In 1816, James Monroe took office and guess what state he was from. Let me give you a hint: Washington was from Virginia, Jefferson was from Virginia, and Madison was from Virginia. Do you have a guess now? Unless you are a wounded turnip, you should pretty much see the pattern. Monroe was the latest Virginian to be in office, thus these early years in America history are known as the era of the "Virginian Dynasty."

You Stay Out of Our Hair, We'll Stay Out of Yours

Monroe probably did a lot of neat stuff during his presidency, but we're just going to focus on the one major decision that affected American policy for years to come. He gave a speech to Congress in 1823. Though mostly written by his Secretary of State, John Quincy Adams, this speech and its subsequent policy became known as the Monroe Doctrine.

Monroe said that he didn't want any more of those pesky Europeans interfering with life in the Americas. America wanted no more European colonies or wars for territory in either North or South America. In addition, America promised to stay out of Europe's business. You leave us alone, we'll leave you alone.

Of course, this didn't mean that America was going to leave our hemisphere untouched. Oh no. America still had the right to get involved in politics up and down the two American continents.

That Annoying Little Slave Situation

If Americans thought the slavery issue would go away in 1808 when the overseas slave trade was finally abolished, they were confused. Not only did slavery remain, it grew from around 700,000 in 1790 to over 3.5 million in 1860. The number of slaves increased through natural birth and the continued illegal slave trade. Watch the great movie *Amistad* to see an example of this illegal slave trade.

Not only was slavery a key element of Southern life, it became a huge political issue. Though it is true that many people felt slavery was evil and thus needed to be abolished, the reason it became an American issue was for political reasons.

If you remember from the Constitution, a slave counted as 3/5 of a human being when calculating the number of representatives a state would have. This is where the Southerners benefited the most. The more slaves they had, the more representatives the South could send to Washington D.C., and the more laws they could be pass to favor the South. The North of course was annoyed because they thought this was unfair. How could the South be rewarded for having slaves, when the slaves didn't ever see any benefits from their supposed representation in Washington D.C.?

Until 1820, there was a nice balance between slave and free states. A perfect tie—11 to 11.

Free vs. Slave States in 1820

Free	Slave
Connecticut	Alabama
Illinois	Delaware
Indiana	Georgia
Massachusetts	Kentucky
New Hampshire	Louisiana
New Jersey	Maryland
New York	Mississippi
Ohio	North Carolina
Vermont	South Carolina
Pennsylvania	Tennessee
Rhode Island	Virginia

But this balance got all messed up in 1817 when Missouri asked for statehood. They wanted to be admitted as a slave state. This scared the North, because then the South would have an advantage in the Senate.

Well, instead of solving the problem, they merely postponed it. They compromised. A guy named Henry Clay molded the solution (get it "Clay"—"molded") that Congress agreed to in 1820. Missouri would be admitted as a slave state. Maine would split from Massachusetts and be its own free state. The balance was kept.

However, the Missouri Compromise was important not merely for the balance it kept, but the precedent set. The second part of the Compromise said that slave states would only be eligible below the 36 degree 30 inch line of latitude. The slave line was drawn. Southern states then pushed for land south of the line to expand slavery, going as far as trying to buy Cuba.

The United States was now a fragile truce between two political groups at odds—the North versus the South.

John Adams Part II: The Quincy Version

Monroe of course won reelection in 1820, which meant that accept for poor little John Adams, every other president had been elected for two terms. And of course, in 1824, what better way to break a winning streak than have good old John Adams Jr. run for reelection.

Once again, there was pretty much just one political party, the Democratic-Republicans. When the election of 1824 rolled along, the Democratic-Republicans threw out a slew of presidential candidates. Because so many guys ran, nobody had the required majority to become president.

Election of 1824

Candidate	Electoral Votes	Popular Votes	% of Popular Vote
Andrew Jackson	99	151,271	43.1%
John Quincy Adams	84	113,122	30.5%
William Harris Crawford	41	40,856	13.2%
Henry Clay	37	47,531	13.1%

Here's the problem when you don't have political parties: people start voting according to who they know best, and it usually becomes a regional battle. As you can see above, the four candidates all got a little bit, but no one won the majority. Sure, Jackson had the most, but the Constitution doesn't say, "The guy that gets the most votes wins." (If so, Al Gore would be President of the United States and now George W. Bush) The Constitution says you need to have a majority of electoral votes, which no candidate had. The election then went to the House of Representatives.

It became an easier choice for Congress when Clay, realizing he had no chance of winning, dropped out, and Crawford got too sick to run. It was down to two. Jackson vs. Adams.

Clay, being the smart politician he was, made a political gamble. Clay wasn't a big fan of Jackson, so he went to his buddies in Congress and asked them to throw their votes to Adams. They agreed, and Adams won. Not surprisingly, Adams appointed Clay as the Secretary of State. Many people thought this exchange was unfair, and it was labeled the "Corrupt Bargain." However, those people that complained are total hypocrites, because you would be, and still are, completely naïve if you don't think Presidents grant appointments to their friends or people who've done them favors along the way.

Whether a deal actually had been struck or not was irrelevant. Adams' election was tarnished and Congress would never forgive him. They turned down all of his ideas, and Jackson was now motivated and ticked off. He'd be back. Oh yes, he'd be back.

And in 1928, he wouldn't lose to the man he labeled the "Judas of the West." Oh no. In 1928, there was no question who would win.

Friends in Low Places

In 1928, America finally had its first non-Virginian, non-Adams president. Andrew Jackson. The hero of the War of 1812 and a man who played up his rags to riches story. He didn't represent old wealth, he represented new America. The America where anyone can be rich if they just work hard.

This election, Jackson won with 178 electoral votes to Adams' 83. This election didn't go to Congress. A few Americans saw Jackson's ascension to the throne as a symbol of things to come. Jackson was a Westerner, one of those rebellious chaps who didn't follow the traditions of England. What would come of America?

While Jackson was giving his inaugural speech, a group of his hoodlum friends and admirers stormed the White House and took advantage of the alcohol and treats. By the time Jackson arrived, his new home-to-be had been thoroughly abused. Adams' supporters could only sit back and chuckle as they saw their predictions seemingly come true.

What is this Jacksonian Democracy?

You might hear a lot about "Jacksonian Democracy." Like Jefferson before him, Jackson was one of the few presidents who had an entire era named after him. Because of his influence on both federal and local politics, the period between

1928 and 1950 is frequently referred to as the Jacksonian Era, or the Age of Jackson.

What made this era so special? Well, we wouldn't be asking that question if we didn't have an answer.

First, Jackson expanded the right to vote to include almost all free white males. Property ownership was no longer a factor for voting. This changed politics, because now politicians had to answer to a wider public and if they didn't make laws that favored every man, even the poorest of the poor. They risked unemployment and losing the next election. However, let's not confuse Jackson as being a huge supporter of equality. Women and slaves still could not vote.

Second, Jackson believed in individual freedoms and the right of every man to get rich. He encouraged westward expansion, even if those pesky Native Americans were still living there. One of Jackson's most disgusting legacies was his harsh policy towards Native Americans. Jackson had already distinguished himself as "Long Knife," the great killer of the Creek Indians. As president, he would not relent. He favored a policy of "removal," in which all Indians would be led on a forced march across the Mississippi River to foreign reservations on nearly unlivable land. Championed by their president, this anti-Indian sentiment would became quite popular at the time and would justify the destruction of Native American civilizations.

Third, Jackson believed in a strong national government, but not at the expense of the individual. Jackson believed private banks should set their own credit and deposit standards, and not have to rely on a national bank. He vetoed National Bank legislation put in front of him, and America followed his lead and hasn't had a national bank since. And no, Bank of America is not actually the bank of America.

Fourth, Jackson also enforced what was known as the "spoils system." Taken from the expression, "To the victor goes the spoils," this was the notion that every president would bring with him his own public servants and kick out all the guys who had worked in the White House and other public offices before. Though Jackson kept some of Adams' people, many were replaced with Jackson supporters.

The Kitchen Cabinet

In forming national policy, Jackson consulted a bunch of his buddies, known as his *Kitchen Cabinet*.

With these actions, Jackson made the Executive Branch far more powerful than anyone had ever imagined. His power and national changes brought him the not-so-flattering nickname, "King Andrew." In King Andrew, America saw a recovery of the two party system. The Federalists might have been gone, but a new party replaced them. This group took the name of the Whigs, the same name given to the men who a generation earlier had tried to overthrow a different king from England.

Remember the Alamo!

Did you know Texas was its own country for almost ten years? Well, if you're from Texas you sure do. In the 1820s, Mexico made the not extremely wise choice to invite Americans down to their state of Texas to live. By 1830, nearly 20,000 Americans had taken them up on their offer and moved down to Texas. Eventually these 20,000 weren't terribly fond of being Mexican and wanted to return to their American roots. That, and they were annoyed that Mexico didn't allow slavery.

When their leader Stephen Austin went down to Mexico City to ask for independence, he spoke to President Santa Anna and left thinking that independence was a possibility. Unfortunately, on his way back to Texas to share the good news, President Santa Anna had him arrested. The Texans weren't pleased with this decision and decided to secede. In response, Santa Anna sent 3,000 troops in to calm down these little rebels.

These 3,000 troops met 187 Texans at the mission of San Antonio de Valero, otherwise known as the Alamo. The men there fought the Mexicans valiantly, but after ten days, the Mexicans defeated the Texan rebels and moved on through Texas. Though this battle was a loss, it gave invaluable moral support to their fellow Texans. In 1836, Texans used the motto, "Remember the Alamo" to will their way to a difficult eighteen minute victory over the Mexicans at San Jacinto while Santa Anna and his men were enjoying a siesta.

Texas gained their independence and became a nation. They applied for American statehood, but their request was put off while the nation decided what to do about the whole slavery issue.

God Told Us To Do It

During the Age of Jackson, America's love affair with the West reached all new levels. Land equaled money and people wanted more of both. Land had already been gobbled up on the east coast, so the only choice was to go west. The only problem was other people already lived on the land Americans wanted. Mexico controlled the Southwest and England still had a claim to the Oregon Territory. Plus, there was the Indians. What to do? What to do?

Fortunately, Americans learned that God had formally ordained their west quest (notice the ryhme). Remember, America was founded by the Puritans who believed God had chosen them to create a "City on a Hill" for the world to model themselves after. In 1845, John L. O'Sullivan put the term "manifest destiny" into America's consciousness as he attempted to justify America's creation of the Mexican War.

Excerpt from "Annexation"
John O'Sullivan
United States Magazine and Democratic Review

Why, were other reasoning wanting, in favor of now elevating this question of the reception of Texas into the Union, out of the lower region of our past party dissensions, up to its proper level of a high and broad nationality, it surely is to be found, found abundantly, in the manner in which other nations have undertaken to intrude themselves into it, between us and the proper parties to the case, in a spirit of hostile interference against us, for the avowed object of thwarting our policy and hampering our power, limiting our greatness and checking the fulfillment of our *manifest destiny* to overspread the continent allotted by Providence for the free development of our yearly multiplying millions.

Generations would use this term, manifest destiny, to justify their drive westward and their destruction of anyone who might interfere with them achieving their divinely inspired goal. Oddly enough, once America became a coast to coast nation, they tried to expand this philosophy to the Pacific Ocean, as America seized islands of interest a little past where Mr. O'Sullivan originally intended.

Those Horrible, Despicable Mexicans! This Means War!!!

Finally, in 1845, Texas became part of the United States. America felt the need to defend its borders. New president James K. Polk sent Zachary Taylor with 3,500 troops down to the Rio Grande. On one side of the river was America's forces, on the other side Mexico's. Now, why were the Americans down there? Just to observe and protect American interests, of course.

Finally, in 1846 Polk would get the catalyst he needed to declare war.

Taylor sent a scout over to the Mexico side of the Rio Grande. And can you believe it? He was shot! What a surprise!

This meant war! America must have revenge!

Some might argue that America pushed Mexico into battle, but this argument did little to convince Congress. The murder of this poor, helpless scout signaled war. Congress declared war and men rushed to join up and get in on the action.

The three year war was not favored by all Americans, but when the Mexicans finally surrendered, America had what it wanted.

So as to not appear imperialistic, America gave Mexico $15 million for the land that today is the American Southwest, including California, the golden gem. Ironically, just months after the sale was final, gold was discovered in California. In the few years that followed this gold discovery at Sutter's Mill outside Sacramento, gold rushers found over $200 million in gold. If you wonder who got the better end of the deal, Mexico or America, merely consider what would have happened in the world if California still belonged to Mexico. Currently, California alone has the fifth largest economy in the world. Add California's $1.3 trillion economy to Mexico's $920 billion economy and you have a country that ranks as the third richest country in the world.

Can you see why Mexico might be a little upset?

Jackson's Indian Legacy

While Manifest Destiny was ruling the day, little thought was given to the plight of the Indians. In the early the 19th century, the goal was simply to push the Indians west, to land not desired by the land hungry Americans.

And if they didn't go peacefully, they would be forced out. For no tribe was this forced migration more painful than for the Cherokees. Ironically, it was these Cherokees who had arguably tried the hardest to assimilate to American ways. They had an alphabet, wore the white man's clothes, created a constitution, and lived in European styled homes. Yet all of this was meaningless in 1835, when two Cherokees signed a treaty that kicked the Cherokees out of Georgia. They had until 1838 to leave.

When the Cherokees didn't leave immediately, Federal troops were sent down to Georgia to kick them out. Under the threat of death, the Cherokees were moved to a filthy, disease-infested prison, and then marched west to Oklahoma. On this "Trail of Tears," over one fourth of the Cherokees, about four thousand, perished.

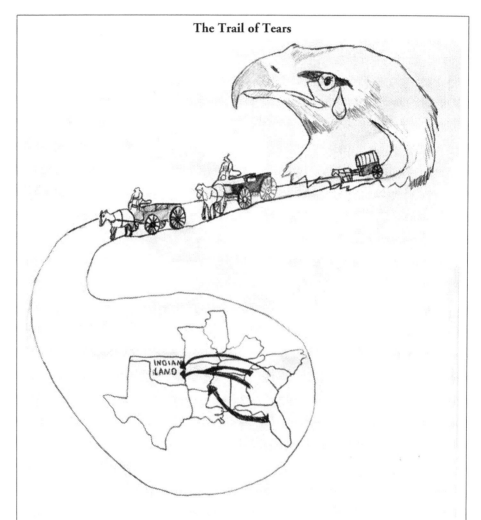

The Trail of Tears

The forced migration of the Cherokees killed thousands and demonstrated the Americans unwillingness to live besides Native Americans.

CHAPTER 12

▼

THE END OF THE UNION: CAUSES OF THE CIVIL WAR

Why Would Brother Fight Brother?

The Civil War is one of the most studied periods of American history. Yesterday, I went to my school library, and there were 47,362 books written about the Civil War.

The Civil War has it all. Battles, love, violence, machines, good guys, bad guys, bearded guys. You name it. The Civil War has it.

But why would a country that had just gained its independence less than a century earlier go to war against itself. Why? The reasons are numerous, my friend. Let me first explain again the difference between two terms—cause and catalyst. The causes of the Civil War were the underlying issues that divided America and created tension. Once this tension had reached dangerous levels, catalysts were the little events that made war erupt. For a war, you have to have both. Without causes, a catalyst is just a random act that both sides can easily pass off as stupidity and would eventually forgive. But when you already are ticked off at someone, catalysts can lead to bloodshed.

In History, Remember Three Words: Social, Political, and Economic

When looking at any historical event, always think of social, political and economic reasons that could have started the event. Social has to do with how people live their lives, what's important to them, how they treat their family and friends, how they think, what religion they practice, and what they do in their free time. Political deals with what the government leaders are doing at the city, state and federal level. Economic refers to anything to do with money, business, and jobs.

First let's start with the social differences that caused the Civil War. The South and the North were different. Duhhh! Northerners looked south and saw a group of backwards farmers holding on to the horrible institution of slavery that was clearly immoral and sacrilegious. In turn, Southerners thought of slavery as a natural component of human relations, and looked at the North as a land of chaos overflowing with ignorant immigrants. Sure, both of these were stereotypes, but that was how a majority of people in each region felt.

Politically, they also differed. First, both sides interpreted the Constitution differently. Northerners believed that the Federal government was the supreme law of the land, whereas Southerners believed states had the right to ignore mandates from D.C. Stability was not a word for this era. After Jackson, not a single president was elected to more than one term until Lincoln. This was amazing considering almost every president had served two terms up until that time. The nation was spiraling out of control, and nobody seemed to know how to fix it.

Money, the thing people cared about most, was a driving factor that caused the Civil War. The biggest economic issue was the tariff. The South had money, and the North wanted them to spend it on Northern products. But why would the South spend all their cash on overpriced Northern stuff, if they could get the same thing cheaper by looking overseas? Northerners wanted to put a tariff on imports, but the South thought that was a stupid idea. Both sides were just looking out for themselves. Another money issue that upset the sides was the distribution of wealth. The South just kept getting richer and richer off of King Cotton, but the North had suffered through two recessions that sent massive amounts of poor laborers angry into the streets. People don't like to see others getting rich when they're losing their jobs.

Most people would agree that the Civil War was fought over slavery. It was one of the issues that affected every aspect of American society during the first half of the nineteenth century. Socially, it defined the power structure of an entire region and firmly placed a small group of elite landowners above all others.

Economically, slavery kept the South as a strictly agrarian (fancy word for farming) economy reliant on bonded labor, whereas the North exploded into the Industrial Revolution using the labor of immigrants unwilling to go to the South where manual labor was filled by slaves. Politically, slavery dominated discussions as both North and South tried to ensure that the congressional balance didn't tip into the other side's favor.

Now Why'd You Have to Go and Discover Gold?

When James Marshall discovered gold at Sutter's Mill in January of 1848, the nation launched into a gold frenzy where "wanna-be" millionaires rushed off to California. After couple years, the Golden State's population had filled with 80,000 "wanna-be" gold miners and their faithful followers. Because it had grown so large, in 1850, California petitioned Congress to be admitted as a state.

Here was the problem. If you look at a map, California is below the Missouri Compromise line, which meant it was open to slavery according to the 1820 law. But if California was admitted as a slave state, the balance in Congress would be all thrown off and the South would gain the advantage in the Senate. The North couldn't allow this, so Congress started throwing out some options.

The "There's No Way the South Is Ever Going to Pass This" option, otherwise known as the Wilmot Proviso, proposed by David Wilmot, from Pennsylvania, stated that all the territories bought/stolen/taken/won (you choose the verb) from Mexico, would not be eligible for slavery. Not at all. The South shot this idea down. Didn't they remember the Missouri Compromise? It said all land below the 36°30′ line, California, New Mexico, Arizona, Nevada, could be slave land.

This problem needed a solution. California needed to be added to the United States to make it a coast to coast nation (plus California is a bit of an impressive state). Other options were brought up. First, the notion of "popular sovereignty," basically let the people of the state take a vote and decide. This idea seemed very democratic, but later you'll see how this experiment didn't work too well in Kansas. The second option extended the Missouri Compromise 36°30′ line all the way to the Pacific Ocean.

The third and best option became known as the Compromise of 1850, proposed by Henry Clay of Kentucky. Both the North and South got something out of the whole California admission situation, but neither side was totally happy. This Compromise solved the problem for the short term, but demonstrated how the slave issue would just not die.

Compromise of 1850

What the North Got	What the South Got
California admitted as a free state	Tough Fugitive Slave Act passed
Slaves can no longer be traded in D.C.	Slavery still legal in D.C.

Secret Trains and a Special Book

Although Northerners were pleased California was admitted as a free state, the Fugitive Slave Act angered a group of Northerners called abolitionists. These abolitionists had been working for decades to abolish slavery. Since 1831, William Lloyd Garrison had been publishing anti-slavery articles in his newspaper, *The Liberator*. Although the abolitionists remained only a small group, their voice was loud and constant.

They were outraged by the Fugitive Slave Act. The law required all citizens to aid in the retrieval of slaves and increased the number of fugitive police officials. It also got rid of trials by jury. Here's the classic part. A set of commissioners would decide the fate of the alleged escaped slave. If they released the fugitive, the commissioners were paid $5, and if he was returned to the South, they were paid $10. Hmmm…now isn't that a clever incentive to have more blacks returned to the South.

After the passing of the Fugitive Slave Act, the Underground Railroad started working overtime. Between 1850 and 1860 abolitionists tried very hard to get the slaves out of the South. The Underground Railroad wasn't your ordinary railroad, but the name given to the secret series of safe houses, known as stations, scattered from the South to the North. Conductors such as Harriet Tubman, the Moses of the slaves, guided many of the slaves from station to station until they were eventually free.

Obviously, the South wasn't terribly excited about this clever little railroad idea. Call it what you want. It was still stealing slaves.

The abolitionist movement angered the South even more after the 1852 publishing of Harriet Beecher Stowe's *Uncle Tom's Cabin*. The daughter of an abolitionist family, Stowe lived in Ohio for a bit and observed the escape of slaves to the North. She heard of their struggles and felt the need to bring their story to the public's attention. Americans were immediately drawn to the story's brutal portrayal of a slave and his treatment in the South. Though some complained it was too hard on slavery, the world took notice and the book became the most popular book of the 19th century.

Because of its popularity, the book became the symbol of a generation. People brought it up constantly when talking about the slavery issue, and for many, this was the first time they had really had a glimpse into the slavery system. Not only did it become a hot topic of discussion, it also drove a deeper wedge between the already divided country. Some might even say it was the KEY catalyst to war. Lincoln believed so. A decade after the book hit the shelves, Lincoln met Stowe and admitted, "So you're the little lady who started this big war."

Did You Ever Want to be a Jayhawker or a Bushwhacker?

The next big North-South conflict started over a Senator wanting to buy some cheap land along a possible railroad line. In 1854, America was figuring out where they wanted to put the first transcontinental railroad. There were pretty much three choices. Take it through the north, following Lewis and Clark's trail. Take it through the middle, passing through Salt Lake City. Or take it through the South, blazing its way across the lovely desert of the American Southwest.

Senator Stephen A. Douglas preferred the middle route. That would take it through Chicago and then Kansas. Two problems. About 32 Americans lived in Kansas and the rest were Indians. Not exactly the place you want to start building a railroad. The second problem was it was in the North, and the South had no desire to put the only East-West railroad through non-slave territory. But Douglas kept pushing the Kansas option. He had a lot of money to gain if it ended in Chicago.

But the South really didn't care about Douglas' financial interests. There was already a clear line paved out in the South where the railroad should be built.

Then came the part where Douglas' proved his greatness as a politician. His Kansas-Nebraska Act of 1854 stated that the Nebraska Territory would be split in half. And here was the important part. Even though both of those states were above the Missouri Compromise 36°30′ slave line, that wouldn't matter anymore. The government would just leave it up to the states to decide. If the people living there wanted slavery, they could have it. If not, then when the time came to decide, they could just vote against slavery. This "popular sovereignty" idea sounded really democratic, but it led to total and complete chaos.

Bleeding Kansas

After the Kansas-Nebraska Act, Bushwhackers and Jayhawkers stormed into Kansas
trying to influence the slavery vote.

The problem with letting the people decide was that Northerners sent down abolitionists armed with anger and guns, known as "Beecher's Bibles," down to help populate Kansas. These "Jayhawkers" were met by Southern "Bushwhackers" from neighboring states. Unfortunately, when these two groups with funny names got together, they enjoyed solving their problems with total violence. They'd burn down each other's houses, tar and feather their opponents and even murder each other. In probably the most dramatic case, John Brown took his sons out one night and in a very twisted type of father-son bonding had them pull a few pro-slavery men out of their sleep and mutilate them in front of their screaming families.

As you can imagine, the Bushwhackers had to get back at the Jayhawkers so they killed a few, and then the Bushwhackers needed some revenge so they killed some Jayhawkers, and then the Jayhawkers…blah, blah, blah. Basically, from

1854 until the end of the Civil War, violence became such a huge part of life in Kansas that the era became known as Bleeding Kansas.

Excuse Me Senator, Can I Whack You With My Cane?

The politicians back in Washington were watching these Kansas acts with a ton of interest. Northerners couldn't believe the Bushwhackers and all the "border ruffians" who crossed into Kansas on election day had started stuffing the ballots. For some reason, on election day, Kansas always had more people in its territory than on any other day. How could that be? Well, those "ruffians" from nearby states would come up, vote for slavery and then return to their homes. So obviously in the first vote for statehood, because the ballots were stuffed by pro-slavery neighbors, slavery was adopted. Unfortunately for the South, eventually D.C. discovered this election was a total sham.

In 1856, one Northern senator, Charles Sumner from Massachusetts, went as far as to openly criticize a pro-slavery politician, Andrew Butler from South Carolina. In his "Crime of Kansas" speech, Sumner insulted Butler by making some fairly damaging comparisons.

Excerpt from "Crime of Kansas"

But, before entering upon the argument, I must say something of a general character, particularly in response to what has fallen from Senators who have raised themselves to eminence on this floor in championship of human wrongs. I mean the Senator from South Carolina (Mr. Butler), and the Senator from Illinois (Mr. Douglas), who, though unlike as Don Quixote and Sancho Panza, yet, like this couple, sally forth together in the same adventure. I regret much to miss the elder Senator from his seat; but the cause, against which he has run a tilt, with such activity of animosity, demands that the opportunity of exposing him should not be lost; and it is for the cause that I speak. The Senator from South Carolina has read many books of chivalry, and believes himself a chivalrous knight, with sentimcuts of honor and courage. Of course he has chosen a mistress to whom he has made his vows, and who, though ugly to others, is always lovely to him; though polluted in the sight of the world, is chaste in his sight I mean the harlot, Slavery. For her, his tongue is always profuse in words. Let her be impeached in character, or any proposition made to shut her out from the extension of her wantonness, and no extravagance of manner or hardihood of assertion is then too great for this Senator. The frenzy of Don Quixote, in behalf of his wench, Dulcinea del Toboso, is all surpassed. The asserted rights of Slavery, which shock equality of all kinds, are cloaked by a fantastic claim of equality. If the slave States cannot enjoy what, in mockery of the great fathers of the Republic, he misnames equality under the Constitution in other words, the full power in the National Territories to compel fellowmen to unpaid toil, to separate husband and wife, and to sell little children at the auction block then, sir, the chivalric Senator will conduct the State of South Carolina out of the Union! Heroic knight! Exalted Senator! A second Moses come for a second exodus!

For those of you who can't understand 19th century Senate-speak, let me help you. Sumner basically says that Butler was a pathetic man who acted like he was a proper, chivalrous Southerner, but in reality he had taken up with a hooker named slavery. Making fun of Sumner's chivalry was one thing, but linking him with a prostitute was too much to handle. Of course, Sumner could have simply turned the other cheek and chuckled at the analogy, but these were tense times.

So what happened was a couple days later, Sumner's nephew, Preston Brooks, entered the Senate meeting, walked over to the seated Sumner and proceeded to pound him senseless. With his cane, Brooks kept banging Sumner on the head. Even after the cane broke, and Sumner fell to the ground unconscious, Brooks still kept banging away.

News of this caning traveled across the country. Southerners saw Brooks as a hero, and sent him new canes in the mail as a present. As Sumner recovered in the hospital, he became a martyr for the North, who saw Brooks as just another example of the barbarians who lived down south. You can be sure that Brooks didn't feel too bad about sending Sumner to the hospital, where he remained for over three years. He joked, "Towards the last he bellowed like a calf. I wore my cane out completely but saved the Head which is gold." Not exactly what my mom would consider an apology.

The Caning of Sumner

Charles Sumner gets his head knocked around after insulting
a Southerner's manhood.

Nice Try

A year after the "Caning of Sumner," the North and South were still headed down a collision course. The next catalyst dealt with a slave whose master. This slave then sued for his freedom. Born around 1800, Dred Scott was a slave who was purchased by Dr. John Emerson and then taken to Illinois, a free state. Emerson eventually died and his wife took over ownership of Scott. Now Scott wanted to be free. He tried to buy his freedom from Mrs. Emerson for $300, but she refused.

He then took her to court to sue for his freedom. The case bounced around Missouri courts for ten years and eventually wound up at the bench of the Supreme Court. After hearing the case, they decided that Scott shouldn't have even wasted his time. First, the Compromise of 1820 which outlawed slavery north of the 36°30' line, was unconstitutional. Second, Scott shouldn't have even have been allowed to sue for his freedom because he was a slave and had no rights.

This decision crippled the North's abolitionist movement. The South cheered. Dred Scott remained a slave and died a few short months later.

The Terrorist Shows Up Again

Remember John Brown? We just talked about him. He was the guy from Kansas who thought it would be a hoot to take his sons out and massacre some helpless settlers. After this lovely experience, he fled to the mountains and plotted his next scheme. This one would be a little bit larger. This one would put the nation on the brink of war.

While hiding in the hills, Brown came up with what his warped mind thought was a brilliant plan. He'd steal some weapons, free some slaves and then invade the South and free the remaining 3.5 million slaves that remained in bondage. Shouldn't be that difficult, he thought. Once all the slaves rise up, the white Southerners will be no match and will have to give in.

That's not exactly how history turned out. In 1858, he began training a group of men for the battles that would follow. On October 16, 1859, Brown along with 20 men, both black and white, crossed the Potomac River and captured the arsenal at Harper's Ferry. He would go no further. A man named Lieutenant Colonel Robert E. Lee was charged with putting down this insurrection. He quickly cornered Brown and his troops, shot many dead and then entered their hiding place and stabbed the rest. Brown survived, was put to trial and was then executed.

Not unlike the Caning of Sumner, Brown's raid at Harper's Ferry was seen differently by the two sides. The South saw Brown as just a symbol of the Northern fanatics who would stop at nothing to end slavery. Many Northerners, though not all, saw Brown as a martyr and a man willing to die for a cause.

At this point, war was a little over a year away.

The South Isn't Too Thrilled About the Man Named Lincoln

The election of 1860 became a battle over the future of slavery. Abraham Lincoln represented the newly created Republican Party. The sole goal of the Republican Party was the abolition of slavery. Lincoln was fairly conservative about the slavery topic and the most electable of the Republican candidates. He believed slavery should not be allowed to spread to the territories, but he also felt the nation must remain united. In 1858 he proclaimed, "A house divided against itself cannot stand." For Lincoln, the United States must stand united.

When voting day arrived, the Democrats proved themselves not too politically intelligent. Earlier in the year, when the Northern Democrats refused to make keeping slavery their number one issue, Southern Democrats left the convention and decided to nominate their own candidate. Bad idea. You never want to split votes. Think of it this way, if you have an election for Homecoming Queen, and you have four super popular cheerleaders versus one dorky band student, who do you think will win? 9 out of 10 times, the band student. The cheerleaders split the votes, while the band student coasts in by dominating the musical vote.

Lincoln was that band student. He won almost all the Northern states, while the two Democrats Stephen A. Douglas and John C. Breckinridge split the Democrat vote. He only received 39% of the popular vote, but it was his total victory in the North that guaranteed him the election.

Once a Republican candidate was in the office of presidency, the South stayed true to its word. Fearing the end of their way of life, one by one, the Southern states seceded from the Union. This means they formally left the United States of America

Order of Secession

Date of Secession	State
December 20, 1860	South Carolina
January 9, 1861	Mississippi
January 10,1861	Florida
January11, 1861	Alabama
January 19, 1861	Georgia
January 26, 1861	Louisiana
February 1, 1861	Texas

The First Shots Are Fired

Once the seven Southern states had seceded, they then drew up a constitution and called themselves the Confederate States of America. But in February there still wasn't a war. Not yet.

Slowly, the Southern states started capturing all of the federal forts and weapons in the South. Why not? The forts were on Southern land, weren't they? Most of the time, the forts would give up peacefully. This all changed at Fort Sumter.

Through the first weeks of April, the South attempted to take over Fort Sumter, an important military post in the middle of Charleston Harbor. Lincoln had had enough. He entered D.C. in March as the new president of a nation that was dramatically smaller since election day. He immediately made a stand. Sumter would not fall without a fight. The Southerners attempted to blockade supplies coming into and out of Fort Sumter. Lincoln then sent down a shipload of materials, but they never reached the fort in time. On April 12, 1861, after numerous warnings, the South opened fire. After a heavy morning of being bombed, the fort finally surrendered and war was on.

Lincoln instantly called up 75,000 troops to put down the "insurrection." Figuring the conflict would be short and young men might not be too excited about a lengthy war, Lincoln asked for only three months of service.

Using your supreme math skills. Three months means May, June, July. The soldiers would go home in July. And guess when the first big battle would be fought? You'll just have to read ahead to find out.

CHAPTER 13

▼

A HOUSE DIVIDED:
THE AMERICAN
CIVIL WAR

It's a Nice Day for a Pretty Little Picnic

In the last chapter we just finished talking about the taking of Fort Sumter by the Confederate States of America, a new country that decided to pop up right after Lincoln was elected. This wasn't the first fort they had taken, but it was the first fort they took by force.

Lincoln had a choice at this point. Do nothing, or step in and stop this rebellion. Remember, he could always just allow the southern states that seceded (broke away from America) to remain another country. North and South could have stayed friends, but then of course you would have had to go through a border crossing at Tennessee. And when you wanted to go to another country for the holidays, you could just pull out your passport and head to Florida.

Lincoln wouldn't accept this option. He felt America must be one nation, united.

So, he requested some troops to put down the insurrection. He had 75,000 troops at his disposal, and he had them for three months. Only three months. May, June, and July of 1861.

Lincoln called up Robert E. Lee and asked him if he wanted to be the general of the American army. Lee said no. He would remain loyal to his home state of Virginia, and fight for the Confederates.

Because of Lee's refusal, Lincoln gave the army to General Irvin McDowell, and he ordered him to attack Richmond, the capital of the Confederacy, right away. Richmond was only about 130 miles away from D.C., so McDowell loaded his troops up with supplies and started marching south.

Unfortunately, McDowell suffered from two fatal problems. His troops were totally inexperienced and unprepared for battle, and, also, everyone knew what he was planning on doing. Some newspapers printed where and how McDowell was going to attack. Also, there was a naughty little lady named Rose Greenhow who used her womanly abilities to get a little extra information. She then passed this on to the leaders of the South.

Instead of McDowell attacking Richmond, he met the Confederacy about halfway at Manassas Junction, a town near Bull Run Creek. A bunch of people from Washington D.C., thought this little battle would be quite entertaining, so they loaded up their stage coaches and headed out to watch. They dressed in their fanciest clothes, brought a picnic lunch, and relaxed on a nearby hill where they could watch all the action.

Unfortunately, the battle didn't turn out as planned. Both sides were pretty inexperienced. First it looked like the North was going to win. The Confederate soldiers were running away, and all appeared lost for the South. But then, out of nowhere, like a Greek god coming down from the sky, General Thomas J. Jackson arrived with his troops and just stood there, looking tough. One guy named Bee pointed to Jackson and told his troops, "Hey guys, check out Jackson. He's not afraid, he's standing there like a stone wall. If he can do it, we can do it! C'mon fellas, let's turn around. Let's go get those Yankees!"

Bee then turned around and was shot.

He died.

But the battle quickly changed. The South pushed back the North, and the Northern soldiers got so scared, they started running back to D.C. Of course, the picnickers were petrified at this turn of events, so they hopped back in their wagons and sped back also. Some soldiers ran so fast, they even passed the spectators.

A Confederate victory! The war wouldn't be short after all. Lincoln was less than pleased and fired McDowell. Both sides learned a lot from this battle. Basically, they weren't ready at all. They returned to the drawing board and started thinking up some new plans.

Yeah Right, Like the South Could Ever Win

It's pretty amazing to think that the South thought they even had a chance to win. In about every category, they had inferior quantities to that of the North. While the South had spent decades perfecting the growing of cotton, the North was producing a cornucopia (cool word) of products. However, the South did have a few advantages, or they never would have started this little conflict. Here's a little sampling of the advantages and disadvantages.

Comparison of War Readiness

Category	United States	Confederate States	Advantage?
War Strategy	Conquer the South	Defend the South	South
Goal	Defeat Rebellion	Gain Independence	South
Knowledge of Land	Unfamiliar	Familiar	South
Officer Experience	Not so much	A bit more	South
Size	Big	Bigger	South
Foreign Help	Europe doesn't care	Europe needs cotton?	South (maybe)
Firearms	Produced 97%	Produced 3%	North
Population	20 million	6 million	North
Manufacturing	More	Less	North
Railroads	Tons of Miles	Not so much	North
Edible Food	A Mountain of Food	Can't eat cotton	North
Money	Super, duper wealthy	Money tied to cotton	North
Government	70 years old	Two Months Old	North
Navy	Have one	Don't have one	North

As you can see from above, the North wins 8-7. Of course, nobody ever listens to me. They had to fight anyway. And fight they did. Over 10,000 battles were fought over the next four year, from the Atlantic Ocean to west of the Mississippi River.

Now, I need your help. We have a choice. I can spend one page each describing each battle, or I can just highlight the main ones. What do you want to do?

I'll give you a chance to decide.

OK...Just the main battles it is. Here we go.

Two Fronts

Even though battles were fought all over the continent, for the most part the battles were confined to two major fronts—the Virginia area and the Mississippi River. Both sides wanted to conquer the other person's capital. Richmond was in Virginia, and D.C. was right on the Virginia border. Subsequently, a ton of battles were fought in this area.

Also, there were a heap of battles around the Mississippi River. If the North could control the Mississippi, they could cut the South in half. No products from Texas could go east. Plus, the South couldn't get their supplies down the river and out to the ocean to trade. The North could slowly starve the South.

Now, you could also say that another front was in the oceans, but after just a few months, the North pretty much controlled the oceans, and had a blockade running all around the coast of the South. Southerners could still get a few products in and out by squeaking through the blockade, but for the most part the North had succeeded in choking the South through this "Anaconda" blockade strategy.

The Rumble for the River

When you think of the Mississippi River Valley battles, think of Ulysses S. Grant. Old U.S. Grant. Old Unconditional Surrender Grant. He wasn't exactly the guy you would think could be a hero. A graduate of West Point, he truly shined during the Mexican War, but because of some issues with alcohol, he had to resign from the army. He ended up selling leather in Illinois. He wasn't the most impressive looking man in the army. On one occasion, he was referred to as, "a short, round-shouldered man, in a very tarnished...uniform....There was nothing marked in his appearance. He had no gait, no station, no manner, rough, light-brown whiskers, a blue eye, and rather a scrubby look withal."

He might have been a slob. He might have been a drunk. But he knew how to win battles.

When the Civil War started he had a chance to redeem himself. Grant's first success was in Tennessee in early 1862. In February, he used both a ground and river attack to capture Fort Henry and Fort Donelson. This allowed the Tennessee River to be opened up to the North all the way to Alabama, a key victory for the Union, both for tactical and morale reasons. The North finally had something to feel good about.

A couple months later, Grant moved an army of 40,000 Union soldiers to the Mississippi border near a church named Shiloh. On April 6,1862, Grant's army was surprised by the Confederates. The South drove them back and back. The person in charge of the Confederate troops was General Albert Sidney Johnston. Because it was still early in the war, both sides suffered heavy casualties. Because they hadn't yet devised a plan for bringing the wounded off the battlefield, hundreds of men lay in agony on the field through the night. Johnston was killed in battle and the North decided it was time to dig in and fight. The North dug in and pushed the South out with help from reinforcements. Grant learned that this would be a war to exhaustion. More men had died at Shiloh than all previous American wars combined. But still, the South refused to quit. He realized then that the Union would need total victory to have any hope of ever defeating the Confederacy.

At New Orleans, an experienced Union officer David Glasgow Farragut captured the mouth of the Mississippi. He was able to take New Orleans by bringing his fleet of ships straight past two forts. Along the way, they sunk eleven Confederate ships and shortly afterwards, captured New Orleans. This was a devastating blow to the Confederates because it meant that the South could no longer support its troops in the West with supplies brought in from the Gulf of Mexico. Under General Benjamin Butler, the North controlled New Orleans for the remainder of the war.

Butler got himself in trouble with the women of New Orleans. Everywhere his troops went, the women of the town picked on them. They spit. They threw insults. One woman even dropped a toilet bowl full of fecal matter on the head of an army captain. Butler had to respond, so he made General Orders #28 that stated, "when any female shall, by word, gesture, or movement, insult or show contempt for any officer or soldier of the United States, she shall be regarded and held liable to be treated as a woman of the town plying her avocation." This wasn't very nice. Basically he called the women of the town prostitutes. That's not very nice at all. Southerners were disgusted, but the South really couldn't do anything about it.

There were still battles to be fought.

The Mississippi River finally fell to the North at Vicksburg on July 4, 1863. Grant's strategy had two main components. First, he took his troops and snuck around the back of the Confederate forces. He then forced Vicksburg to surrender after a six-week blockade in which no supplies were allowed in or out. Once Vicksburg fell, the Mississippi was again property of the United States of America.

Grant had succeeded. Lincoln would soon take Grant away from the Western campaign and bring him to the East. There was still a lot more war to be fought.

The Beasts of the East

When we last left off talking about the East, the Northern troops were running scared little puppy dogs back to Washington D.C. A total embarrassment.

Eventually, Lincoln settled on a new general, General George McClellan, or you might just want to think of him as Chicken George. He was one of the best generals in the Union Army. However, because McClellan wanted to run for President in 1864, he didn't want to lose any battles and ruin his presidency. So, he would only fight battles that he was sure to win. Lincoln wanted him to march down and attack Richmond.

McClellan had another idea. He could take tens of thousands of men, tons of supplies, hundreds of horses, put them all on a boat, sail them down below Richmond and then slowly fight their way up the peninsula and attack Richmond from the South. Of course Lincoln, who was taught the shortest distance between two points was a straight line, wondered why McClellan didn't just go directly to Richmond and torch the city. But Lincoln eventually gave in and let McClellan do his little peninsula idea. McClellan's idea became known as the Peninsular Campaign of April and May of 1862. Surprise, surprise, it failed. Lincoln got a bit upset, fired McClellan and then appointed John Pope the new leader of the army.

While McClellan was trying to implement his brilliant Peninsular Campaign, a critical battle occurred, not on land, but on sea. On March 1862, a Southern ironclad, a ship made of metal, named the *Merrimac*, started to bombard and destroy some of the Union ships trying to blockade the Southern coast. In response to this, the Union sent out their own ironclad called the *Monitor*. The *Monitor* was a small boat that had a pivoting gun on its deck, while the *Merrimac* was a fairly large boat that had numerous guns jutting out of its sides. For hours they rammed each other and shot tons of cannonballs, but they just bounced off the metal plated sides. The battle between these two ironclads was the first ironclad battle ever and it changed the way modern naval battles were fought. In the end, neither boat was willing to give up and the crew inside the ironclads was getting dirty and exhausted. So the battle ended in a draw.

Back to Pope. Unlike McClellan, Pope attacked Richmond directly. Unfortunately, he got caught up at a town that you've already heard about, Manassas Junction. This became known as the Second Battle of Bull Run. Before Pope could organize and attack Richmond successfully, Lee and Johnston of the Confederate Army attacked Pope and his troops on August 1862. General John Pope was defeated. Maybe that was why McClellan didn't attack directly.

Subsequently, Lincoln put good old Chicken George back in charge. It was because of this reverse in position that enlistments fell off and desertions increased. Why would people want to fight for McClellan? People hesitated to buy Union war bonds. Even Britain started to consider recognizing the Confederacy as an independent nation. With the Union army stinging from defeat, the Southerners were in high hopes.

Here was where the South took the offensive. After turning down Lincoln's request to head the American army, Lee had accepted Confederate President Jefferson Davis' request and organized the Army of the Potomac. After Bull Run, Lee quickly moved his army of 50,000 men into Maryland on September 4, 1862. He was now on the attack. He was invading the North.

He thought this invasion would drop Northern morale even further and the Union would give up their fight to reunite the country. He never had a chance to find out if this strategy would work.

His troops expected some reinforcements, but they never showed up. A copy of Lee's orders, showing where all his soldiers were located, were left behind in a cigar case and fell into the hands of McClellan. Lee and McClellan met at Sharpsburg, near Antietam Creek. They fought all day, each side advancing a little bit here and there and retreating a little bit here and there. To that point, it was the bloodiest battle in the war. At nighttime, Lee retreated back to Virginia. The battle was a draw, but Lee's invasion of the North had reached its farthest point.

He would have to retreat.

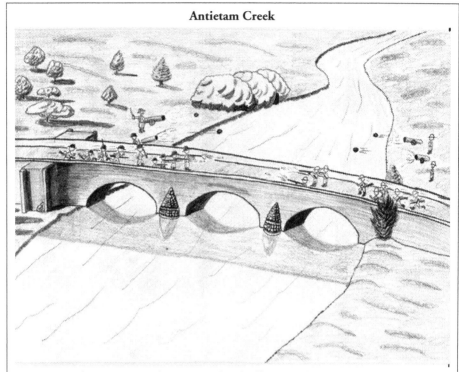

Antietam Creek

On September 4, 1862 Robert E. Lee faced off against the Union forces in his first attempt to invade the North.

A Better Reason to Fight

Finally, the North won. For the first year, it looked like the South would actually win the war. Now, that the North had a victory. They had momentum. The morale of the soldiers went up and it looked like the United States would again be united.

Lincoln had been waiting for a victory. He needed a victory for two reasons. First, it would keep the Europeans out of the war. For a brief period, England and France actually considered helping out the South. But now that they had lost, no way would either country help out a side that wasn't assured victory.

But more important than keeping the Europeans out of the war, it gave Abraham Lincoln the opportunity to raise the stakes of the war to a higher cause. Before, the Civil War was fought to reunite America. But Lincoln had a greater vision. He wanted the war to be a war to change the course of American history.

He wanted to make it a war to end slavery, and create a nation where Americans could feel proud saying "all men are created equal."

To this point, he had hesitated to make the slavery issue a primary issue in the war. If he did, he risked having the border states that owned slaves (Maryland, Kentucky, West Virginia, Delaware) secede and join the Confederacy. So he waited. He waited for a victory. Antietam was that victory.

And finally, on September 22, 1863, just five days after Antietam, Lincoln announced the Emancipation Proclamation. This declared that on January 1, 1863, all slaves that lived in states that had seceded from America would be freed. This was a big deal. Not because any slaves were actually freed because of it. None were. Remember, what authority does Lincoln have to make laws for another country? However, it was important because the goal of the war became freeing from over three million human beings from bondage. After the Emancipation Proclamation, once America defeated the South, all the slaves would be free.

Now all the Union had to do was defeat the Confederacy. A task that would take another couple years to accomplish.

Beginning of the End

I know. I'm starting to lose you. If I bring up any more battles, drool will start to form in the corner of your mouth and your mind will zone off to Happy Land. So, why don't I speed things up a bit.

After the loss at Antietam, Lee retreated to the South to strengthen his forces. He had to do something to force the North to surrender. He would have to invade the North again. This time he would go through Pennsylvania.

As Lee moved up through Pennsylvania, he hoped that a decisive victory would force the Union to agree to peace negotiations. This would be the last chance to defeat the North. The Confederacy was running low on supplies and men, and another loss could signal their doom.

The battle's location—Gettysburg.

Gettysburg was a small town in southern Pennsylvania. A Confederate unit had entered the town looking for shoes, but instead of foot apparel, they found Union soldiers. The most important battle would begin the next day, July 1, 1863.

The first day of fighting looked bad for the Union. They were pushed back and almost overrun at a lovely little hill called Cemetery Ridge. However, the Union did not surrender. They held the higher ground and fought back hard as the Confederates approached. In one final, last ditch effort to win the battle, Lee ordered Major General George Pickett to send his division across an open field to attack the Union. This strategy failed and Lee was forced to surrender.

This was the turning point of the war. The war would end in April 1865, but the fate of the South was determined at Gettysburg. The Union wouldn't surrender, and they would accept nothing less than unconditional surrender from the Confederacy.

The Gettysburg Address
Abraham Lincoln
November 19, 1863

Fourscore and seven years ago our fathers brought forth on this continent a new nation, conceived in liberty and dedicated to the proposition that all men are created equal.

Now we are engaged in a great civil war, testing whether that nation, or any nation so conceived and so dedicated, can long endure. We are met on a great battlefield of that war. We have come to dedicate a portion of that field as a final resting-place for those who here gave their lives that that nation might live. It is altogether fitting and proper that we should do this. But, in a larger sense, we cannot dedicate—we cannot consecrate—we cannot hallow—this ground. The brave men, living and dead, who struggled here have consecrated it, far above our poor power to add or detract. The world will little note, nor long remember what we say here, but it can never forget what they did here. It is for us the living, rather, to be dedicated here to the unfinished work which they who fought here have thus far so nobly advanced. It is rather for us to be here dedicated to the great task remaining before us—that from these honored dead we take increased devotion to that cause for which they gave the last full measure of devotion—that we here highly resolve that these dead shall not have died in vain—that this nation, under God, shall have a new birth of freedom and that government of the people, by the people, for the people, shall not perish from the earth.

Lincoln made a trip to Gettysburg a few months later and delivered an address to dedicate the opening of a national cemetery in honor of all those that died in the historical battle. His ensuing speech went on to be one of the most famous speeches in American history. The Gettysburg Address outlined America's future. Those who died for their country did so to make a better America. Their supreme sacrifice would make America a better place.

The End

After Lincoln's Gettysburg Address, a ton of battles still needed to be fought. Ironically, Gettysburg was fought on the same day as Vicksburg, that Union victory on the Mississippi River. This was a quite fortunate coincidence because Grant was able to then move to the East where he would face Lee's forces.

Grant's strategy was to move south and keep pounding Lee until he finally surrendered. He was benefited by William Tecumseh Sherman whose "March to the Sea" idea totally destroyed morale in the South. Sherman took 100,000 men, invaded Georgia and then kept moving to Atlanta, destroying everything along the way.

Lee's Surrender

At Appomattox Courthouse, Robert E. Lee surrendered to U.S. Grant, symbolically ending the Civil War.

By September 1864, Atlanta had fallen to the Union and everyone awaited Lee's reaction. Lee continued to fight gallantly, but eventually he realized he was in a no win situation.

And finally on April 9, 1865, with his 9,000 troops totally surrounded by Union forces, Lee surrendered. Totally dressed up in his finest uniform, Lee met Grant at the McClean house in a town called Appomattox Courthouse (it wasn't actually a courthouse, that's just the weird name of the village). Lee agreed to surrender his army, but not the entire Confederate Army since he had no control over the rest.

However, the South saw the writing on the wall. Lincoln had been re-elected again. France and England weren't going to help. Sherman had destroyed morale with his March to the Sea. Southerners were starving to death because of the blockade. Northern forces only seemed to be getting stronger.

Though there was still fighting going on for the next few months, the war symbolically ended with the signing of Lee's surrender. To this day, the American Civil War is America's costliest war, both in lives lost and in destruction of morale. From this point on America would be again legally united, but for many, America remained two philosophically separated nations for decades to come.

With the war behind them, the United States faced an even larger task— rebuilding a shattered nation.

Civil War Battle Timeline

Date Battle Ended	Battle	Theater	Importance
April 14, 1861	Fort Sumter	East	First shots of the war
July 21, 1861	Bull Run	East	Proved war would not be short
April 7, 1862	Shiloh	West	Grant continues push to Mississippi
August 30, 1862	Bull Run II	East	Richmond saved, Union loses again
September 18, 1862	Antietam	East	Pushed back Lee's first invasion
July 3, 1863	Gettysburg	East	Pushed back Lee's second invasion
July 4, 1863	Vicksburg	West	Mississippi River falls to the Union
November 1864	March to the Sea	East	Sherman destroys morale of the South
April 2, 1865	Richmond	East	Lee leaves Richmond

CHAPTER 14

▼

REBUILDING A NATION: RECONSTRUCTION

Kory Aldous
Junsuke Fukuda

The Beginning of Reconstruction

Reconstruction. The time period that followed the destruction. President Lincoln now had the privilege of restoring the United States of America. Would the North punish the South, or forgive it? It seemed that the South had already been punished. They lost a quarter of a million people in the Civil War. The war-torn South was basically destroyed and ruined.

Lincoln tried to help rebuild the South. The sooner America became a united country, the sooner it could move on. In contrast to Lincoln's view of reconciliation, there were the Radical Republicans. They wanted to penalize the Southerners, and make them pay so that they would never have the nerve to rebel again.

The Radical Republicans happened to be led by two oddballs, one of which was Thaddeus Stevens. Stevens, who can be compared to Scrooge, was a very bitter man who essentially had a grudge against the world. Well, what can you say for a man who was born with a club foot and whom some say was raised on sour milk? No wonder he was grumpy. And his counterpart? He happened to be the well known Charles Sumner. Remember this guy? It's been three and a half years since he was caned for making fun of Preston Brooks' uncle. Though still not thoroughly recovered, he was back in his Senate seat. And he too, was mad at the

Southerners. He had taken this Civil War pretty personally. This is what months in a hospital will do to you.

Well then, as you probably already figured out, both Lincoln and the Radical Republicans came up with opposing plans. Lincoln's plan was the Proclamation of Amnesty and Reconstruction, which he sent out on December 6, 1863. This plan stated that Lincoln would pardon all Southerners who fought in the war if they would take an oath to support the Constitution of the United States. Furthermore, he would identify their state government as a loyal one if only one-tenth of the voters took the oath of loyalty.

This plan didn't please the Radical Republicans. Thus, they created the Wade-Davis Plan. This plan was fairly complex. It said that each state needed a majority vote under an oath, instead of Lincoln's one-tenth vote. Also, a separate oath had to be taken to just allow you to vote or become a delegate. However, in-order to take this "ironclad oath," you had to testify that you had never held an office in the Confederacy, or fought for its army. Wow, how many men do you actually think could become a voter or delegate? How many Southerners had nothing to do with the Confederate secession? Pretty much no one. And that was the point. The goal was that with this provision, the South couldn't take part in democracy until the next generation came along. On July 2, 1864, the Wade-Davis Bill was passed by Congress and then sent to Lincoln to become a law. Here was where Lincoln proved what a master compromiser he was. He signed the Wade-Davis Bill into law, but also gave the South the choice of which plan they wanted to accept—his sensitive 10% plan or the Radical Republicans rather unpleasant option.

Assassination and the New President

On April 14, 1865, Lincoln was in a meeting with his Cabinet. He discussed reconstruction and how they needed to accept the South as equals. It was going to be pretty hard to succeed in getting the North as a whole to become charitable towards the South. So you think President Lincoln could pull it off? We'll never know. That night, President Lincoln and his wife went to Ford's Theatre to watch a play, *Our American Cousin*.

While watching, tragedy struck. John Wilkes Booth, an actor, entered the President's box and shot Lincoln through his left ear. He then jumped down to the stage screaming, *"Sic semper tyrannis!"* (Thus ever to tyrants!). Being the stupid man that he was, he didn't realize how far that jump was, and he broke his leg when he landed on the stage. He then hopped on his horse but didn't get very far in his escape. Lincoln eventually died across the street at Petersen's Boarding House, and two silver dollars were placed on his eyes. The man who had guided the nation through its darkest hour lay dead, with his work not yet completed. Would the man that replaced him be able to finally unite the country?

Andrew Johnson then became the new President. He was a Democratic Senator from Tennessee, and was the only Southern senator to side with the Union during the Civil War. President Johnson suggested that the Southern conventions get together and nullify their ordinances of secession (basically say that the Southern states never really broke away from America) and adopt the Thirteenth Amendment. The Southern states, however, ignored the suggestion.

The Confederates in Office

The Southern states immediately started to work their way back into the Union. They proceeded to elect former Confederates to Congress. By 1865, every Confederate state excluding Texas had fashioned together new governments.

Congress decided to set up a Committee of Reconstruction. This committee was set up to solve issues in the North, and to help re-admit the Confederate states. Oh yeah, and by the way, remember that Thaddeus Stevens guy? Well he became the leader of this committee.

To start things off, the Freedmen's Bureau was re-instated. This bill gave free meals to refugees, built hospitals, treated illness, and helped find jobs for people. Most importantly, it provided schools with teachers. This helped give the blacks an education. The Freedmen's Bureau Bill was brought up to President Johnson, but he decided to veto the bill. Since there weren't enough Republicans to override his veto, they had to move on.

The Civil Rights Bill was next. Ideally, it was supposed to protect blacks in the South. Not only did Johnson veto the Freedmen's Bureau, he decided to veto this bill as well. As a result, many frustrated conservative Republican members gave up and joined the Radicals, which then allowed them to override the President's veto on not just the Civil Rights Act, but also the Freedmen's Bureau Act. Congress could override anything that Johnson now vetoed.

Soon afterwards the Fourteenth Amendment was constructed. It declared that if you're born in or had immigrated legally to the United States, you automatically became a citizen. Tennessee ratified this Amendment while the other states refused. This set up quite a dilemma between the Republicans and the President.

The Radical Republicans decided to make things a little tougher. They passed the Reconstruction Act of 1867. It split the South into five districts, with each of them under military rule. This forced the South to ratify the Fourteenth Amendment. What do you think Johnson once again did? Yes indeed…he vetoed the bill, but this time, the Radicals overrode it. This meant that the old South would have no say in this new government.

From 1867, the South then went under a period known as Radical Reconstruction where a new government reigned. Scalawags (white Southerners), carpetbaggers (Northerners who went south), and blacks made up this new government. For the first time, African-Americans held official government offices. As part of these governments, the South gradually rebuilt itself. Railroads, schools, and public services all provided to help reorganize and set up the war-torn South. As a result though, debt continually increased. However, most of these governments didn't last long, and by the 1870s everyone in the south seemed to be voting Democrat again.

Now, Congress was out to get Johnson. They were tired of his vetoes and wanted to fire him, but first they had to push him into a corner and force him to do something illegal. The Radicals passed many laws that took away the power of the President. The final straw came with the Tenure of Office Act, which said the President couldn't fire any federal official without approval from the Senate. President Johnson ended up firing a guy named Stanton. This was what Congress had been waiting for! He broke a law. He could be impeached. Or could he?

Johnson was then sent before the Senate under impeachment charges. The formal reason for impeachment was he ignored the Tenure of Office Act. However, everyone knew the real reason was Congress' differences with Johnson over Reconstruction. Although the House impeached Johnson, the Senate fell just short of convicting and removing him. The required two-thirds vote was off by one vote! One vote was all that saved Johnson.

Scandal in the White House

In the election of 1868, the Republicans nominated Ulysses S. Grant, the war hero, for President. Going up against Horatio Seymour, he had little chance of losing. Though Grant was a great general, he knew little about politics. He was easily manipulated and at a time when America needed a strong leader, he failed.

During his second term in office, the public exposed two major government scandals that showed the corruption of America. Basically, some people were greedy enough to cheat the nation and make money. I know it comes as a big surprise, but there are people out there who like to make money without having to work for it.

The first scandal was called the Credit Mobilier Scandal. The story began in 1862 when the Congress decided to build the Pacific Railroad, extending it from the Missouri River to the Pacific Ocean. The company who contracted to build the 667 miles of railroad was the Union Pacific Railroad. This naughty company invented a fraudulent plan that eventually brought those involved $30 million. Here was their plan. The Union Pacific Railroad created another railroad construction company named Credit Mobilier of America. They then used federal funds to pay the Credit Mobilier for the construction; construction that sometimes never existed. Essentially, the Union Pacific used America's tax money to pay themselves for work that was never accomplished. This scandal made the people angry and because the people who approved this plan, or had invested in the Union Pacific, were close to the president, Grant's reputation suffered.

Another scandal further soiled the reputation of the government. Congress not only passed a law raising their own salary, but also the salaries of the President and Supreme Court justices. Congress was seen as a bunch of self-serving politicians who cared little about the citizens they were elected to represent. It was all about money. Democracy had been forgotten.

If the nation thought corruption in the government would end once Grant left office, they were about to be disappointed. After two terms under Grant, the election of 1876 would bring another candidate to office. Unfortunately, this election became known as the "disputed election." For some reason, every 40 years America seems to have an election where something semi-illegal happens. You'd think America would figure out how to do this whole voting thing.

In 1876, the Republicans chose Rutherford B. Hayes from Ohio as a candidate. The Democrats, who had not won an election since 1856, chose Governor Samuel J. Tilden from New York. Here's a key difference in their platforms (a fancy word for their positions on issues). The Republicans called for continued control of the South. The Democrats called for an end to reconstruction.

Election day was a mess. Both parties were desperate to gain control. People were interested in the result, too. In fact, 81.8% of eligible voters participated in this election, which is exceptionally high compared to the pathetic 40% we regularly get today. On the last day of the election, it seemed like Tilden was going to win. Even Hayes was sure about it. Tilden needed just one more electoral vote to win the majority. However, South Carolina, Louisiana, and Florida had sent in two separate envelopes, with two separate results. One envelope voted for Hayes. The other voted for Tilden. Please notice how Florida made an election boo-boo way before the lovely Gore-Bush election of 2000.

Without these states, the electoral score was 184 for Tilden, and 165 for Hayes. Again, Tilden needed only one more vote.

Whichever envelopes were chosen would decide the next president of the United States.

To solve this problem, Congress formed a group called "the electoral commission." They were given the authority to decide the president. The commission had a total of 15 members. Five from each house, and the other five from the Supreme Court. If they were fair, they would have gotten seven members from both the Republicans and the Democrats, and had one independent. But no, since a lot of things in politics don't seem to be fair, they had eight Republicans and seven Democrats. So hmmm….I wonder who won? Why yes, since the Republicans had more people, Rutherford B. Hayes became the new president. The results from each of the three states that favored Hayes were opened and entered into the books. The envelopes that favored Tilden were thrown in the trash.

Hayes won 185-184. Amazing.

The reaction of the Democrats in 1877 was interesting. They did not whine saying, "It's not fair…" That would have caused another conflict. But instead, a group of conservative Southern Democrats came up with a new idea…a compromise! The Compromise of 1877. They accepted the victory of Hayes, and asked three favors in return.

1.   Withdrawal of federal troops from the South

2.   Appointment of at least one seat in the Cabinet for the South

3.   Economic aid to industrialize the South

The Republicans agreed to these terms and the disputed election had come to an end. More importantly, Reconstruction officially ended and the South was able to once again run its world however it saw fit. From this point, any gains made from the Civil War and Reconstruction would be destroyed.

Race Relations in the South: Why Did We Fight Again?

While the United States wanted to unite the nation and bring equality to the former slaves, the South had a different idea. They wanted to return life to the pre-Civil War days when blacks knew their place and whites reigned supreme. The 13th amendment might have outlawed slavery, but the South was going to do everything under their power to keep things just the way they had always been. "Black Codes" were soon approved in the South. These laws controlled the work blacks could do, where they lived, and how they acted out in public. Harsh vagrancy laws also existed. These stated that if a black man was found wandering about without a job, he could then be fined $50 and put in jail. If he could not pay the fine, another man could then pay the fine and bail him out of jail. This man would then own the black man. So it seemed like slavery had been reconstructed once again, just in a different form. So now, why again was the Civil War fought?

On to a more sensitive topic. Some old Confederates began organizing secret armies down in the South. And of course, this wasn't helpful in uniting the country and ending persecution. A former Confederate leader, Nathan Bedford Forest formed the Ku Klux Klan, otherwise known as the KKK. Other white supremacy organizations were formed to punish blacks and "keep them in their place." All throughout the South, Klan members, dressed in white hoods and robes, victimized the blacks. In just one year, around the area of New Orleans, more than 300 were murdered. Thousands of blacks were brutally tortured, kidnapped, and or tarred and feathered. Before he left office, President Grant actually did something worthwhile and passed acts to outlaw these clans. However, these laws had little effect and were impossible to enforce.

During Reconstruction, blacks were somewhat protected by their Northern neighbors. However, once Reconstruction ended in 1877, the segregation of the blacks became a huge problem. Minor segregation grew larger, and "Jim Crow" laws were enacted. "Jim Crow" was a term used to describe black people, and these laws originated from the Black Codes. They became part of Southern society and their goal was to control black movement and prevent their admittance into Southern society. These laws separated blacks and whites on railroads, in public parks, in hospitals, in schools, in theaters and in a host of other public settings. The concept of "all men are created equal" had been forgotten.

To make things worse, the Supreme Court began promoting segregation. The Supreme Court overturned legislation passed during Reconstruction that protected freed slaves. For example, it said the Civil Rights Act of 1875 was unconstitutional.

The idea of segregation gained momentum. In 1890, Louisiana passed a law saying that blacks were required to ride on separate railroad cars. These types of segregated facilities were called, "separate, but equal." Blacks protested, but it didn't change anything.

Jim Crow laws became officially sanctioned in 1896, after the landmark case of *Plessy vs. Ferguson*. Homer Plessy was a carpenter in Louisiana, and was 7/8 Caucasian. On June 7, 1892, Plessy boarded a train and sat in a car reserved for whites. He was then arrested because he wouldn't move from his seat. Eventually the case went all the way to the Supreme Court. Well what did the Supreme Court do? They upheld the law because "separate but equal" was not considered racist. In fact, it guaranteed equality.

Or did it. In the decades that followed, blacks would soon learn that "separate but equal" actually meant "separate and inferior."

40 Acres and a Mule

When blacks were first freed, they dreamt of receiving "40 acres and a mule" to start off their new lives. However, this turned out to be nothing but a dream as sharecropping and black codes essentially returned them to a state of slavery.

In addition to the plague of segregation, the labor of freed blacks looked remarkably similar to that during slavery. After being freed, blacks had to look for work. However, they had no money, no clothing, and few marketable skills. When they went looking for jobs in the cities, they were turned away. They eventually had to go to white landowners and ask for a job and a place to live. Most of the time, they went to work at their farms as "sharecroppers." When sharecroppers were short on money, they had to borrow from their landowner at high rates of interest. Initially, they also had to borrow farm equipment, seeds and living supplies to get them through their first harvest. Then, guess what happened? The sharecroppers had to work for the landowner until they could pay them off. So how long do you think that took? Well, each year their debt grew bigger as drought and bugs ruined the harvest. These free blacks now became permanently indebted to the white landowners. And their children. No, they weren't slaves, but they were tied to the land with no hope of ever escaping.

After a few short decades, the South had succeeded. Slavery had been recreated, just under a different name.

CHAPTER 15

▼

LOOKS GREAT, SMELLS BAD: THE GILDED AGE

Oh What a Beautiful Country

If you were to look at America at the end of the 19th century, you'd see two totally different countries. On one hand, you had people richer than anyone could imagine. They wore the fanciest clothes, lived in the most opulent palaces, and threw parties that lasted for days. Then there was the rest of the nation, the 90% of Americans who lived below the poverty line in conditions that would make a rat vomit, working in factories that could steal their life in a moment.

This was the Gilded Age. The age where things might have looked pretty, but the reality was they pretty much stunk. Mark Twain coined the term "Gilded Age" in his 1873 book of the same name. "Gilded" means to cover something with a thin layer of gold so that it looks more impressive than it really is. That was the late 19ᵗʰ century. While a select few got richer than anyone in the history of America, the rest labored away in total despair.

The Gilded Age affected every area of society. America's government was supposed to be the model democratic nation, but in reality it was simply a den of corruption where city, state and federal governments sold out to the highest bidder. Our economy was supposed to be the ideal economic system, but the notions of capitalism and competition were replaced with monopoly and all out destruction of competitors. Our people were supposed to be most diverse and opportunistic in the world, but more and more Americans started to realize that the American dream was nothing more than a spun fantasy.

America was heading down a dangerous path of corruption and despair, and the same men that held the responsibility for the industrial revolution also had to be blamed for pushing America toward self-destruction.

Just Call Me Mr. Robber Baron

At the heart of the Gilded Age were the "Robber Barons," a group of guys who became chiefs of their industry by wiping out competition while creating efficient companies that produced the maximum amount of profit with the least amount of expense. The four big guys were Jay Gould, John D. Rockefeller, Andrew Carnegie, and J.P. Morgan. Each of these fine gentlemen became millionaires a hundred times over, but each also used business practices that were unethical. They justified their actions with their own view of Social Darwinism. Just like a strong gorilla survives because he is evolutionarily better, the Robber Barons believed they had risen to the top because they were simply the chosen people who had survived in the jungle of capitalism. Interesting logic, but if it worked, maybe it was true.

Jay Gould started off by investing in small little railroad companies. As each railroad prospered, he extended his holdings until he had a stake in most of the railway lines. Of course, what's the fun of being rich if you can just keep getting richer. Gould thought of an ingenious plan in which he would trade a ton of his money in for gold. He then talked to his good old friend President Grant and convinced him to not let out any gold into the market. And if you know anything about supply and demand, this made the price of Gould's gold skyrocket. He became a rich, rich man. Grant looked like an idiot for agreeing to this deal.

When the American economy hit a brief depression in the late 1860s, another Baron, J.P. Morgan swept in and bought a ton of the railroads that were almost going out of business. He made millions. Even when he was younger, Morgan was an opportunistic chap. During the Civil War, he bought a bunch of broken rifles from the government and sold them back to the American Army. Unfortunately, every time they fired, they blew off the finger of the poor guy who was doing the shooting. Other than that, they worked great. Anyway, by the dawn of the 20th century, Morgan owned more than half of America's railroads.

On these railroads went one of the most important supplies of the industrial revolution—oil. And who controlled all the oil—John D. Rockefeller. He owned the men who found the oil, the drills that got the oil, the companies that refined the oil, and he even controlled the men that shipped the oil. When Rockefeller threatened to take his oil off the railroads, companies were forced to give him money just so he'd keep transporting his products using their trains. With his domination of the oil industry and his ability to manipulate the railroads, he became the richest man in America.

Liquid Gold

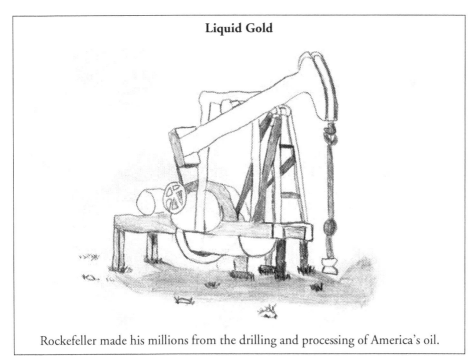

Rockefeller made his millions from the drilling and processing of America's oil.

Yet another Robber Baron was Andrew Carnegie, the king of the steel industry. America was growing like a football player on steroids, and Carnegie was there to furnish all the steel for the buildings. Though Carnegie also drove out his competition, he became well-known for his lovely philanthropy. Worth over $5 billion, he was able to buy a ton of libraries and even a few institutions around the nation.

Wealth of Robber Barons

Name	Industry	Estimated Wealth
John D. Rockefeller	Oil	$1 billion
Andrew Carnegie	Steel	$400 million
John Jacob Astor	Railroads	$300 million
Frank Weyerhaeuser	Lumber	$200 million
J.P. Morgan	Finance	$119 million
J. Ogden Armour	Meatpacking	$100 million

* Oh and by the way, $1 million dollars in 1900 is the same as $22 million today.

Business 101

Now that you know the main players, here's some background on how they made their money. Feel free to use these as you get older. You might not make any friends, but you can get rich beyond belief. And as Mark Twain once said, ""What is the chief end of man?—to get rich. In what way?—dishonestly if we can; honestly if we must." The goal of America? Don't fool yourself. It's to get rich.

Strategy #1: The Trust—Start a company that makes toilet paper. Everyone needs it, so you have a great product. Then, go talk to all your buddies and agree to set up the toilet paper trust. Once everyone is in agreement, you can totally control prices. You could even agree to sell a roll of toilet paper for $5. And you know what, you'd get the money. What are people going to do? Not buy TP. Yeah right.

Strategy #2: Pinkerton Detectives—If those pesky little unions try to strike, send out some Pinkerton Detectives to go solve the problem. Now, if these "Detectives" accidentally break a few people's legs or burn down a house here and there, don't be too upset. Amazingly, in just a few days, your little strike problem will go away.

Strategy #3: Destroy Competition—If another company is competing against you and their prices are a little cheaper, just get rid of them. This might hurt for a bit. You drop your prices super, super low. Then, your competition can't afford to keep up by slashing their prices, so you just have to wait until they declare bankruptcy. Then, you buy their company and raise prices again. And, if that doesn't work, just blow up their company or destroy their products. See John D. "Reckafeller" for further clarification.

Strategy #4: The Rebate—Want to make some more money? Tell the railroad companies you won't use their railroad unless they give you a "rebate." Amazingly, the companies will start paying you a rebate to use their railroad. Great deal!

Strategy #5: Bribery—Buy a politician. They're great buys. And as long as you get an honest one, one that stays bought once bought, you're in good shape. City politicians are great, but you can also try buying a Congressmen or someone on the president's staff. See U.S. Grant for additional details.

Those are just a handful of strategies. Feel free to try them out and let me know how it went.

Johnny, Did You Throw Your Poop Out the Window?

Ahhh. The tenement. What a lovely little place to live. Nothing like fourteen families living on a floor that has two windows to the outside world and smells like a pigsty after its owner has had a bad case of diarrhea.

Tenements, or slums, were the cramped apartments where immigrants and poor laborers lived. They had one toilet per floor and the odor was improved with the feces from animals, the lack of bathing by the tenants, the uncollected trash, and the leftover poo from Johnny's morning visit to the porcelain god. Now, you can't live in poop, so tons of people got sick and died. Some moved out of the cities to nearby "bedroom communities" or "garden cities" (affluent suburbs of the major cities), but most just hung around and hoped for the best.

Voting Is Cute and All, But Bribery Works Far Better

At every step of the government ladder, there was corruption. Sure, the majority of people were still honest, but the minority who broke the law gave politics a bad name. This totally differs from today, where everyone thinks politicians are the most honest and honorable people in the nation.

At the city level, there were the bosses. Bosses controlled both economic and city life. They would help immigrants and the poor get jobs and housing, while at the same time pressuring them to vote for candidates favorable to corruption. Once in office, the bosses would then manipulate the elected leaders. For example, Boss Tweed from New York had the mayor give building contracts to some of his buddies. They would charge $500,000 to build a bridge, even though it only cost $100,000. And guess what happened to the leftover money? It slipped into the pockets of Tweed and his cronies. This is what is called "graft." For decades, bosses controlled life in the cities, and anyone who dared oppose them could expect to be given the choice of taking a bribe or being killed. Not exactly the way democracy was written up in the Constitution.

At the state and federal level, bribery, graft and fake elections also popped up. President U.S. Grant ruled over one of the more corrupt governments. Almost his entire cabinet was in the pocket of one type of business interest or another. The biggest scandal of his presidency was the Credit Mobilier scandal of 1867. The railroad company United Pacific Railway charged way more money to complete tasks than was needed to complete the task. Even though it took only $30,000 a mile to build a railroad, they felt pretty comfortable charging $50,000. And where did the extra $20,000 a mile go? To the railroad and to government officials who might step in to block the money making scheme. Yet again, the American people lost out so that a few men could get rich.

And Liberty and Justice for All

America promised a paradise to immigrants and the poor, but in fact delivered a land of misery and suffering. Blacks saw the promise of freedom granted by the 13th amendment broken and their lives returned to that of slavery. They returned to the fields where they labored away their lives only to survive in a world where they were not wanted. Men were lynched for any action that might be seen as messing with the prescribed social system and again the government did nothing. In fact, in 1896, the Supreme Court even encouraged the separation of the races. In the landmark case, *Plessy vs. Ferguson*, the Supreme Court deemed it perfectly appropriate for two separate worlds to exist, one for blacks and one for whites. Blacks thought they'd achieved equality in 1865, but little did they know that they'd have to wait another hundred years before they would be recognized as equal citizens.

If the blacks were treated unfairly, the Native Americans were handled simply atrociously. With the presidency of Andrew Jackson, America's policy towards the Indians changed dramatically. Before Jackson, Indians were allowed to settle west of the Mississippi. This land was thought to be useless, so no one really cared if the Indians settled there. This changed however with the coming of Manifest Destiny and the non-stop western migration. It became apparent that the only way Indians would survive was if they moved off their homelands to allow for Western migration and then settled on reservations of barely usable land.

Sitting Bull

Sitting Bull tried to unite the Sioux to attack the incoming settlers and soldiers.

In the decades that led to the gradual annihilation of the original occupants of America, Indians saw their land destroyed, their buffaloes slaughtered, and their people massacred. At first, the Indians tried to fight back, but the Americans eventually killed both their warriors and their will to fight. The symbolic ending of the Indian struggle came at Wounded Knee when Indian men, women and children met death at the hands of American soldiers.

The Sand Creek Massacre
Excerpt from *Bury My Heart at Wounded Knee*
Dee Brown

"I saw the American flag waving and heard Black Kettle tell the Indians to stand around the flag, and there they were huddled—men, women and children. I also saw a white flag raised. These flags were in so conspicuous a position that they must have been seen. When the troops fired, the Indians ran &. The warriors put the squaws and children together and surrounded them to protect them. I saw five squaws under a bank for shelter. When the troops came up to them they ran out and begged for mercy, but the soldiers shot them all. I saw one squaw lying on the bank whose leg had been broken by a shell; a soldier came up to her with a drawn sabre; she raised her arm to protect herself, when he struck, breaking her arm; she rolled over and raised her other arm, when he struck, breaking it and then left her without killing her. There seemed to be indiscriminate slaughter of men, women and children…. Everyone I saw dead was scalped. I saw one squaw cut open with an unborn child lying by her side &. I saw the body of White Antelope with the privates cut off and I heard a soldier say he was going to make a tobacco pouch out of them. I saw quite a number of infants in arms killed with their mothers."

—Robert Bent, man riding with Colonel Chivington

Is There Anyone We Can Pick On Outside of America?

During the Civil War and the decades that followed, America was so focused on keeping the nation together, that it really didn't have time to worry about the outside world. Plus, the Industrial Revolution was being fed by the need to build up the nation. Everywhere you looked cities were growing higher, railroads were extending further, and companies were getting richer. However, toward the end of the 19th century, American businesses faced a problem. Consumers were buying less and the huge railroad and expansion boom of the post-Civil War years was slowing down. America needed more markets for its products.

So, where did we look—around the world. Some Americans adopted an attitude of Manifest Destiny that extended past the east and west coasts and to nations far, far away. People felt the need to expand Christianity and democracy to all the heathens of the world. Also, some believed we needed to make a military presence that would be felt around the world, so no one would ever risk hurting us. Some just hadn't had a war in a while and were getting bored.

That takes us to Cuba. Cuba is an island off the coast of Florida and it had been a colony of the Spanish Empire for years. In 1895, those pesky Cubans declared their independence, which then set off a war between Spain and Cuba for the dominance of the island.

America jumped at the chance to help their southern neighbors. For years America had been pretty excited about the possibility of adding Cuba as yet another state. Cuba had a ton of sugar, timber and mineral resources that American businesses could definitely use. Plus, the Cubans were fighting for independence, something America could definitely relate to their own struggle against England a century earlier.

When the Spanish sent troops into Spain to control the rebellion, America sent its own navy down to Cuba. Why do you ask did we feel the need to send our navy down to Cuba? That's none of your business. I'm sure we were just trying to show that we cared for the health and well-being of all humans around the world. Having our navy down in Havana Harbor turned out to be a problem. On February 15, 1898 the American battleship *Maine* exploded and sank to the bottom of the ocean killing 260 seamen.

Immediately the "yellow journalists" (newsmen who wanted to sell papers by printing sensational articles) from America ran headlines across their newspapers claiming "Spain Attacks America!!!" and "Poor, Little Innocent Soldiers Slaughtered by Horrible Spaniards." The funny thing was, the journalists forgot to actually look at the facts. Even though the New York Herald and many of the other international papers knew that the explosion was due to a fire in the engine room, that didn't matter. Who cares about silly little facts when you're trying to sell a newspaper? And both William Randolph Hearst and Joseph Pulitzer knew that wars sell papers.

In a few days, America had its war. Assistant Secretary of the Navy Teddy Roosevelt got a little bit too excited and immediately sent out a telegraph to the US fleet in Asia telling them to attack the Philippines. Teddy then also got together a band of adventurers known as the "Rough Riders" and headed down to Cuba. Within a few months, Spain was defeated and the future of America would forever be changed.

By 1898, America had the beginnings of an empire. Spain forfeited Puerto Rico, Guam and the Philippines. America could now be seen as a colonial ruler. The 19th century was spent building a nation. The 20th century would be spent expanding our power around the world.

With President McKinley's assassination in 1901, the Gilded Age was set to come to an end. The spunky little Teddy Roosevelt came to power and though he would continue McKinley's precedent of intervention in foreign affairs, he would also spawn a new period in American history—the Progressive Era.

CHAPTER 16

▼

REFORM AND WAR: THE PROGRESSIVE ERA AND WORLD WAR I

This Smells Like Muck

The decades that followed the American Civil War weren't exactly highlights in American history. The corruption and abuses of the Gilded Age left a few select men rich while the majority of the nation sat in utter poverty. Attempts had been made during the Gilded Age to fix the problem, but with a government in the back pocket of the Robber Barons, and a nation that really didn't seem to care about the plight of the working man, America didn't seem to be getting any better.

That would all change with the coming of Teddy Roosevelt, a president who ushered in the Progressive Era, the period between 1902-1920 in which America started to right some of these wrongs and put the nation on a path towards prosperity for all.

But the credit can't all be given to just one man. Much of the credit for changing the nation has to be given to the journalists who stirred up national attention by disclosing all the horrible atrocities that were present in the capitalist system. These journalists knew their audience. People love to read about things that are disgusting. People watch *Fear Factor*. People strain their necks to look at the car accident on the side of the road. People go to movies where blood oozes out of body parts. People love gore.

The journalists knew it, which is why Roosevelt would call these journalists "muckrakers," people willing to stand in the filth, stir it up for everyone to smell, but never really offering any solutions to the problem. The muckrakers did their job well. Never before had Americans known exactly what was happening to the masses of laborers around them, and many probably wished some of the facts had been kept hidden.

The first muckraking article appeared in October 1902 in the magazine *McClure's*. Lincoln Steffens's "Tweed Days in St. Louis" launched the muckraking genre with his attack on corruption in the city of St. Louis. In the years that followed, many other articles, historical accounts, and novels made their way to bookshelves and newspaper stands around the country; the people loved them and couldn't seem to get enough. Even Upton Sinclair's depiction of the horrific conditions of the meatpacking industry did little to satisfy America's appetite for rank and raunchy revelations. In his novel, *The Jungle*, an Eastern European immigrant named Jurgis learns quickly that capitalist America has no problem putting profit before health.

Excerpt from *The Jungle*
Upton Sinclair—1906

Jonas had told them how the meat that was taken out of pickle would often be found sour, and how they would rub it up with soda to take away the smell, and sell it to be eaten on free-lunch counters; also of all the miracles of chemistry which they performed, giving to any sort of meat, fresh or salted, whole or chopped, any color and any flavor and any odor they chose. In the pickling of hams they had an ingenious apparatus, by which they saved time and increased the capacity of the plant—a machine consisting of a hollow needle attached to a pump; by plunging this needle into the meat and working with his foot, a man could fill a ham with pickle in a few seconds. And yet, in spite of this, there would be hams found spoiled, some of them with an odor so bad that a man could hardly bear to be in the room with them. To pump into these the packers had a second and much stronger pickle which destroyed the odor—a process known to the workers as "giving them thirty per cent." Also, after the hams had been smoked, there would be found some that had gone to the bad. Formerly these had been sold as "Number Three Grade," but later on some ingenious person had hit upon a new device, and now they would extract the bone, about which the bad part generally lay, and insert in the hole a white-hot iron. After this invention there was no longer Number One, Two, and Three Grade—there was only Number One Grade. The packers were always originating such schemes—they had what they called "boneless hams," which were all the odds and ends of pork stuffed into casings; and "California hams," which were the shoulders, with big knuckle joints, and nearly all the meat cut out; and fancy "skinned hams," which were made of the oldest hogs, whose skins were so heavy and coarse that no one would buy them—that is, until they had been cooked and chopped fine and labeled "head cheese!"

It was only when the whole ham was spoiled that it came into the department of Elzbieta. Cut up by the two-thousand-revolutions-a-minute flyers, and mixed with half a ton of other meat, no odor that ever was in a ham could make any difference. There was never the least attention paid to what was cut up for sausage; there would come all the way back from Europe old sausage that had been rejected, and that was moldy and white—it would be dosed with borax and glycerine, and dumped into the hoppers, and made over again for home consumption. There would be meat that had tumbled out on the floor, in the dirt and sawdust, where the workers had tramped and spit uncounted billions of consumption germs. There would be meat stored in great piles in rooms; and the water from leaky roofs would drip over it, and thousands of rats would race about on it. It was too dark in these storage places to see well, but a man could run his hand over these piles of meat and sweep off handfuls of the dried dung of rats. These rats were nuisances, and the packers would put poisoned bread out for them; they would die, and then rats, bread, and meat would go into the hoppers together. This is no fairy story and no joke; the meat would be shoveled into carts, and the man who did the shoveling would not trouble to lift out a rat even when he saw one—there were things that went into the sausage in comparison with which a poisoned rat was a tidbit. There was no place for the men to wash their hands before they ate their dinner, and so they made a practice of washing them in the water that was to be ladled into the sausage. There were the butt-ends of smoked meat, and the scraps of corned beef, and all the odds and ends of the waste of the plants, that would be dumped into old barrels in the cellar and left there. Under the system of rigid economy which the packers enforced, there were some jobs that it only paid to do once in a long time, and among these was the cleaning out of the waste barrels. Every spring they did it; and in the barrels would be dirt and rust and old nails and stale water—and cartload after cartload of it would be taken up and dumped into the hoppers with fresh meat, and sent out to the public's breakfast. Some of it they would make into "smoked" sausage—but as the smoking took time, and was therefore expensive, they would call upon their chemistry department, and preserve it with borax and color it with gelatine to make it brown. All of their sausage came out of the same bowl, but when they came to wrap it they would stamp some of it "special," and for this they would charge two cents more a pound.

However, Upton Sinclair wasn't the only muckraker. In *History of the Standard Oil Company*, Ida Tarbell wrote about how John D. Rockefeller used his power to destroy his competition and buy influence in the government. She knew this story quite personally as her father was driven out of business by the oppressive Rockefeller. Lincoln Steffens wrote *Shame of the Cities*, which exposed government links to crime. Though it focused on the mayor of Minneapolis, Americans quickly learned that the boss system existed all over America. The leaders had been bought and democracy was in the hands of criminals. In addition to exposing corruption in business and politics, the muckrakers also attacked the inhumane conditions of those living in the tenement buildings of major cities. In *How the Other Half Lives*, Jacob Riis uncovered the sad lives of the poor as they struggled to survive.

Excerpt from *How the Other Half Lives*
Jacob Riis

Hear the pump squeak! It is the lullaby of tenement-house babes. In summer, when a thousand thirsty throats pant for a cooling drink in this block, it is worked in vain. But the saloon, whose open door you passed in the hall, is always there. The smell of it has followed you up. Here is a door. Listen! That short hacking cough, that tiny, helpless wail—what do they mean? They mean that the soiled bow of white you saw on the door downstairs will have another story to tell—Oh! a sadly familiar story—before the day is at an end. The child is dying with measles. With half a chance it might have lived; but it had none. That dark bedroom killed it.

The muckrakers did their job uncovering the filth. Now all America needed was someone to do something about it.

Cleaning Up the Filth

The successes of the Progressive Era often times get credited solely to the presidents—Roosevelt, Taft, and Wilson. Much of the changes however, came from progressive citizens who were simply tired of seeing the pitiful lives of the poor and disadvantaged. One progressive, Jane Addams, made children her first priority. Kids were wandering the streets, either dying slowly or committing crimes to survive. Jane Addams pushed for playgrounds, medical care at schools, and a juvenile court system so ten year old kids wouldn't be tried as an adult. Before 1900, if a child committed a crime, he'd be sent to jail where he'd then learn from his elders all the wonderful skills it takes to be a really good criminal. Not exactly the education system our founding fathers envisioned. Jane Addams also fought for child labor laws so eight year olds wouldn't be working in factories for sixteen hours a day. Jane Addams' great idea for Settlement Houses became the model for community centers and YMCAs that still exist today.

And then there's the sausage. Remember that yummy little delicacy of rat hair and borax that was being cooked in America's kitchens? Well, the government didn't look too favorably at the meat packing industry and just six months after Sinclair's *The Jungle* was published, Congress passed the Pure Food and Drug Act. They later passed the Meat Inspection Act. Both of these told manufacturers that it was a pretty naughty to put fungus in food and then sell it as tasty vittles.

Then there were monopolies. Nobody likes a monopoly except for the guy that owns the monopoly. Roosevelt had had enough with Rockefeller and all his buddies who had pretty much destroyed capitalism. In America, there's supposed to be this fun little thing called competition, but the Robber Barons got rid of it. Since Rockefeller was the only guy producing oil, he could pretty much charge whatever he wanted. Weren't there any laws to stop this type of behavior? Yes, there was, but because the government was so darn corrupt, they never enforced the laws.

Ending the Trusts

Roosevelt tried to end Rockefeller's dominance of the oil industry through his "trust busting" legislation.

Theodore Roosevelt changed that. With the Hepburn Act, the Interstate Commerce Commission (ICC) could finally start attacking any business that broke laws and then carried their supplies across state borders. See, the federal government can't touch companies if they only operate within a state. For example, let's say Bob's Deli in San Francisco, California makes hamburgers out of poison and then sells them to small children. Because the food was eaten in the state and the product never left the state, the federal government couldn't do anything about it. It was the state's problem; but if the state governments were corrupt, these laws could never be enforced.

That's where the ICC came in. The moment a product crossed state lines, it came under the jurisdiction (fancy word for authority/power/control) of the federal government. For the big companies that moved their products on pipelines, trains, ferries, or over bridges, that meant they could now be punished by the federal government. And punished they were. By 1911, Standard Oil was broken up into 34 companies. You now know these companies by the names of their gas stations—Exxon, Mobil, Chevron, Texaco. If not for Roosevelt and his "trust busting," you'd be driving down the street and only seeing gas stations with the name "Standard Oil."

While Roosevelt was attacking the trusts, he was also saving the nation's prettiest land. He reserved land so companies couldn't use the resources. Many of these reserved tracts became the National Parks some visit during the summers—Yellowstone, Yosemite, and Grand Canyon. So, whenever you go camping think of the good old Teddy bear himself, Mr. Roosevelt.

One Great Idea, and One Not So Great Idea

Two of the main results from the Progressive Era were the 18th and 19th amendments. The 18th prohibited the manufacture, sale and trade of alcohol and the 19th gave women the right to vote.

For decades, prohibitionists had been trying to outlaw alcohol. They were tired of seeing men waste their wages at the local bar and breaking the law because they were a bit tipsy. These prohibitionists believed that once you outlawed alcohol, a decrease in crime would follow. Slight problem with that idea—people needed alcohol. They had to have it. Instead of getting rid of crime, America plunged into its largest era of organized crime. Crime families organized to produce and sell alcohol illegally at "speakeasies" around the country. Eventually, the 18th amendment was repealed because too many people were breaking the law.

The 19th amendment also came after decades of struggle. Women first were given the right to vote in states, and later, after they had proven themselves in World War I, they were given the right to vote at the national level. This amendment was a monumental shift in the Women's Rights Movement.

Carrying Around My Big Stick

While the nation was caught up in the Progressive Movement, America continued to have a role in overseas affairs. Throughout the 20th century, America had tried to remain semi-isolationist and stay out of other people's business. However, with the Spanish American War and the coming of Teddy Roosevelt, a new era in American politics was started.

Teddy Roosevelt's motto was "Speak Softly and Carry a Big Stick." Translated this means, "I have a lot of really cool weapons and if you cross me I'll beat you up." America became more involved in the affairs of South America. If you remember back to the early 1800s, James Monroe implemented the Monroe Doctrine that said no European countries had the right to bother the American countries. Roosevelt added to that by saying that even though Europe couldn't interfere with business in the Americas, the United States could.

Roosevelt used this philosophy to justify his actions in the Panama area. Those pesky Colombians, for some reason, refused to let us a build a canal through the northern part of their country. America's solution was to give money and arms to the Panamanians and have them revolt from Colombia. Once Panama was an independent country, America could build a canal through Panama cheaply. This canal would save money because now ships didn't have to go all the way around the southern tip of South America. America ended up paying Panama a $10 million dollar deposit and $250,000 a year. Not a bad deal considering it would save American companies hundreds of millions of dollars.

Roosevelt was also able to show off America's power by sending the navy to Asia. This Great White Fleet went to Japan and China, parked in the harbors of these two countries and then just sat there for a bit. The goal was to intimidate the countries so that they would keep an Open Door Policy and let American companies trade freely with them. There's nothing like a little military persuasion to get countries to cooperate.

Roosevelt's successor, the ever plump William Howard Taft, had a different idea. He called it "dollar diplomacy." The idea behind this is that instead of using the military to get your point across, you send a ton of money to the governments and hope the money trickles down into the hands of the citizens of the country.

Then, everyone would be happy and countries would all love America. The problem with that was, that when America gave the money to the government—surprise, surprise—they forgot to pass it down to their citizens. They "accidentally" kept all the money for themselves.

The War to End All Wars, Until the Next Big War in Twenty Years

At the turn of the century, Europe was in a period of transition. For centuries, kings and queens had ruled the continent, and the masses had simply bowed down in subservience to their masters. These same kings and queens wanted to extend their empires and dominate as much of the world as possible. However, times were changing. The industrial revolution meant that money was being made, but the workers weren't benefiting like they thought they should. Tempers were flaring and conflict was inevitable.

Causes of World War I

Cause	Description
Arms Race	Armies and navies grew, technology advanced, no one wanted to be left behind
Nationalism	People see self worth tied to success of nation, don't want to be humiliated
Imperialism	Competition for markets for their industrial revolution products
Triple Entente	Great Britain, France Russia
Triple Alliance	Germany, Austria, Italy
Self Determination	Members of shared ethnic group should be able to decide future

Tension had been building for decades, but a catalyst was needed. The catalyst for this war happened on June 28, 1914, when the Archduke of Austria, Franz Ferdinand and his wife, the Dutchess Sophie were visiting Sarajevo. Sarajevo was located in the province known as Bosnia-Herzegovina, a province under the control of the Austrians. For those of you geographically impaired, that's the bottom right hand part of Europe. Ferdinand knew the trip would be dangerous because the locals weren't happy that they were being ruled by the Austrians. However, he went anyway.

Bad idea.

At about 10:00 in the morning, while his royal car cruised through the streets, a guy jumped out and threw a grenade at Ferdinand's car. The driver saw the grenade coming and sped up to avoid it. It ended up injuring people in the car behind him and some nearby spectators. Ferdinand had avoided the first attempt.

Minutes later the car sped through the streets, but had to slow down to make a sharp turn. As it slowed another assassin jumped out, put a bullet in Sophie's head and then put a bullet straight through the heart of Ferdinand.

Europe now had its catalyst.

Dominos, Submarines and a Secret Letter

After the assassination of Ferdinand, war was imminent. One by one nations declared war on each other. Because of all the "entangling alliances," once a nation was declared war on, its buddy nation had to then declare war also. Austria-Hungary declared war on Serbia. Russia then declared war on Austria-Hungary. Germany then declared war on Russia. France declared war on Germany. Germany declares war on Belgium. Great Britain declares war on Germany…and so on…and so on. Until eventually, all of Europe was involved.

And that ladies and gentlemen was the domino effect. One falls, they all fall.

But as you can see, this only involved Europe. Where does America come in? If you look back at the "Causes" chart, none of the causes had anything to do with America. If you look at the alliances, America wasn't part of any of them. So America really had no interest in the war. Right?

Well, that's what Woodrow Wilson believed, so he tried to keep America isolated from the war as long as possible. But, just because America was staying out of the war didn't mean they couldn't make a ton of money from the fighting. If Europe was so involved with fighting wars, they wouldn't have time to produce the necessities of life and the weapons of war.

Enter America. America became the grand industrial supplier for the world. At first, we traded with everyone, both sides, we didn't care. As long as you had money, we'd send ships to you. However, eventually, the Allies (France, England, and their buddies) blockaded shipments to the Central Powers (Austria-Hungary, Germany, and their friends). America had a choice. Do they ignore the blockade and keep trading with Germany? Doing this would anger the Allies and block off a huge market for U.S. supplies. So, America chose to stop trading with the Central Powers and trade exclusively with the Allies. This wasn't that hard of a choice since we already had far stronger economic ties to Britain than any other country.

This turned out to be a great idea. In the first two years of the war, our trade value to the Allies increased from $825 million to $3.2 billion. Before the war, America was in huge debt to the world, but not for long. American banks started loaning money to the European powers. This worked out perfect, because the money we loaned them would then be spent on American supplies, bringing money straight back to the U.S. By the end of the war, everyone owed us money. So much for a recession. America was doing great.

Germany, however, wasn't too pleased about this whole deal. America was claiming to be neutral, but to the Central Powers it looked a lot like they were supporting the Allies. Germany got fed up and started a policy of using their fancy underwater boats, U-boats (we call them submarines) to start bombing any ship that was carrying military supplies to the allies.

America warned the Germans that they better not touch any American ships or hurt any Americans. However, it was only a matter of time before the wrong ship was sunk. That ship turned out to be the British passenger ship, the *Lusitania*. On May 7, 1915, U-boats torpedoed the ship and over 1,200 people died, 128 of which were Americans. Germany said though the *Lusitania* was a passenger ship, it was carrying military supplies. Even if there were weapons, the damage was done. Anti-German public opinion swelled. How could those nasty Germans attack poor, innocent tourists on a boat? Something must be done.

Woodrow Wilson still kept America out of war. When another U.S. ship, the *Housatonic* was sunk in 1917, Wilson shut off diplomatic ties with Germany, but still kept America out of war. This would change with the March 1, 1917 publishing of the Zimmerman Note. Alfred Zimmerman of Germany sent a coded message to the German ambassador to Mexico proposing a deal. If Mexico agreed to be Germany's ally, Germany would get back the land Mexico lost from the Mexican-American War.

When the U.S. heard that Germany was thinking of taking the war to America's soil, that was enough. On April 2, 1917, Wilson went to Congress and demanded war. Congress agreed and on April 6, 1917, America formally entered World War I.

Trench Warfare

World War I became the war of the trenches. Each side made trenches on two opposing sides of a big chunk of land, and then spent the next months bombing the heck out of each other and trying out all the new weapons. Millions of people died in these trenches, both from weapons and horrific trench conditions.

If a bomb or a bullet didn't get you, you had to worry about a host of other issues. The trenches filled up with water easily and the soldiers ended up living in a perpetual pool of filth. This could sometimes result in trench foot, where soaking wet feet eventually got infected and might even have to be amputated.

Then there were the rats. Rats hung out in the trenches, feasting on the dead bodies and the bits of food scraps left behind. One of the less lovely parts of war were the piles of dead bodies filled with rats that had burrowed through the eye sockets and were making their homes inside. Yuck!!!

Food was also scarce. The first couple years of the war, soldiers lived on dried beef and biscuits. But as flour started to run out, the biscuits were then made from ground turnips. It took over a week to get the food to the trenches so the soldiers could pretty much be guaranteed that the food would be stale. The food and water also were saturated with germs and soldiers often caught dysentery, a disease where you have diarrhea for days upon days. Great way to die.

Then there was the gas. Using chemical weapons was new in World War I. Before the war, armies had always considered chemical weapon usage to be uncivilized. However, when the French fired tear gas grenades against the Germans during the first months of the war, the precedent had been set. Over the next five years, everything from mustard gas, to chlorine gas, to nerve gas was thrown at the opposition. In total, nearly 100,000 soldiers died from gas attacks and over 1 million spent time in hospitals.

Peace at Last

The war was long and brutal. Millions died on battlefields that stretched across Europe. Those that didn't die on the battlefield risked falling prey to the spreading influenza epidemic or starvation due to lack of supplies. Europe was a mess, for a while it appeared the Allies might lose, but the entrance of the Americans changed the tide of the war. The Allies finally started pushing the Germans back to their homeland.

On June 28, 1919, exactly five years after the Archduke had been shot, both sides gathered at the Palace of Versailles outside of Paris and signed the Treaty of Versailles. This treaty reorganized empires and forced the Germans to accept full responsibility for the war. The German, Austrio-Hungarian, and Ottoman Empires were all divided up and new nations were created. Poland, Finland,

Czechoslovakia, Romania, Yugoslavia, Bulgaria, Syria, Iraq, and Palestine. The age of empires had ended and the age of nations had begun.

Rebuilding Europe

Based on the terms of the Versailles Treaty, Germany would have to assume the primary responsibility for rebuilding the destroyed nations of Europe.

The most important factor of the Treaty of Versailles was the issue of reparations. Germans had to accept full responsibility and this meant they had to pay money to the victors in the form of reparations. These reparations would cover the total cost of the war. Everything. Military weapons and ammunition, clothing and salaries for soldiers, and the civilian buildings, farms, and factories that were destroyed. Even the cost of paying retirement and medical benefits to soldiers and their families. Basically, the entire cost of the war was to be covered by the Germans.

Now, how do you figure out a price tag for that. Is it $38,365,321,412 or $54,987,326,124? The point is no one knew. So instead of agreeing to a number, they just told Germany they'd have to pay a chunk of money until the Allies got tired of taking their money.

The Treaty of Versailles marked the end World War I, and really ticked off the Germans. They ended up hating their government for agreeing to such horrific terms and as their economy sunk deeper and deeper, they were willing to listen to any nutcase who promised them a better life. And that was what made Germany ripe for a guy like Adolph Hitler to come in and take over.

Aside from leading Germany down the pathway to yet another war, the meeting at Versailles had another result—the League of Nations. President Woodrow Wilson presented his Fourteen Points to the European nations. These dealt with how to treat the new nations, how all nations should work together for peace in the world, and the manner in which all of these would be overseen. It was this last idea, Wilson's Fourteenth Point, that led to the creation of the League of Nations. Though the League eventually failed, it did set the precedent for nations working together. Following World War II, again the world would try to create a governing body for maintaining peace in the world, but this time it would be called the United Nations.

▼

CHAPTER 17

ROARING INTO THE DEPRESSION: THE ROARING TWENTIES AND THE GREAT DEPRESSION

Elise Nilsson
Elizabeth Hunter

Life Couldn't be Finer

World War I was over. It had lasted from 1914 to 1918. During these four years of commotion in Europe, America got rich. Very rich. For America, one of the few positives of war is that the economy improves. That's one of the benefits of not fighting a war on your own soil. Nothing of yours gets destroyed and everyone wants to buy products from you. It's a win-win situation.

Throughout the war, America became the chief provider to Europe. You name it, they made it—tanks, boats, guns, bullets, uniforms, cars, and bandages, even food and beverages. They made it like never before, and Europe just kept buying. Even when Europe ran out of money to buy their products, American bankers came up with a great idea—loan them money. See if you understand this: American money was given to other countries which in turn was spent on American products. And in the end, they had to pay America back for the money they borrowed. You can see how America benefited.

To everyone's joy, this industrial expansion continued even after the war ended, thanks to raw materials and high tariffs in America. With such high tariffs on foreign products, people were naturally drawn to purchasing American goods. Some industries in the United States were even given help from the government, called subsidies, which increased their income even further. While European nations recovered from the mass destruction of the first world war, America kept on rolling and never missed a beat.

Put that Drink Down!

Before the nation entered the 1920s, Americans approved the 18th amendment, the final step in the prohibition movement. The amendment made consumption and possession of alcohol illegal. To many, it may seem like a "weird" act. It was a poor decision but had good intentions. For decades, too many men were blowing their money at bars, and not spending quality time at home with their families. Plus, people associated alcohol with drunkards. Drunkards often committed crimes, right? So by prohibiting alcohol, the country would be able to eliminate crime!

Nice idea. What a shame that it didn't work out the way the government hoped it would. In fact, instead of reducing crime, prohibition plunged America into one of the most criminal eras in its history. Think about *The Godfather* and the hundreds of other movies that deal with the mafia. The mafia wasn't fighting over who made the prettiest quilt. No, they were fighting over alcohol; who could make it, and who could sell it.

Something that the prohibitionists didn't consider was that people like their booze. Masses of people were furious and rebelled against not being able to drink. Illegal bars called "speakeasies" were formed. These "speakeasies" were set up all over the nation for people who "required alcohol." But these alcohol dependant people obviously welcomed the idea (Not to mention the delighted gangsters who made loads and loads of money from smuggling alcohol across the country and distributing it to illegal businesses). Hopefully you've heard of Al Capone. If not, he was a famous gangster at the time that made around $105 million per year for smuggling alcohol into the United States. That's not a bad salary!

It's About Time

As the country entered the 1920s, the 19th amendment was also passed. Women in America *finally*, after decades of struggle, received the right to vote. Before, politicians had been able to claim that women were inferior to men, couldn't make key decisions about politics like men, and were best suited making babies and sweeping the floor. World War I changed all that nonsense. When over four million men went to Europe, someone had to step in to fill their shoes in the factories and on the farms. Not only did women take these jobs, but they proved they could do the jobs just as well as the men. When the war ended, the women were asked to give their jobs back to the men, which they did. Even though they'd been kicked out of the workplace, their contribution couldn't be ignored. They'd proven themselves. So, they finally got the right to vote, thus ending the women's suffrage struggle that had been going on since the mid-1800s.

But guess what? They still showed very little interest in politics and often weren't taken seriously. True equality was still a long way away, and some people would say that it's still not there today. Making people treat each other as equals never occurs just with the passing of a law. It's similar to when the 15th amendment was passed. African Americans got the right to vote, but even after they received voting rights, they still had a long way to go before they would be treated equally. Still, the 19th amendment surely gave women a little more power, which, naturally, was a momentous step forward for the nation.

The Booming Years of the 1920s

The 1920s was a wonderful decade. Food was plentiful and cheap. Businesses were making a ton of money, and the middle class was able to buy really fancy toys like cars, radios and refrigerators. People also started having this odd little thing called "free time." Finally, workers looked forward to Saturday and Sunday where they wouldn't have to be in a factory from dawn until dusk.

However, it is important to note that this decade was known as the "Roaring Twenties" for only a select few. After a period of progressive reforms, American business turned back into a series of trusts and large corporations that controlled the marketplace. A miniscule fraction of the American population was extremely rich and only a slightly smaller percentage could be labeled as the middle class. The majority of Americans lived in poverty.

However, with a little more time on their hands and a bit more money in their pocket, entertainment became a big deal. This is where America started to develop its identity. This era was also called the "Jazz Age." Sources of entertainment increased, as people started listening to singers, jazz bands and even "Vaudeville" acts. Furthermore, the number of radio stations increased rapidly. Even with the rise of radio stations and alternate music sources, the most popular form of entertainment was movies. Hundreds of black and white films were made during the decade and millions of movie tickets were sold each week. The movies were *silent*, but no one cared about it because they had no idea that colored movies with sound would be available in the future. Poor them.

The Great Depression by the Numbers

- Richest 1% owns almost half of America's money

- 15%-20% of all Americans can be considered "middle class"

- 200,000 workers a year are fired because machines can now do their jobs

- 30%-40% drop in value of farmland

- 200 companies control over half of American business

- 600 banks on average folded each year

Entertainment is great, but what makes people really happy?
Money.
And nothing makes people happier than making money without having to work. This was where the stock market came in. The New York Stock Exchange became the primary system of investment. Thousands of people bought and sold stocks, or "shares," as they came to be called. The owner of a share owned part of the company. As the company's profits increased, the profits of the shareowners increased, as well. Investing in shares became almost addictive for a large percentage of the population. The stock market became a mania. People started borrowing on "margin" to buy stocks. Here's how the system works. A person borrows money from the brokerage, which is a firm that buys and sells stocks for people, to put towards an investment. An individual puts up part of the cash to make the purchase, while the brokerage loans them the remaining cash. Eventually they have to pay back the loan, plus interest on the loan, known as the "margin rate."

Pay close attention to the word "loan." These people were getting into debt with the hope that they would make back their investment, plus so much more. This was a bad idea.

What attracted so many to this system was the fact that it gave you the opportunity to get a greater return on your investments. But it was a risky business. Yes, you could increase your investments, but you could also lose *a lot* of money and that's why only skilled investors were advised to borrow on margin. Of course we all know that people tend to ignore what others tell them. For some reason when the stock market goes up, people can't imagine it ever coming back down. It's as if the stock market demon hijacks your brain and takes away your ability to make intelligent decisions. People were warned that the bubble would burst, but they simply ignored the warnings.

The Bubble Bursts

The nation's prosperity survived for a decade and a decade only. In September 1929, the stock market came close to a full halt due to the massive amount of unwise investments. Some of the markets later reached new highs, but overall, the stock market began to decline bit by bit.

A month later, on October 24th, prices fell dramatically. Margin buyers had to abandon their stocks. This incredible rush to sell their stocks made prices fall even faster. This day was soon identified as "Black Thursday", which was followed by "Black Tuesday" on October 29th. Now unlike "Pink Wednesday" and "Violet Friday" which are always a hoot, "Black Tuesday" brought tears to the eyes of even the most confident investor. On "Black Thursday," Wall Street collapsed. The well-known Robber Baron by the name of J.P Morgan got together with a bunch of businessmen to try and save the stock market. They collected a total of $30 million, which was a great aid for the market. Prices moved upward and for a while the market was recovered. Unfortunately, the prices dropped soon again, so you could actually look at it as $30 million right out the window. But I suppose it's the thought that counts! Thanks J.P.

This rapid drop proved that bankers could not do much to help the collapse. Soon, the average price of the fifty leading stocks fell by fifty percent. But the stock market collapse was just the catalyst. The causes of the Great Depression went much deeper and would prove difficult to fix.

Overproduction of consumer goods, tons of debt, and a weak farm economy were just a few of the additional roots of America's despair. During World War I, Americans couldn't make enough products to meet the demands of their European customers. More factories were opened, and more products came piling out the door. When the Europeans stopped buying all their stuff, Americans picked up the slack by buying tons of these new products with their rising salaries. The problem was not everyone was wealthy, or even in what we would today call the middle class. So, after a family bought their first refrigerator, their first car, and their first radio, they probably wouldn't be buying their second for awhile. But the factories ignored this reality and kept pumping out the products. The problem was, there was no one to buy them. This is overproduction. The same thing happened on the farms. Farmers got rich during World War I, selling a ton of food to America's starving European allies. They made so much money that they bought more land and started planting more crops. Again, when the demand for these crops went down, the farmers found that their prices dropped a ton. Another tough lesson in supply and demand.

For awhile the problem was solved by allowing people to buy on credit. Can't afford to buy a car? Just buy it on the installment plan. You can pay back little by little and just owe a ton of money to the bank for the rest of your life. You'll see in a second though that buying things on credit is great when you have a job and the money's flowing in. But what happens when you miss a monthly payment and you can't pay the bank? The bank gets a bit unhappy. But what would happen if millions of people started missing their payments?

You'd have a problem.

The 1920s might have been "roaring," but the 1930s would be described with a different adjective.

From Poor to Poorer

You've seen a few of the causes, now see how the cycle of misery played out. The stock market crashed. People and businesses lost money on their investments. These people couldn't pay back their loans. They stopped buying products. Companies started losing money. Companies fired people. People still couldn't buy products. More people get fired. People start getting scared and take money out of banks. Banks run out of money. People start hiding money and stop spending it. Nobody's buying anything. More people get fired.

A Web of Sorrow

The stock market crash of 1929 pushed America into its greatest period of decline, and forcing millions of Americans into a unbeatable depression.

And that ladies and gentlemen is the cycle of a depression.

Problems during the depression were not scarce. The huge percentage of unemployment caused anxiety, as those who actually still had their jobs were constantly in fear of losing them. One out of four of individuals seeking work were not able to find it. Thousands of people went hungry and tons of poor children suffered from the many long-term effects of malnutrition. Families in the countryside started surviving on nuts and berries, while people in the cities started selling apples and pencils to make a bit of money. Aside from the physical effects, psychologically people got tremendously depressed. Men couldn't hold down a job and felt useless. Families had to move to find work.

One benefit was that divorce rates decreased. Couples could not afford separate households so they just continued living with their enemy. Those who *were* getting married had to postpone their wedding plans. Children went to the streets to sell anything they could get their hands on.

You know those stories about how your grandfather walked barefoot to school, uphill, in the snow. Those stories are probably true. They pretty much summed up the Great Depression. If people wanted to survive they had to work together and they did everything they could to keep alive. People were fighting and stealing in the streets for food. Farmers had to kill their own livestock because they needed food. People wore hand-me-downs or homemade clothes. Some people didn't even have any shoes to wear. Many people didn't have even the basic necessities to survive. Many people couldn't pay rent so they lost their houses and had nowhere to live. People weren't getting married because they didn't have enough money. Even people who had done well previously had to stop buying new and expensive things and use the things they already had hoping they would last for a while. Lots of children suffered from malnutrition. People couldn't afford medical help. People died from starvation and disease.

When the whites suffered, the blacks and other minorities were suffering even more. Most of the blacks lost their jobs. "Last hired, first fired," became the motto of minority groups.

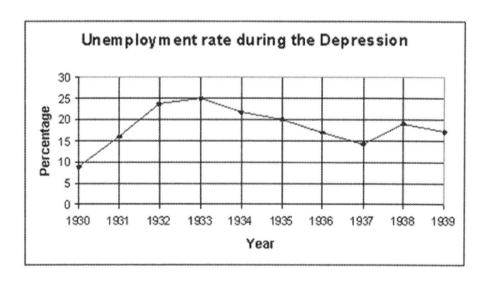

Who's Up for a Challenge?

Let's go back in time a little. In 1928, which was about a year before the depression occurred, a new president was elected. His name was Herbert Hoover. America was still pretty well off at the time of the election and Hoover really had no clue he would soon be up for an incredibly challenging presidency. On "Black Tuesday," Hoover realized that the stock market crash was seriously affecting the economy, as well as international business. He knew it was up to him to save the country. He announced that while he would cut taxes and expand public works spending, he would still try to keep the federal budget balanced.

One of Hoover's strongest beliefs was that aid for the hungry and unemployed should come from the local governments, NOT from the federal government. People need to feel the pride of standing on their own two feet without asking for handouts from their government. Wasn't America built on effort and independence? Hoover believed giving handouts would be insulting. Hoover once said "Every time the government is forced to act, we lose something in self-reliance, character and initiative." It was a noble thought, but when people were starving to death and couldn't find work, they quickly learned that pride can't put food on the table.

One of his responses to the collapse in the economy was the Hawley-Smoot Tariff, an attempt to make raise the import tax on over 20,000 items. At first Hoover was against the proposal, because it clashed with his personal beliefs. Hypothetically, this would increase federal revenue and encourage Americans to buy only American products. Not only did it totally fail to accomplish its goals, but it can be credited with sinking America deeper into depression. In retaliation, other countries then imposed high tariffs on American products which basically meant that the whole world was now having to pay more for products when they didn't have enough money in the first place. Subsequently, Mr. Hawley and Mr. Smoot are not remembered as the two brightest men in American history.

Hoover made additional efforts to try to pull America out of the Depression. He called upon cities, states, and private charities to feed the hungry. Didn't that go against his attitude towards charity? Oh well I guess he changed his mind. Instead of being Mr. Anti-Charity, he started pushing to help out those in need. Hoover persuaded Congress to cut incomes taxes. Unfortunately it didn't help much as incomes were still so low. He brought business and labor leaders to the White House and then "advised" them to keep up wages and keep the factories going despite the state of the nation. Not all the businessmen shared Hoover's desire to take a loss for the sake of the masses. However, Hoover put his money where his mouth was. He cut his own salary by 1/5. (Of course, that wouldn't be *that* difficult of a task for a President. I doubt he ever went hungry.) The immortal baseball player Babe Ruth even made a quip at Hoover's success and salary during this time. After earning $80,000 in 1930, a reporter noted that Ruth earned more than the President of the United States, Herbert Hoover. Ruth replied, "So What? I had a better year than he did."

As if the economic problems weren't bad enough, the country was hit by a drought in 1930. Half a million farms in eighteen states were affected. Crops withered and cattle died. In a desperate attempt to help out, Congress offered $20 million in farm aid. The drought, along with the failures of many programs upset and irritated farmers and unemployed workers deeply.

One group, former veterans of World War I, organized in 1932 and decided to do something about the situation. About 20,000 went on what was called the "Bonus March" to Washington D.C where they protested by sleeping on the lawn in front of the Capitol Building and marching through the city. They demanded compensation for time served in the military. Some of the thousands of "Bonus Marchers" spent the nights in tents and shacks. They named these little camps "Hoovervilles" in an attempt to mock the president. The Hoover administration worried that this large group of people would turn into a mob. On July 28, 1932, a policeman killed a marcher who was causing disorder. President Hoover got extremely frustrated with these rebels so he sent the army to drive them away.

Looking back, you have to wonder if Hoover developed an ulcer. Life wasn't going too well for Americans, and he was taking a great deal of the blame. The country had enough of Hoover and in 1932 they would have pretty much elected any Democrat that had a heartbeat.

To the Rescue

The man chosen by the Democrats was the governor or New York, Franklin Delano Roosevelt, who from now on will be referred to as FDR, because his name is way too long.

FDR was the distant, distant, distant cousin of Teddy Roosevelt, one of the most hyper presidents in America's history. FDR had an equally endearing personality. He had survived polio, and even though he never regained the usage of his legs (even though the movie *Pearl Harbor* has him standing up), his smile never failed him. He was a master compromiser who wasn't afraid to make difficult choices when necessary.

In 1932, difficult choices were definitely necessary. America was only sinking deeper into recession. Something had to be done.

Once in office, FDR got to work immediately. His "First 100 Days" were some of the busiest of any president in history. Just like Hoover, he had various ideas for solving the country's economic issues. It's almost impossible to name all the programs that he pushed through Congress during his Presidency, as there were so many. Feel free to check out the chart and see if through some gift of memory, you can remember them all. There was the CCC, the PWA, the CWA, the AAA, the NIRA, not to mention many more. No wonder they became known as Roosevelt's "alphabet soup" plan. These laws were formed to create jobs, provide relief and to speed up the economic recovery.

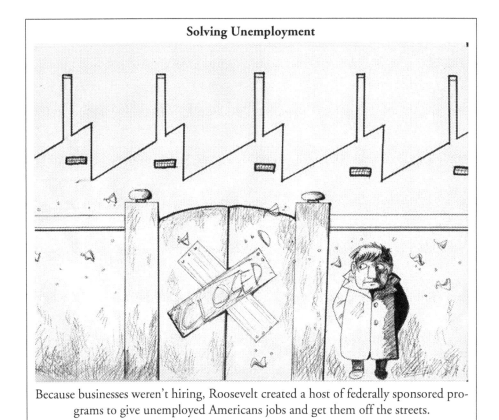

Solving Unemployment

Because businesses weren't hiring, Roosevelt created a host of federally sponsored programs to give unemployed Americans jobs and get them off the streets.

On March 4, 1933, FDR spoke to Congress about his New Deal, which he said aimed at the three R's—recovery, relief, and reform. One of the things he asked for was a bank holiday, which would last for four days starting March 6. People had been getting a bit tense about their money in the bank, so they had all panicked and withdrew their money simultaneously. Bad idea. If there is no money in the banks, no money can be loaned out, no money can be invested, and the economy starts crashing further. Roosevelt got on the radio the Sunday before the holiday and explained what he was doing and why. The people listened and understood. For the first time in awhile, it appeared they had a president listening to their needs.

FDR quickly surrounded himself with a group of educated advisers. This group came to be called his "Brain Trust." He even invited people from universities and the business world. He would listen to almost any idea, and then make a decision after weighing all the pros and cons. Fortunately, he had an advantage other presidents don't always have. He was a Democrat. Congress had a majority of Democrats. So any law FDR wanted to get through would pass through Congress without much difficulty. Most of these acts gave the government far more power than it had ever had. Not only were people not expected to get out of the depression on their own, everyone started looking to the government for help. This then started a new phase in America's history, where the government could be counted on to help out its citizens.

Play By My Rules

One problem. Though the Democrats ruled Congress and the White House, they didn't control the Supreme Court. After awhile, the Supreme Court started shooting down these laws as unconstitutional. The Supreme Court thought this was giving too much power to the government, especially the president.

This was a problem for Roosevelt, because the Supreme Court justices were pretty much serving for life. What to do? What to do? FDR tried to convince them of the greatness of his programs, but they weren't buying it. He wanted to add judges and force retirement on Justices over a certain age. You see, by doing so, he would have eliminated three of his opponents in the Supreme Court. This certainly wasn't the wisest thing he thought of during his presidency. The Supreme Court was upset, Congress, who had always been on his side, now saw his actions as very manipulative. Was he the president or the king?

Back to his programs. Basically there were three different kinds of programs set up: those for financial recovery, those for relief for the unemployed and those for industrial recovery. Here's an idea of the kinds of acts passed from each category. The Emergency Banking Relief Act was passed to provide financial recovery. As for the relief for the unemployed, one of the acts passed was called the Tennessee Valley Authority. It gave hydro-electricity, plus jobs, to residents of a large part of Tennessee. As you can imagine, such an act was incredibly helpful for those seeking work. The National Recovery Administration and the Agricultural Adjustment Administration were two of the industrial recovery programs. He also set up the FDIC. What's that? Well, next time you go to the bank, look on the door and you'll see a sign that says "FDIC Insured." That means if the bank burns down, your money is insured and the government will pay you back. Probably the most lasting of his ideas was the Social Security Act, in which both workers and employees paid money to the government and, in turn, the government would provide them with unemployment money if they ever didn't have a job and monthly retirement checks once they got old. But Social Security probably doesn't sound that important to you, because it will probably run out in about thirty years.

	Name	**Year**	**Definition**
TVA	Tennessee Valley Authority	1933	Build dams, power plants in Tenn.
FERA	Federal Emergency Relief Administration	1933	Helped take care of unemployed
CWA	Civil Works Administration	1933	Jobs repairing roads and parks
HOLC	Home Owners Loan Corporation	1933	Helped people get loans
NIRA	National Industrial Recovery Act	1933	Companies have to compete fairly
FDIC	Federal Deposit Insurance Corporation	1933	Insured bank deposits
AAA	Agricultural Adjustment Act	1933	Farmers paid to make less
PWA	Public Works Administration	1933	Jobs for buildings, schools, dams
CCC	Civilian Conservation Corps	1933	Jobs making National Parks pretty
FCA	Farm Credit Act	1933	Loans for farmers

FHA	Federal Housing Administration	1934	Bank loans insured by government
SEC	Securities Exchange Act	1934	Stock traders can't be naughty
IRA	Indian Reorganization Act	1934	Organized Indian reservations
WPA	Works Progress Administration	1935	Money for works and the arts
REA	Rural Electrification Administration	1935	Loans to make power in countryside
NYA	National Youth Administration	1935	Gave jobs to young adults

Dealing with Criticism

The Supreme Court was still very against FDR's New Deal and they confronted him by saying that both the NIRA and AAA were unconstitutional. Again the President responded manipulatively. He proposed a court-reorganization plan, which would have increased the number of judges. He justified this by saying they needed new judges because their lives were just too darn busy. Really, he just wanted to be able to swing the vote in his favor.

However, the Supreme Court was not FDR's only opponent. Liberals and Socialists teamed up to criticize his New Deal. They didn't think it was effective enough. They were angered by the fact that it did not do enough for the unemployed. Even an Anti-New Deal American Liberty League was formed by a bunch of conservative critics. Poor FDR. What was he supposed to do now?

During the time period when the President was working hard to try and fix the many problems America was dealing with, labor unions rose up once again. The events that stimulated the rise of these unions were mainly the passing of the National Industrial Recovery Act in 1933 and the National Labor Relations Act in 1935. These acts both restarted the labor movement in the nation. Whereas in the 1920s companies pretty much did whatever they wanted under Republican presidents who favored big business, the 1930s saw a labor comeback. Various strikes were organized, and as a result the labor unions saw improvement in 1938. This was when Congress passed the Fair-Labor Standards Act, which allowed a minimum wage of $0.40 an hour, a maximum workweek of 40 hours and limited child labor on those less than sixteen years of age.

Times Are Getting Better… Or Are They Really?

Towards the middle of the decade, the nation ultimately achieved some measure of recovery, but bankers and businessmen were turning against the New Deal, as they were not making as much profit as they wanted. They disliked FDR's concessions to labor and were appalled by the fact that the nation had been taken off the gold standard. You could say they were getting a little scared of the president's "experiments" and feared losing their wealth. So guess what the president decided to do? Create a new program of reform, of course! This new program included social security, heavier taxes on the wealthy people, new controls over banks and public utilities, along with a huge work relief program for the unemployed. Sounds kind of like what he did earlier? Probably was, too, but since his old attempts mostly frustrated people, he attempted new ones out of sheer worry.

All the same, the country seemed to be approaching some kind of end to this drawn out depression. There was a noticeable improvement in the economy around 1937. Oh, the joy! But no. When the president noticed an improvement, he decided to cut down the payments and programs offered by the government. Bad idea. Unemployment now rose from $6 million to $10 million in less than a year. America just couldn't pull itself out of the Great Depression on its own. Only another world war could accomplish that.

A Long Awaited Resolution

Luckily, in 1940 business was strong again, as it had reached the levels of early 1937 when times were prosperous (until *someone* messed that up). Of course, the depression was far from over. Millions were still unemployed. In fact, most Americans believe the Great Depression did not end until World War II and I will attempt to explain why. When France fell in 1940 and Britain was blockaded, Roosevelt sent all possible aid (except military involvement) to Britain. This was sort of like the first step to wealth, as Britain now started purchasing supplies from the United States, which surely was a helping hand for the American economy. America entered the war soon after the Japanese had attacked Pearl Harbor on Dec 7, 1941. Here is where America pulled itself out of the most horrible recession in its history. Tons of products had to be made for not only America but for all its allies. Everyone had a job. Americans invested in the country by buying war bonds. Factories worked day and night to fulfill the war demand. By the end of World War II, America was the richest nation in the world, producing more than any other country. It had also emerged from the war relatively free from destruction and with a huge military. America would spend the next fifty years as the dominant nation in the world.

But that's another chapter.

CHAPTER 18

▼

THE SECOND WAR TO END ALL WARS: WORLD WAR II—EUROPE

Akshay Balsubramani

The Making of a Madman

Now we've come to the largest war in the 30,000-year history of humankind—World War II. In order to understand the war, we have to first look into the life of Adolf Hitler, the most powerful man in Germany during WWII and one of the cruelest dictators in history. If there were no Hitler, there would have been no World War II.

Hitler was born in Braunau, Austria on April 20, 1889. He hated his father, who was supposedly quite cruel to young Adolf. Adolf was an excellent student in elementary school (imagine Hitler being a good young boy) and loved art, but he started to become rebellious by college prep school, and was failing when he dropped out. Since his childhood, Hitler wanted to become an artist, so he tried to join the Viennese Art Academy in 1907; he was rejected. This was probably when the ordinary guy started to become one of the world's great villains. He was very depressed and extremely angry at being rejected, and lived a poor life in Vienna trying to get his pretty little painted postcards sold.

Then he met the mayor of Vienna, Karl Lueger. Lueger used the press to manipulate the public. Adolf loved this idea of manipulating the public, and he later borrowed Lueger's ideas when he became the German leader. Lueger and Hitler shared a hatred for Jews, also known as anti-Semitism.

As you hopefully now know, World War I started in the early 1910's. What was Hitler doing around that time? Well, we already covered the contact with Lueger. Hitler then moved to Germany in May 1913 because he didn't want to be drafted into the Austrian army. Actually, "drafted" isn't the word for it; young Austrian men were conscripted into the army, which basically involved the government coming to your home, putting a gun to your head, and forcing you to leave for the war. So Hitler moved to Munich, Germany, and was then caught there and forced back to Austria. This next part is really surprising—Hitler managed to get in front of a bunch of Austrian draft officials and somehow convince them that he had been a good boy and was not actually trying to get past the draft. Well, they were convinced, and he wasn't punished.

Unfortunately for him, because he said he wasn't trying to dodge the draft, he had to take the army entrance exams. It didn't really matter, because Hitler failed the physical test and went back to Munich, legally this time. Strangely enough, Hitler volunteered for the German army and fought decently in the war. Although he was injured twice and didn't get promoted to any rank beyond corporal, which is a pretty low rank, he won an award called the Iron Cross First Class, for showing his courage in battle.

Adolf Hitler: Rookie Nazi Recruit

After World War I ended, Hitler eventually got the job as a political officer in Munich. Remember Lueger's anti-Semitism and his other ideas? Well, Hitler joined the small German Workers' Party, which had the same ideas. We already know that Hitler was a great speaker and was really persuasive...after all, he escaped punishment for draft dodging. When he spoke for the German Workers' Party (NAZI), people listened, and Hitler soon became one of the most important party members. It was no surprise when in April 1921 he became the leader, or Führer, of the National Socialist German Workers' Party, the new name for the German Workers' Party.

So now we have Hitler leading the tiny Nazi party, and looking to spread his ideas by expanding the party. Up to 1923, this was pretty easy for him—Germany was suffering from a terrible depression. Let's try and find out why:

Cast: Germany, Allies
Time: just after WWI ended
Germany: Okay, so I lost. What are you asking me to do? I surrendered already…
Allies: Just pay us a lot of money since we lost many men and lots of equipment during the war, and it's all your fault…pay $100 trillion up front and a few trillion per year for the next century…that doesn't include the 50% interest, of course.
Germany: WHAT! That is going to ruin me!
Allies: Too bad, so sad. You should have thought of that before you attacked us. You lost, didn't you? You have to do what we tell you.
All quoted money values are completely made up

So Germany had to pay massive reparations—sort of like damages in a lawsuit—and therefore went virtually bankrupt. Of course, the German people suffered the most. Some of the common people wanted a change of government. They couldn't imagine it getting any worse. Hitler was only too happy to make great speeches insulting the German government and blaming all of Germany's problems on the Jews, the government leaders who signed the peace treaty, and the horrible Allies who continued to oppress them. This strategy worked really well. Everyone loves someone to blame for their problems.

After hearing about an Italian called Mussolini take over his government, Hitler became inspired to do the same. He and his followers surrounded a beer hall as part of a plan to try to take over the German government during November 8-9, 1923, and in the end he got arrested. He was sentenced to many years in jail but only spent one. This was actually a pretty light sentence for someone who wanted to overthrow the government—people today can be jailed for a year just for stealing a TV from Radio Shack. Anyway, the government outlawed the Nazi party, and people stopped supporting it.

Meanwhile, Hitler was in jail, dreaming up new and evil ways to conquer the world. During his stay behind bars, Hitler went through 4,732 pencils and eventually completed *Mein Kampf*, a massive book outlining his views and his life—the title means "My Struggle." This book was a Nazi follower's dream. Imagine having a book that condemned the Jews, declared Germans to be the master race, and demanded a German revolution, all in one convenient, easy-to-carry book written by their leader! For this reason, *Mein Kampf* became the Nazis' Cookbook from that point onward.

Finally the year was up, and Hitler stepped outside the prison walls, tasted freedom…and immediately started rebuilding his weakened party. For a few years, nothing much changed about the Nazis, but suddenly, the Great Depression hit America and the world. Hitler, as we know, absolutely loved depressions, and the Nazis started to grow again, this time dramatically. In the elections of September 1930, Nazi representation in Parliament increased by almost *ninefold*, from 12 to 107. Two years later, he came in second behind a guy named Hindenburg in the presidential elections. The stage was set for Hitler to come into power and start arming Germany.

Who Let This Guy Be Leader?

On January 30, 1933, Hitler was appointed Chancellor of Germany by Hindenburg (who, incidentally, didn't really like him—this was just the only way to keep German politics stable). On February 28, 1933, something very important happened—Hitler somehow persuaded Parliament to pass the Enabling Act, which declared that Germany was in an emergency state. It then stated that the constitution could be ignored because of the emergency and gave Hitler special powers to deal with the situation. The rest is history—Hitler eliminated every one of his opponents, and President Hindenburg died in 1934, leaving Hitler to enjoy his new position as Führer, or leader, of Germany.

Hitler then spent time getting Germany ready for the war, which he would start. We need to stop here for a moment. Aside from the ridiculously huge reparations, the Versailles Treaty also said that Germany couldn't have a military. Hitler ignored this. He built up a militia 3 million men strong known as the Sturmabteilung, and employed 6 million more Germans by putting them in factories to strengthen the country. So, while the other European nations sat back with their twenty year old weapons, Hitler set out to create the most powerful military in the world. Hitler realized that England and France were really afraid of another world war, so they were willing to do just about anything for him, in a process known as appeasement, so long as it would keep him from starting a war. Pretty interesting, isn't it—just a few years back, Germany had to pay those countries a ton of money, and by the mid-1930s Hitler was calling all the shots. Military force scares people.

Hitler

Hitler only rose to power because the climate of Germany was ripe for change.

America Before the War—This is a US History Book, Remember?

America was being pushed away from war by a group of people called the isolationists, who wanted America to remain more isolated from world affairs. Not everyone agreed. FDR (that's Franklin Delano Roosevelt, the US President, for all those who didn't read the previous chapter) was against this isolationist policy and felt that if America didn't get involved, it would be Hitler's next target. Get it? Good, then we can continue.

The isolationists pushed for a bunch of Neutrality Acts to be passed in the years leading from 1935 to Pearl Harbor in 1941. These Acts prevented exporting weapons on American ships to countries who were at war; the isolationists thought that this was a good policy to keep America out of war. Good idea, but a really popular president like FDR had his way anyway. He couldn't stop the Neutrality Acts from being passed, but he did get the "cash and carry" arms policy passed in 1937, which basically said that any country at war could buy weapons from America if they paid cash up front for the weapons and transported them on their ships, not America's. Kind of sneaky, but it worked—FDR was able to keep helping democracies like England and France from the war's beginning. FDR got his way in another thing, too. He managed to stop a proposed constitutional amendment which banned war without the American population's popular vote—as you might have guessed, the public was not pro-involvement like FDR. In November of 1938, FDR really started getting jumpy when Hitler increased the Holocaust's intensity. FDR demanded that the arms embargo—the banning of weapons exports—be lifted, but it wasn't...not then, at least. We'll leave US policy for right now and move on to Europe.

Europe—See, We Finally Got to the Point

Like the previous section, all we really need to know is a couple of simple facts to understand this section. Firstly, how would you feel in 1938 if you were England or any of the other countries which won WWI? Well, let's consider: Germany was on the rise again, you were generally having a decent time with a recovering economy, and your people definitely didn't want war. You would probably dislike the idea of war, especially if the only thing Hitler said he wanted was a small piece of land in what is now the Czech Republic. The democratic European nations, led by England and its Prime Minister Chamberlain, adopted a policy called appeasement; they said that if Hitler or Mussolini (Remember him from early on in this chapter? He became the dictator of Italy) wanted something, they could have it if it prevented war. Or, to use a slightly confusing figure of speech, "No war at all costs." The second thing we should remember is that Hitler quickly realized this and thought, "So they'll give me just about anything if I say there won't be war—how interesting, they seem to be really trusting and truthful."

The rest of the section should be no surprise. Hitler was given Sudetenland on September 28, 1938 in an attempt to prevent war. On March 15, 1939, Hitler broke his pledge and took Czechoslovakia by force; the European countries still didn't react. Hitler and Stalin, the USSR's leader, signed a non-aggression pact in 1939:

Hitler: Okay, Josef...that's your first name, right?
Stalin: Yah. My name is Josef Stalin and I was born on...
Hitler: Shut up. I forgot what I was going to say...ah, here. (*digs out written speech from his pocket*) Here we go...what I was going to say was—I consider

the master race to consist of men that are tall, blond haired, German born with blue eyes and an athletic physique able to—

Stalin: Umm…let me ask you something my friend. Do you own a mirror?

Hitler: I don't know what you're getting at. Anyway, here's the deal Joe. I won't attack you if you don't attack me. I also want western Poland for Germany. Agreed?

Stalin: Yah. What do I get in return?

Hitler: You can have all that land just west of Russia.

Stalin: Fine then…

Note: "All that land" is now Finland, Estonia, Lithuania, Latvia, Ukraine, Belarus, and a few other countries in the area.

A few dates: On September 1, 1939, Hitler invaded Poland. On the 3rd, because England had promised to defend Poland if attacked, a domino of European countries declared war on Germany. On September 17, Stalin invaded Poland, and 12 days later, it was conquered.

Date	German Events That Led to War
Aug. 2, 1934	Hindenburg dies, Hitler takes over absolute power
March 16, 1935	Hitler announces he's ignoring Versailles Treaty and will make a ton of weapons
March 7, 1936	Troops enter Rhineland to take land back from France
March 12, 1938	Hitler invades Austria one month after signing an agreement saying he wouldn't
Sept. 30, 1938	Munich Agreement: Great Britain, France, and Italy give Sudetenland to Germany
March 30, 1939	France and England agree to support/defend Poland if attacked
May 1939	Denmark signs non-aggression treaty; Hitler breaks treaty one year later
Aug. 23, 1939	Germany and Russia sign non-aggression pact; Hitler breaks treaty 2 years later
Sept.1, 1939	Germany invades Poland
Sept. 3, 1939	Britain and France declare war on Germany

April 9, 1940	Germany invades Denmark and Norway
May 10, 1940	Germans invade Holland, Luxembourg, Belgium, France
June 14, 1940	German troops enter Paris
July 10, 1940	Germany begins air attack on London

Wow, A New German Word—Blitzkrieg

What? Blitzkrieg? It's not as hard to understand as it sounds—just a new way of making war pioneered by the Germans in WWII. It means "lightning war" in German, and it basically concentrates on striking fast and hard at the enemy, tearing down the defenses against you and quickly conquering your goal.

The whole idea of blitzkrieg started back in World War I, when the German army tried using "stormtroopers" (just a long word for the best of the infantry, or foot soldiers; sound familiar from Star Wars?) to quickly break through enemy lines and destroy them. They forgot that even the best foot soldiers get tired, especially when they have to carry enough supplies for days or even weeks on end and move quickly. So anyway, the German plan failed, and they lost WWI.

Then, tanks were made really powerful and efficient—more so than anywhere else in the world—by the Germans after World War I. They called these tanks Panzers, and they were pretty deadly. Imagine a whole mass of roaring, fast tanks charging at you as opposed to a yelling mass of people running at you. Which would be more intimidating and powerful? The tanks, of course. So Germany tried to make its army as tank-based and mechanized as possible before even starting WWII. They had a nice chance to test the Panzers in the Spanish Civil War in 1936, supporting the Spanish rebels. No prizes for guessing who won. Spain was a supporter of Germany, Italy, and Japan (the Axis powers) after that war.

Here's more on the strategy of blitzkrieg. A good way to soften up enemy lines before using your tanks is to send out planes to strategically bomb places, which are important to the enemy. These include airfields (so that the enemy can't bomb your tanks or refuel, land, etc.), communication centers (it's great if you hit a major one; the enemy cannot coordinate attacks, and information can't be relayed for defense; some places might be totally undefended), and transportation arteries like highways and railroads. If there are extra bombs or planes left, the enemy defense lines, especially the rear portion (which will normally be undefended) can be considered targets. Another nice way of causing confusion to prepare for the tank strike is to send masses of infantry at the enemy without trying to actually attack in earnest and thus losing few men. If you were an enemy general, already in some confusion due to widespread bombings of your territory, wouldn't you rearrange your defense lines and pull certain men off certain spots to defend against other spots which are being swarmed by infantry? This is exactly what the attackers are looking for; they can now send in the tanks.

Ah, the part we've all been looking forward to: the tank strike. Let's dramatize the situation:

> *Scene: Hitler gives orders over the phone during one of his blitzkrieg campaigns, general advising him.*
> Hitler: *(on phone)* Send in the Panzers! Let's put one every kilometer or so, strung out in a line.
> General: Why? That's suicide, sir!
> Hitler: *(to general)* It looks nice on the paper…like a pretty little caterpillar dancing on the road…
> General: Sorry, sir, but in blitzkrieg, the Panzers are used in tight formations. That way, if the enemy attacks even one Panzer, all the other Panzers are close enough to fire back along with the Panzer under attack.
> Hitler: *(on phone)* Tight formations, then! *(to general)* Okay, fine, just don't talk back again, boy.
> General: Yes, sir! *(under his breath)* Man, this guy isn't the sharpest crayon in the box.
> Hitler: Tanks are enough for this little assault…aren't they?
> General: I'm sorry, sir, but generally, other mechanical units like planes or maybe motorcycles are sent in to generally harass the defenders and prevent them from taking a hill or some place from which they can defend. I recommend keeping the infantry in, too…they're just there to make confusion, anyway, and there's no point in telling them to stop.
> Hitler: Someday I'll order you executed for being a smart aleck…but you're useful for now. We seem to be winning.

And here's how the blitzkrieg actually worked when put into practice. I'll just give it to you all at once: Hitler used blitzkrieg to rip through Denmark, Norway, the Netherlands, Luxembourg, Belgium and much of France in less than three months, starting in April 1940 and going until June 14, 1940, when Germany took Paris. That's six countries in three months, invading France by going around the Maginot Line by breaking through the Ardennes Forest. By the way, the Maginot Line was a line of trenches and forts covering eastern France which the French military thought was impossible to break through. They got a huge surprise when it was pretty much flattened by German Panzers as part of the blitzkrieg (too bad we couldn't have seen the looks on the French generals' faces).

Blitzkrieg was used in a couple of other places, too. Hitler used it a bit in Poland, and one of Hitler's generals, Rommel, used it for a while to take much of North Africa. It's been copied by other countries in many wars since WWII. For example, America used it in the Gulf War, which didn't even last two months. America also used it in the Iraq War. It was, of course, extensively modified to include "smart" missiles, advanced bombers, and other bits of technology, but the concept remained the same. Basically, blitzkrieg is a great idea, which has worked really well many times, so everyone wants to use it—that's not too hard to remember.

Enough About Blitzkriegs, Get on With the War

Now that I've taken you through a brief little lesson on military strategy, let's get back to the war. We'll pick up in the second half of 1940, when Hitler, Mussolini, and Co. were feeling great. Using a new war tactic which nobody had heard of and even less people could pronounce, Germany and the Axis powers had taken just about all of mainland Europe besides southern France, which they didn't really care about anyway. Except for one thing…there were still two strong and annoying countries to take care of—America and Britain. For Germany and Italy, America was too far away to think about attacking, especially since England was in the way. Well, there was only one country left: England.

Between July and October 1940, Hitler sent huge numbers of bombers to large British cities. Of course, the British didn't just take it lying down—they tried to fight back. The only problem was that their RAF (Royal Air Force) didn't have half as many planes—literally—as the attacking Luftwaffe, the German air force. So the British tried to use a new technology called radar to spot the German bombers before they came. Did it work? What do you think? Of course it worked, and radar has been used ever since for this kind of wartime stuff and also for peacetime air traffic. The British also had another trump card to play which the Germans never expected: Ultra.

> *Scene: British forces defending London from bombers. Private 1 does not know about Ultra yet, while Private 2 does. "Private" is a very low rank in the army.*
> Private 1: So let me get this straight: they have 1000 bombers operational right now, we don't know how many are being sent today to bomb London or even to bomb England, we have 200 planes to spread out among all the cities of England, and you're smiling?

Private 2: Sure, why not?

Private 1: *(saying each syllable slowly and ominously)* Be-cause they are go-ing to mur-der us…

Private 2: Every day's a happy day with Ultra!

Private 1: Have you gone crazy or am I missing something?

Private 2: Don't you know about Ultra? It's this amazing decoding system. The Nazis send ultra-secret coded messages where we can intercept them; they don't care too much, because they think the messages have an unbreakable code. But we use Ultra to decode the messages, and we know where they're going to hit next. Since we know what cities they're going to bomb today, we can send our planes to only those cities and fight them off with the help of radar.

Private 1: But why is it called "Ultra"?

Private 2: You know, the messages are "ultra-secret".

Private 1: *(sarcastically)* Wow, I couldn't have come up with a better name.

Even though some British targets were destroyed, the Ultra and radar aided British defense was for the most part really successful. Hitler eventually got tired of having bombers destroyed by the RAF, and he decided that the invasion of England could wait, thus ending what was called the Battle of Britain.

America During the War—Again, This is a US History Book

Fine, fine, let's get back to American history. America still hadn't joined the war—we had to wait for Pearl Harbor in 1941 for that—but there were definitely enough people giving the government advice on how to fight the war if America got involved. One guy who made his predictions and suggestions nearly two decades before Pearl Harbor but was very foresighted was Billy Mitchell, an ex-WWI pilot. He said that America should be the first to realize that air power was the future of war. He even arranged a demonstration in which airplanes sank "unsinkable" heavy battleships easily. Is spite of this, you know what happened to him? He was court-martialed and basically wasn't allowed to keep his military job for five years. He did manage to get something done, though; he influenced another guy called Moffett, an admiral (really high rank), who tried to get more airplane research done using his power in the military.

Let's move on to the most important person in America—President Roosevelt. He wanted to protect the "free nations" including England, France, and the other Allies. During the Battle of Britain, he desperately wanted to help Britain, but at first, he didn't know how to get this kind of a bill past the isolationists in Congress without declaring war and destroying his reputation. Then, he managed to sneak in a couple of non-war bills which would help Britain. One of these was the "Destroyers for Bases" trade, in which America would give Britain some warships in exchange for some unimportant naval bases in places like Central America. Essentially, America was just giving the British destroyers since neither America nor Britain really thought that the bases were important. Like Hitler, FDR had great persuasive powers (funny how all these leaders are like this), and he got the Lend-Lease bill passed using these. This stated that America could lend or lease supplies to other countries if this would protect America's security. The bill, of course, gave FDR the power to really start helping Britain out, because helping Britain could be viewed as helping American security, and America could "loan" equipment to England on a larger scale.

The 1940 presidential election in America was kind of close, unlike the other two FDR elections. This time, the Republican opponent was Wendell Willkie. The only real issue in this election was whether people liked what FDR had done so far or not, since Willkie didn't find a deciding issue to really make his position unique. To understand who won and why, put yourself in the mind of a typical voter. Would you have really wanted to avoid reelecting the guy whose policies had guided America through the Depression pretty successfully and instead elect a guy whom you barely know about in the middle of the biggest war in history? "Probably not," said most voters, and FDR won for the unprecedented third time in a row—nobody ever did that before or has done it since. Although the election may look like a total landslide at first with the electoral vote split 449-82, the election was much closer than that—if less than a million Roosevelt voters had voted for Willkie instead, he would have won. Hmmm…it would be interesting to think how history would have changed if that had happened. I just can't imagine Wilkie sitting down to talk with Churchill and Stalin.

If you were a typical American living in the last half of 1941, you would have been pretty worried about the war reaching America; many events put America on the brink of war. First, we have to understand that starting from September 1, 1940, America started sending ships to convoy British shipments—in other words, guard against their capture and defend them by sailing alongside them. Hitler wasn't too happy with this, because sinking tons of British supplies would have made it much easier for him to invade England and finish off the whole European takeover plan. So a year and three days later (that's September 4, 1941, for anybody who can't think today), Germany attacked the *Greer*, an American ship. And for the 9,642 time the catalyst for America entering a war was a boat being sunk. FDR, who had been looking for an excuse to help the Allies out, declared that American ships could shoot German subs on sight. In October, two more American ships were hit, and America was basically fighting an undeclared war with the Germans in the Atlantic.

Hitler Makes His Mistake

Everyone who's reading this probably knows that winning a match in sports is usually all about capitalizing on the other guy's mistakes. In war, it's the same: when you are losing and the opponent makes a mistake, you have a chance to turn things around. Hitler made his mistake on June 22, 1941, when he invaded Russia. Even non-military people like us can tell that that's not very smart; Hitler made the Nonaggression Pact with the USSR so that he wouldn't have to fight a war on two fronts, and then he broke it? Stupid idea! The Nazis overcame the Soviets by pure force for a few months and advanced to within a few miles of several major cities. Then winter struck, and the German invasion was stalled; equipment froze and men suffered. The end result was that several German armies were pinned down in Russia for months on end, giving the Allies time to get their second wind and go on the offensive. If you can't picture this, rent *Enemy at the Gates*. It's a good movie and describes how the Russians refused to surrender Stalingrad and eventually pushed back the Germans.

Simultaneously, the war started to turn the Allies' way in the Atlantic. Through luck or hard work at the right time—call it what you like—radar and sonar were invented and used by Allied ships, which were able to avoid and even attack German submarines successfully for the first time. This opened up a more stable supply line between America and England, which in turn let the Allies strike back while the Russians held down large German armies to the east. Another event which really helped the Allies was the Pearl Harbor attack on December 7, 1941. After Pearl Harbor, America officially joined the Allies, which allowed America to full its full support behind England.

Yes, WWII was Fought in Africa

Meanwhile, the Axis powers were trying to conquer North Africa. The head commander there was Erwin Rommel, an amazingly successful general nicknamed the "Desert Fox." Rommel was born in Germany on November 15, 1891, and wanted to become an engineer—he was good at math in school. From the beginning, he was a military man; he enrolled in military school, fought in WWI, and, through a strange coincidence, was awarded the Iron Class, First Class, just like Hitler. He was noted as really outstanding by his commanders, though; in 1917, he was awarded "Pour la Merite," which was normally given to generals only— and Rommel was about five ranks short of general.

His rise up the ranks continued until in September of 1939, he was promoted to Major General and appointed commander of Hitler's bodyguard until the Polish campaign ended. How much of an honor was this? Well, the old greeting "Grüss Gott" (Greet God) had been replaced with "Heil Hitler" (Hail Hitler) in Germany, so Hitler was pretty much a god there, and being in charge of defending him was an unbelievably high honor. Rommel caught Hitler's attention as a good commander, and Hitler granted his request to command a Panzer division for the first time. Rommel's group helped to take over France, and he became famous among the military for doing what he wanted—which almost always worked—without paying attention to how things were normally done. For example, Rommel didn't send regular communications to his commanders (which was required), and moved around so much that neither the Germans nor the Allies knew where he was, only to resurface and capture a target using perfect blitzkrieg tactics.

Rommel eventually was appointed to be the commander of the Afrika Korps, the German force in Africa. He used incredible improvisation and ingenuity to defeat the Allies repeatedly. An example of such tactics was a diversion. Rommel tied bundles of wood and bushes to a bunch of light trucks, with a few tanks in front. The Allies were totally fooled into thinking that this was the main force by the massive dust clouds generated as the bushes were dragged across the sand and by the few tanks in front. As they turned to chase the "force," Rommel's real force appeared from behind and totally destroyed them.

Rommel would have taken Egypt—he had marched all the way from Libya to western Egypt with barely a pause—except that he didn't have enough supplies. Hitler's not-so-smart decision to attack the USSR had made that the first-priority supply destination and had pulled supplies from everywhere else. When Rommel reached El Alamein, Egypt, he had to wait for a while for more supplies to reach him. The Allies under General Montgomery took advantage of the German mistake in sending inadequate supplies (remember the sports analogy) and finally beat Rommel at El Alamein on November 4, 1939. The Afrika Korps finally had to retreat to Tunis in Tunisia. On November 8, a large Allied group landed in Vichy-controlled northwest Africa. In case you're wondering, Vichy France was essentially southern France—the part which the Axis powers didn't take. They lived in fear of the Axis powers and had to support them, but when the Allies came in, Vichy France was happy to support them and defect from the Axis side. The two Allied forces, Montgomery chasing Rommel from the east and the later arrivals coming in from the west, cornered the Afrika Korps at Tunis. Rommel was recalled to Germany, the Axis army in North Africa surrendered, and the Allies were really starting to turn this thing around.

Then the Allies started taking everything back. The successful landing at Normandy allowed them to take back France, and the USSR was pressing on Germany from the east. But instead of surrendering, Hitler starting behaving—not very normally, as we covered earlier. Rommel didn't like this too much, and he was possibly one of the people involved in the 1944 assassination attempt on Hitler. The German government realized that Rommel didn't agree with Hitler anymore—well, we all know the punishment for disagreeing with Hitler. Rommel was given a choice: either commit suicide (to the public, death with honor through wounds he had suffered) or be executed on charges of treason, which could have made his family accomplices. On October 14, 1944, one of the greatest generals of the century committed suicide as the only alternative to save his family. I said it before, and I'll say it again: ouch.

The Holocaust

It would be stupid to discuss World War II without discussing the Holocaust. Hitler's attempted annihilation of the entire Jewish population has become so synonymous with World War II, that you must know some background.

First, there were two basic stages of Hitler's camps. First came the concentration camps. To these camps, Hitler sent anyone who threatened his power or he felt was an outcast of society. Intellectuals, Gypsies, homosexuals, the disabled, Jews, Christians. Anyone Hitler didn't like, he ordered to these concentration camps. At these camps, the prisoners worked non-stop and were also forced to be the guinea pigs in demented scientific experiments.

The second stage of Hitler's plan were the extermination camps. In each country Hitler conquered, Jews were rounded up and secluded in a controlled area of a city. They were stripped of all possessions and forced to survive on what they could find on the ground. Then, Hitler started sending these Jews to extermination camps where the primary goal was murder. Once at these camps, the Jews waited for their turn to die as millions of their brethren were gassed, shot or burned to death.

Eventually, some of the Jews were freed when the Allies broke through the German lines. However, the damage had been done. Millions were murdered and generations of Jews would have to deal with the suffering of losing a loved one for such a despicably insane idea called ethnic cleansing.

The Holocaust

Hitler attempted to exterminate an entire population due to his warped view of the hierarchy of peoples.

Allied Turnaround—This'll be Fast

So the Allies were done with North Africa, and the war was a two-front war, with the USSR attacking from the east and the rest of the Allies from the west. On July 10, 1943, the Allies made what was the largest parachute landing in history, with 250,000 troops landing in Sicily, an island off the coast of Italy. Unfortunately for the triumphant Allies, the Axis army there retreated to the mainland. The Allies eventually took Rome and overthrew Mussolini, although the Axis army fought them every step of the way. Then, they started to bomb Germany, causing massive damage to vital targets—we covered those in the theory of blitzkrieg, remember? And more importantly, they kept Germany on the back foot so that they couldn't make a major attack again. Meanwhile, the Soviets defeated the German armies in Russia and moved west over 400 miles, reaching the eastern front of Germany in late 1944. Now the Allies were really taking it to the Axis powers.

D-Day—What was That?

What? D-Day? No, that wasn't doomsday or anything like that, just the name for the day on which the invasion of France started—June 6, 1944. But the ball started rolling a few months earlier in December 1943, when all the Allied leaders agreed in a conference in Tehran, Iran, that they had to start invading mainland Europe—France and Germany—in May 1943. The campaign was soon given a new, cool code name by the military—Operation Overlord. They also chose General Dwight D. Eisenhower—yet another military hero who would become an American president—as the "Supreme Allied Commander" for the invasion.

Then, they came up with a plan for the invasion. Their plan was for three divisions to be shipped to Normandy, on the northwest French coast, at the beginning. In two weeks, eleven more would come, and the divisions would keep trickling in until 100 divisions would eventually attack Germany from the west. A new and improved plan called for five divisions to land initially, with two being American, two British, and one Canadian. It also required the Allies to come up with 13,000 aircraft to support the invasion…they were really serious about this, weren't they? (An interesting side note is that the Nazis only came up with 400 aircraft to fight the landing force at D-Day. Kind of a mismatch). This plan, like many military campaigns, called for a diversion—false leads like radio messages and bomb droppings were constructed so that the Germans would believe that the invasion was coming from Calais, which was relatively far away from the main invasion.

As the date of the invasion approached, inefficiency by several countries caused it to be postponed to June 5, 1944. However, Eisenhower had weather concerns on that day, so the next day—June 6, 1944—actually turned out to be D-Day. The actual operation went basically without a hitch, mostly because of the diversion, which worked perfectly. D-Day was extremely significant because it enabled the Allies to get a foothold on mainland Europe, which they used to the fullest; they ended up attacking Germany from the western front, which would not have been possible without the carefully planned and successful Operation Overlord.

D-Day By the Numbers
• June 6, 1944 first troops land
• 200 yards of beach
• 5,000 ships
• 13,000 fighter, bomber, and transport aircraft
• 150,000 servicemen
• 195,000 tons of bombs
• 10,000 casualties
• 4,000 dead
• 200,000 vehicles eventually landed
• 600,000 tons of supplies in the first three weeks
• May 8, 1945 Victory in Europe (V-E) Day

Allies Win—I Knew That Anyway, Why Make me Read the Chapter?

With huge armies approaching from both sides, Hitler started getting desperate; wouldn't you? His last, desperate move was called the Battle of the Bulge on December 16, 1944. Hitler figured that if he could take Antwerp, a city right in the middle of the Allied attacking lines, he might be able to cut the Allied army in two and maybe go on the offensive again. He tried it with Panzers on December 16, but unfortunately for him, an Allied commander called McAuliffe at Bastogne, a key railroad junction, refused to surrender, even when his forces were getting pounded and worn down by Panzers. This bought enough time for the Allies to come to his rescue and defeat the Germans.

Soon after that battle, the "Big Three" allied leaders—FDR, Churchill, and Stalin—met at an obscure place called Yalta for an immensely important convention. Stalin, a crafty old guy looking out for his country's interests, tried to bargain with FDR and Churchill, who were looking out for the good of the world. Is this true? NO—everyone looks after their country's interests! Anyway, Stalin bargained with the other two, arguing that Russia had lost the most lives and equipment. What did he get? Half of all the reparations and the breakup of Germany in return for his promise that the countries adjacent to and west of Russia—the eastern bloc—could be democratic. Did he keep this promise? No, but what fun is having a treaty if you can't break it.

After the Yalta Conference, FDR died, and General Eisenhower took his time mopping up the Germans, allowing Russia to get to Berlin and Prague first and claim them. This, by the way, was crucial for the cold war which lay ahead. Anyway, May 8, 1945 was a day of celebration for the Allies—Germany finally surrendered on that day eight days after Hitler committed suicide. This day was called V-E Day—Victory in Europe Day. WWII in Europe was over, and it didn't seem to teach the Allies much—they (especially America) kept on getting involved in wars and violence in the decades after 1945, starting with the atomic bombs being dropped on Japan. But that's another story.

▼

CHAPTER 19

ISLAND HOPPING: WORLD WAR II—PACIFIC

Patrick Wong

Not Over Just Yet

With V-E Day behind them, America could now focus on the war in the Pacific. Even though Germany surrendered on May 8, 1945 and Japan was on the defensive, the end of war in the Pacific did not appear close at hand. Since 1942, America had fought to push Japan out of Asia, while simultaneously trying to devise a plan to eliminate Hitler's forces. This two-front war would prove to be the most difficult task in American history, but Americans, both at home and abroad would rise to the challenge and end the imperialist giants' attempts to take over the world.

But I'm getting ahead of myself. Let's assume all you know about World War II in the Pacific was what you learned watching Ben Affleck and Josh Hartnett fly around in *Pearl Harbor*. Good special effects, but not entirely accurate.

Before the war even started, Japan had been trying to create what they called the Greater East Asia Co-Prosperity Sphere. Penned by Japanese Prime Minister Matsuoka Yôsuke in 1940, the idea behind this "sphere" was that Japan would unite Asia and head the region while pushing out those nosey capitalists from the West. And as much as "Co-Prosperity" makes it sound like everyone would benefit, Japan interpreted the phrase to mean they could take over other countries and then benefit from the resources of that nation. Not exactly sharing like we were taught back in kindergarten.

America Steps In

During the 1930s, Japan was governed by a group of militarists, guys who think they can make their country powerful by taking over the world through brute force. In 1931, Japan invaded Manchuria. In 1937, they invaded China. While in China, Japan used a scorched earth policy in which they burned, destroyed, or looted everything that might be of use to the Chinese. In addition, their atrocious brutality, including rape and decapitation, forced America to take a stand.

While President Franklin Delano Roosevelt (FDR) tried to convince the isolationists that something needed to be done, Japan continued its march through Asia. In September 1940, Japan took over Northern French Indochina (Laos, Cambodia, and Vietnam). The US finally acted. FDR signed a trade embargo that would prohibit the sale of steel, scrap iron, and aviation fuel to Japan. Because of Japan's limited natural resources, this embargo angered them greatly. Fearing having to eventually fight a two-front war, Japan signed a neutrality treaty with Russia. With that worry tucked safely somewhere, two months went by and Japan took over Southern Indochina.

Japan Gets Frustrated

By the end of 1941, Russia was on the verge of defeat by the Axis powers (Germany, Italy, Japan, Hungary, Romania, Bulgaria). Seeing this happening, the shrewd Japanese took this opportunity to take oil resources in Southeast Asia. Once again, the US intervened. However this was to be different; the US were furious, and demanded that Japan withdraw from China and Indochina and promise not to conquer new territory.

Japan ignored these threats, and worse, started developing a secret plan.

What were the Japanese planning? Well, obviously Japan wanted to conquer more countries. Their shopping list included Burma, Malaya, East Indies, and the Philippines. Then they were going to establish defensive borders in the central and southwest Pacific. Japan was still worried about the beast to the east— United States. They expected that after spreading their empire across Asia, the US would declare war. Japan realized it couldn't win an extended war with America. Its only hope was a sudden, crushing strike. The Japanese predicted that the

United States would not be able to put their heart into the war, especially if they had lost their Pacific Fleet.

Over the second half of 1941, Admiral Isoroku Yamamoto and his generals created a secret plan to wipe out America's navy and morale in a single blow. Their target—Pearl Harbor.

That Horrible Sunday Morning

Nobody, not even the best writers, can describe the events in Pearl Harbor as vividly as actually observing the real situation. That includes me, but then I will try my best to describe the situation in detail anyway. At 6:10 am, the first waves of Japanese planes took off towards Pearl Harbor from their aircraft carriers. There were 183 fighters, bombers, and torpedo planes that took off. Truly awe-inspiring for so many planes to bomb one small part of the United States, isn't it? Contrary to popular belief that the Japanese attacked first, it was actually the US that struck the first blow, though a minor blow at the Japanese when at 6:45 am, the U.S. destroyer Ward sank a Japanese submarine. However, it was the Japanese that indeed initiated the war with the US, and it was they who mounted the first offensive.

Tension built as the crucial moment drew closer. At 7:02 am, a radar station in Oahu, Hawaii (Opana Radar Station) detected an unidentified aircraft. It was received eighteen minutes later (7:20 am, for those who are too lazy to do math), by an officer at Fort Shafter in Hawaii but he ignored it, thinking that it was just a US bomber. This assumption proved fatal.

The first real confirmation that the Japanese were going to attack was at 7:33 am, while Japanese diplomats at Washington were 'pretending' to negotiate peacefully. All of a sudden they were ordered to break off talks. Immediately they sent a warning to Lieutenant General Walter Short (commander of the US army in Hawaii). Ironically Short was pretty tall, but anyway, unfortunately for the US, communications was impossible in Hawaii due to atmospheric static, so they had to use a conventional telegraph. The message would reach Short at 11:45 am, which was hours after the attack.

At 7:40 am the first wave of planes arrived at Oahu. At 7:49, the commander, Mitsuo Fuchida ordered the aerial attack. So the Japanese shouted their war cry, and started attacking Pearl Harbor and other parts of Hawaii six minutes later.

The ensuing battle caught the awakening sailors totally by surprise.

Japanese airplanes raced through the harbor that housed "Battleship Row," raining down a fire of bullets on the vulnerable ships. By 8:10, the U.S.S. Arizona exploded after a bomb crashed through its hull. It sank less than ten minutes later, killing over a thousand sailors. Other battleships suffered similar fates as the planes took their battle elsewhere, destroying air bases and docks across the island of Oahu.

Bombing of Pearl Harbor

The Japanese sneak attack on Pearl Harbor killed over 2,000 Americans, but united the nation toward war.

This first wave eased up around 8:40 and then the second wave came in, however this time they were met with more American resistance as American aircraft took to the skies. By 10:00 the last planes of the second wave, withdrew to the north. The battle had ended.

The Japanese pilots wanted another strike, but the more calculating superiors opposed the idea because their objective had not been achieved; none of the US carriers were found. They were out at sea.

Time passed and the damage reports mounted. Trucks become temporary ambulances. Places such as schools, barracks, dining halls, and even churches became makeshift hospitals. In all 2,403 Americans died that day, 188 planes were destroyed and eight battleships were damaged or destroyed.

But the battle was not a total loss. The shipyards and fuel bases suffered minimal damage, and, more importantly the vastly important aircraft carriers were out to sea. Of most significance, the surprise attack helped secure public opinion for a war. The voice of isolationists died. America wanted revenge. They wanted war!

Excerpt from Franklin D. Roosevelt's Pearl Harbor Speech December 8, 1941

Yesterday, Dec. 7, 1941—a date which will live in infamy—the United States of America was suddenly and deliberately attacked by naval and air forces of the Empire of Japan. The United States was at peace with that nation and, at the solicitation of Japan, was still in conversation with the government and its emperor looking toward the maintenance of peace in the Pacific.

As commander in chief of the Army and Navy, I have directed that all measures be taken for our defense.

Always will we remember the character of the onslaught against us. No matter how long it may take us to overcome this premeditated invasion, the American people in their righteous might will win through to absolute victory. I believe I interpret the will of the Congress and of the people when I assert that we will not only defend ourselves to the uttermost, but will make very certain that this form of treachery shall never endanger us again. Hostilities exist. There is no blinking at the fact that that our people, our territory and our interests are in grave danger. With confidence in our armed forces—with the unbounding determination of our people—we will gain the inevitable triumph—so help us God.

I ask that the Congress declare that since the unprovoked and dastardly attack by Japan on Sunday, Dec. 7, a state of war has existed between the United States and the Japanese empire.

Ummm…Maybe We Shouldn't Have Bombed Pearl Harbor

Admiral Isoroku Yamamoto perfectly summed up the true effect of the battle, "I fear all we have done is to awaken a sleeping giant and fill him with a terrible resolve."

No one could have said it any better. Japan had awoken the sleeping giant, and he was furious. Never before in American history had the country united to overthrow an enemy. Decades of labor turmoil, racial tension, and political squabbles were put aside and the entire focus of the nation went on preparing for war and defeating Japan, and its primary ally, Germany.

At first, companies were a bit hesitant to dedicate all of their industry to the war effort. But with a little "convincing" from FDR, they eventually changed their mind. Night and day factories roared, and the military equipment just kept rolling out. In the four years that followed the attack on Pearl Harbor, America turned out over 250,000 planes, 100,000 armored cars, 75,000 tanks, and millions of tons of ammunition. In that same short time, America went from the sixteenth largest military in the world, to the most intimidating power on the planet, a status they have kept for the last sixty years (and a status that is being tested at this very moment as American troops head toward Baghdad).

They're Unstoppable!

After the attack on Pearl Harbor, the Japanese were truly on a roll. They did not know defeat in the months ahead. By March 1942, they held all the waters from the Solomon Islands to mainland Asia—4500 miles! They also held every island on the range except for the southern part of New Guinea and the Bataan peninsula of Luzon, Philippines. On the mainland (and below), they had Malaysia, Singapore, and Thailand as well as Burma. During the battles themselves, they completely crushed navies, with their losses no larger than a single destroyer. That white flag with the red circle was becoming a common sight those days.

The Allies main priority, however, was just to not get knocked out of the Pacific while they attempted to contain Hitler. They stayed on the defensive, until they were prepared to launch an attack. They needed to keep Hawaii and Samoa and protect the sea-lanes from the US to Australia. Supply ships were at risk from the Japanese, but fortunately for the US, the Japanese had few submarines, and those they did have weren't really used to destroy supply ships.

Doolittle and His Little Raid

First thing's first, we are not talking about the doctor who can speak to animals, Besides, his name is Dolittle, not Doolittle. And second, yes, this is the final scene in the movie *Pearl Harbor*. Man, you guys watch way too many movies.

Something important to note is that Doolittle did not plan this attack. The planner was most likely a naval officer named Captain Francis Low. It was planned soon after Pearl Harbor, as retaliation for what the Japanese had done to the US. This raid would be the first attack on the Japanese mainland. The first step in crushing the Japanese had just started.

The pilots and crew that joined this mission were only told that it was a "dangerous secret mission." They didn't even know the destination until the planes were loaded and the raid commenced. The obvious reason was to prevent leakage of information in case there were spies in the US.

The time came for the raid to start. On April 18, 1942, 16 B-25 bombers were to take off from the USS Hornet to attack Japan. US intelligence had spotted a small fishing boat 600 miles from Japan. Instinctively they destroyed it, thinking that the people in the boat might know something about the carriers or the impending attack. Because of this, Doolittle ordered the raid to start ahead of schedule to stop any possible Japanese preparation. This however created problems. The planes had previously been modified to adapt to the low flying altitudes, but because of this sudden change, the people knew there wasn't enough fuel. They took away various non-essential parts of the planes and either left them that way or replaced them with dummy replicas, just to deter the Japanese from fighting back. With that solved, the US attacked.

Although the attack was successful (all 16 bombers took off successfully and bombed their targets), none of them actually reached China. Because of the fuel problems and resistance from the Japanese, all but one crash-landed. The one that did land landed in Vladivostok (find that one on a map for eight bonus points), and the crew members were interned (detained). They were freed May 29, 1943, almost a year after the raid. Seven people were wounded, three died, eight were taken by the Japanese (among those eight, four survived the war). The damage inflicted was minimal, but the consequences were great.

Americans had attacked the heart of Japan. American morale took a huge leap, while the Japanese faced their first big defeat. It also revealed a weakness to bomber attacks on Japan's mainland. America would use this knowledge to their advantage three years later, when a fat kid and a little boy were dropped from the skies. It also made the Japanese reorganize their battle strategy; four first-line fighter groups were kept in Japan rather than being sent to the Solomon Islands where they were urgently needed.

Coral Sea and Midway

The Japanese sure knew how to fight, and they didn't mind testing their mettle against the daunting Allies. Admiral Yamamoto was one of the people who wanted to fight the US through their navy, partly because of ego, and also partly because of necessity. He needed to destroy the Pacific Fleet or else by the next year the Allies would be strong enough to truly attack Japan, not like the minor little attack Doolittle launched. Two opposing carriers (*Lexington*, the US carrier) collided northeast of Australia in the Coral Sea on May 7 and 8, 1942. Scientific development had grown such that the two enemy ships did not even see each other, instead they relied on their technology to destroy the opposition. During the battle, both made mistakes and suffered many losses. But the Japanese eventually sunk the Lexington. All right, if you're reading this and you're soon to have an English class, here are two words of the day you may find useful:

Tactical victory   =   a victory in a particular battle

Strategic victory   =   a victory in the long run

The Japanese scored a tactical victory, because they sank US's Lexington. However because of their heavy losses and also because they wanted to keep the advantage in Coral Sea they had to withdraw those involved in the invasion of Port Moresby. There, the US scored a strategic victory, since it prevented the Japanese from invading Australia, which was one of their goals.

In the Battle of Midway, the US was going to score both a tactical and a strategic victory! The Japanese wanted the island of Midway since they thought it was the key to their conquering scheme. Admiral Yamamoto wanted to fight with the US again in a "showdown" against US's Admiral Nimitz, who was still recovering from the "tactical" disaster at Coral Sea. Unfortunately for the Japanese, the US had something called a "Magic" decoder. This decoder intercepted and decoded the Japanese plans, so they knew in advance. But I guess that's what war is all about. Espionage, decoders. "All's fair in love and war." So when the Japanese attacked, the US was ready and waiting, and a terrible battle took place. The Japanese were defeated, losing four of their best carriers and some of their best air groups. The US lost only one carrier. The Allies now had the upper hand in naval battles, and Japan had absolutely no hope of taking over Midway, Samoa, and Fiji. The tide had turned.

Island Hopscotch

Guadalcanal was interesting because it introduced a few 'firsts' in World War II, mostly in favor of the US, and vice versa for the Japanese. Not long after the battle of Midway, the Japanese were ready to attempt to conquer again. They needed to find a location at the southern Solomon Islands to build an airfield. This way, the Japanese could disrupt supply and communication lines between Australia and their Allies, making Australia vulnerable to Japan's attack. Eventually they found a place at the northern coast of southern Solomon Islands and prepared to build their air base. Unfortunately for the Japanese, their plans were known to the Allied Forces.

Taking of Iwo Jima

In their "island hopping" campaign, American forces took over Iwo Jima, a key island base for the landing and supplying of American forces.

The ensuing air, sea, and land battles for Guadalcanal lasted from August 1942 to February 1943. This was the first time America was on the offensive, and a victory would push Japan back a bit to the Asian mainland. Both sides lost numerous lives and a ton of equipment. However, with the American military machine back home building weapons at an unparalleled rate, the Americans could afford the losses. Eventually, America was triumphant and forced the Japanese to retreat. This was a huge turning point.

Although Guadalcanal was an important tactical and strategic victory for the US, it wasn't enough just to get Guadalcanal. Japan was still a far, far way away. That's like saying that just because you take over Mexico City, you can now start attacking Alaska. It's just not possible.

What followed after that was a two-year struggle between the opposing forces to regain those islands the Japanese had conquered. The general in charge was Douglas MacArthur. The navy would also have to go through the central Pacific in operations of the Gilbert, Marshall, and Mariana islands. However, the Japanese were extremely resilient and put up a good fight. Eventually the US did regain the islands in the central Pacific, with the cost of over 16,000 Americans. By June 1945, the US was ready to strike the Japanese homeland.

"Fat Man" and "Little Boy"—The Deadly Duo

Whew! You've done well, reader. You've gotten this far, and now is what is probably one of the most famous, yet controversial parts of the war—the atomic bomb.

First, let me give you a rough idea of how the bomb works. And if you don't understand, don't take it personally; very few people in the world actually can explain it, and they are kept under lock and key.

Now the huge explosion means there were vast amounts of energy involved. Where would they get that energy from? It gets energy from fission (splitting) of the nuclei (core) of isotopes uranium-235 and plutonium-239 (they would use one or the other, not both on one bomb). Simply put, splitting a core is extremely difficult to do, unless you can find the energy to accomplish such a task. The good thing about splitting atoms is, once you get one, you can set off chain reactions and make the other nuclei split. How is this done? When the nuclei is split, it releases large amounts of energy, as well as two or three neutrons which whiz around, colliding with other nuclei, thus creating the chain reaction. Here's an interesting fact of the day: If you convert one kg of matter into raw energy, it could create 22 megatons of TNT power. That equals

22,000,000,000,000 kg of TNT power…yikes! Imagine being next to it. You wouldn't just blow up, you'd be vaporized! Now here's the sick (or interesting, if you're bloodthirsty) part: the effects of the bomb, on the human body and surroundings. Depending on how close you are to ground zero, where the bomb detonates, you can have a range of symptoms.

Damage Capabilities Based on Distance from Ground Zero

Miles	Zone	Description	Fatalities
0 – ½	Total Destruction	Vaporization/Burned beyond recognition	98% dead
½ – 1	Total Destruction	All buildings above ground destroyed	90% dead
1 – 1¾	Sever Blast Damage	Large structures collapse	60% dead
1¾ – 2½	Severe Heat Damage	Everything has burn damage	50% dead
2½ – 3	Severe Fire/Wind Damage	Homes damaged, $2^{nd}/3^{rd}$ degree burns	15% dead

Now this terrible invention was part of the Manhattan Project. It was soon heavily funded after Einstein reported to the President that Germany and Japan might have been making a super-powerful bomb of a type never seen. This scared the US because if they had weapons like those they could wreak total destruction with their bombs, so the government funded the $2 billion Manhattan Project in 1939 that brought a select group of scientists together. It became a race to see who had the first atomic bomb. The US won—not very surprising considering that both Germany and Japan were not exactly in peak condition.

Remember the two atoms used to make the bombs? The uranium-235 and the plutonium-239? If not, that's ok. The US created two bombs; one was a uranium bomb, nicknamed Little Boy, and the other was the plutonium bomb, named Fat Man. Because plutonium was discovered quite recently, they were uncertain about success. So they tested the bomb on July 16, 1945, and it was a resounding success. The testers did not regard their safety, instead jumping with excitement to see that it had succeeded. The reason why the plutonium bomb was named Fat

Man was because it was bigger, and more powerful. The plutonium isotope was more stable, so it required more energy to split the atom.

Now with the scientific information all set, we must retrogress back into history. After the technical questions were answered, questions concerning humanity arose. Many people were in favor of using the bomb, many others were against it. Here's a chart of their arguments.

Arguments for Using Atomic Bomb

For	Against
• Feared USSR would spread their influence after war	• Why not just test it first publicly and give Japan an ultimatum
• Have to get rid of Japanese once and for all	• How can any country trust America again, a nation that secretly created this bomb
• Japanese refuse to surrender, threatening suicide	• It is immoral
• Cost in price and lives of invading Japan to get them to surrender just too high	• An arms race followed

The US did use the bombs, both Fat Man and Little Boy. August 6, 1945, in Hiroshima, was a day Japan and the world would never forget. A lone B-29 "Flying Fortress" dropped Little Boy, the uranium bomb over Hiroshima. The target was Aioi Bridge, but he missed by 550 feet. Nevertheless, the sheer power of the atomic bomb made the miss irrelevant. It destroyed Aioi Bridge and a lot of the city, instantly killing 66,000 people, and injuring 69,000 others. The fallout that resulted killed even more people. By the end of 1945, there were about 145,000 deaths, and between that time until 1951 60,000 more died of radiation illnesses.

To the surprise of the US, Japan still resisted. Three days later, another B-29 dropped Fat Man, the plutonium bomb over Nagasaki. The target was a city, but it missed by over a mile. The reason was that the plane had too little fuel so it could not reach the designated point, and there were also too many clouds blocking the pilot's aim. Once the clouds broke and fuel was on the verge of running out, the pilot had to drop the bomb so as to avoid anti-aircraft fire. Because the plutonium bomb was more powerful than its brother, it still managed to decimate half the city and some nearby mountains. There were less casualties; 39,000 deaths and over 25,000 injured. By the end of 1945, 70,000 people died from the lingering effects of the awesome A-bomb.

The destruction in terms of lives was unparalleled. A week later, Japan received the terms of surrender and on September 2, 1945 Emperor Hirohito officially surrendered.

Japanese Surrender

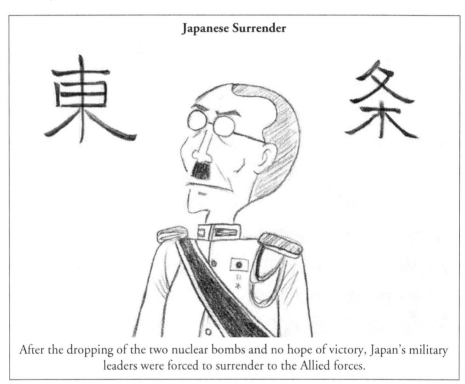

After the dropping of the two nuclear bombs and no hope of victory, Japan's military leaders were forced to surrender to the Allied forces.

World War II had ended, but the way the war ended set an ominous tone for future decades. The creation of the atomic bomb, and the arms race that followed, foreshadowed that the next world war would not be over the ownership of pieces of land, but over the survival of the planet.

CHAPTER 20

▼

SCARED TO DEATH: THE COLD WAR

Aaron Rubin
Jake Emerson

I'd Rather Have My Wars Hot

The second portion of the twentieth century can best be described as the struggle between capitalism and communism. This was known as the Cold War, a half-century long feud between the world's two superpowers, the United States and the Soviet Union. Beginning at the close of the Second World War, the Cold War was provoked by three issues: the formation of the Soviet Bloc, the plague-like spread of communist beliefs throughout the world, and the development of weapons of mass destruction.

The result was two major wars between the United States and the communist threats, a "Red Scare" that spread through the United States, and diplomatic problems between America and the Soviet Union that thrust the two world powers of the day to the brink of nuclear war. The chaos of the Cold War resulted in the ultimate breakup of the Soviet Union. However, the Cold War also gave the world an industrial and technological boost, as well as constructed diplomatic agreements amongst world powers as to how to deal with weapons of mass destruction. The half-century long war defined the era and laid the course of events into the next century.

The Cold War's origin can be roughly traced back to the formation of the Soviet Bloc. The Soviet Bloc was a group of communist Eastern European nations that were officially independent, however were under an incredibly imperialistic influence of the Soviet Union. During the later stages of World War II, as the USSR was on the offensive, it systematically grabbed nations in its way and put them under the control of the Kremlin, the USSR's military headquarters. When World War II ended, the nations occupied by the Soviet were declared "independent." However it was clear that the Soviet Union was the true governing body in each bloc state. From East Berlin to Hungary to Azerbaijan to Kazakhstan, Eastern Europe and parts of the north Middle East were said to be behind the "Iron Curtain." A supposedly classless society, a society without the freedom of speech, free government or free trade, had covered half of Europe; according to the United States and a collection of its allies, this problem needed to be eradicated.

In 1949 the North Atlantic Treaty Organization (NATO) was put together and it originally consisted of all the Allies from Western Europe, and also the U.S. and Canada. Its main purpose was to Europe against a possible attack by the Soviets, and an attempt by them to spread their ideology.

Excerpt from the North Atlantic Treaty (NATO) Washington D.C.—April 4, 1949

The Parties to this Treaty reaffirm their faith in the purposes and principles of the Charter of the United Nations and their desire to live in peace with all peoples and all governments.

They are determined to safeguard the freedom, common heritage and civilization of their peoples, founded on the principles of democracy, individual liberty and the rule of law. They seek to promote stability and well-being in the North Atlantic area.

They are resolved to unite their efforts for collective defence and for the preservation of peace and security. They therefore agree to this North Atlantic Treaty.

American distaste for the communist world increased with the construction of the Berlin Wall in 1961, a Soviet-built wall made to prevent residents of East Berlin from defecting to the west. Since World War II, tension between West and East Germany had always been hot. A democratic government was set up in West Germany, while a communist government was set up in East Germany. Then you had tiny little Berlin isolated way in the far eastern part of East Germany. Berlin was likewise divided into two sections, half democratic and half communist. Initially, back in 1948, East Germany had tried to prevent supplies from entering West Berlin. This attempt was foiled by the Americans who for more than a year flew over 270,000 flights delivering millions of tons of food and fuel.

Berlin Air Lift

For over a year, citizens of West Berlin survived the Soviet blockade on food and materials flown in by Western nations.

So, when the Germans started the construction of a 29 mile long, concrete wall, the Americans saw this as a formal imprisonment. The wall became a symbol of the "Iron Curtain" which forbade the freedom of expression. In addition, for people attempting to flee Soviet-controlled Europe without authorized permission, punishments included capture, torture, imprisonment and execution.

Communist citizens must not be allowed to experience democracy.

Dominos and Bombs

The popularity of communism after World War II seeped to all parts of the world, alarming the United States. With the Soviet Union growing, the Soviet Bloc slowly forcing itself west, and the spirit of Karl Marx in the air, proletariat revolutions began happening in states where class struggle was the greatest and oppression of the working class was the harshest: China, Korea, Vietnam, and Cuba. The climate was always ripe for change in places where life really wasn't that enjoyable. The introduction of more communist nations to the global community drove fear into the heart of the United States. If too many nations converted to the commune-based government, eventually capitalism would cease to function. If there is no capitalism anywhere, where would America sell its products? Americans feared that the communist world would eventually take over the "land of the free". With the spread of communism throughout the world, tension between the USA and the USSR began to escalate thus leading to the development of vastly more destructive weapons.

The Cold War can best be recognized and described as the period that could have turned into a nuclear holocaust resulting in an unimaginable outcome. Starting at the end of the Second World War, both the United States of America and the Union of Soviet Socialist Republics captured former German scientists and forced them to create weapons for their own interest. Learning from Einstein's findings and theories that atoms have the potential to cause great damage, scientists working for both superpowers began developing weapons of mass destruction. Fission bombs, hydrogen bombs, and nuclear missiles all became standard issue in the arsenals of both nations. These nuclear arsenals kept getting larger and larger, more and more destructive with each breakthrough weapon. To both sides, the other nation appeared to be a threat that could not be overlooked. When two superpowers have the most destructive weapons in the world, the outcome is either peace by diplomacy or war.

Unfortunately the face-off between the communists and the United States erupted into war. On June 25th, 1950 the northern part of Korea, under communist control, invaded the south in an effort to unite the Korean peninsula as a united Korean socialist state. The UN Security council disapproved of this move seeing it as a Chinese-USSR collaborative effort to take over the peninsula. Thus, defensive forces for the south, led by the United States, attacked northern troops. Many troops who had just finished defeating the Japanese empire now had to fight a new battle against a new foe.

Along the 38th parallel, a line of latitude that divided the north from the south, troops from both sides were being pushed back and forth. Then communist China came to the aide of their communist Korean brothers. The United States was pushed far south below the 18th parallel; but with some quick regrouping and importing of reinforcements, U.S. General MacArthur was able to push the stampeding Chinese and communist Korean troops back up north. Eventually a ceasefire was arranged and a demilitarized zone near the 38th parallel was established. The communist north formed its own nation while the south formed a democracy. The Korean War was the first official war that the United States had fought in its attempt to halt the spread of communism in the world.

Spies Like Us

Espionage became a common form of warfare between the USA and the USSR. Though no official war involving tanks and planes and submarines had been declared or happened between the two nations, both were immensely involved in spying on each other. It was simple for the Soviets to infiltrate the United States due to its relatively free and open society, and loose border restrictions. Therefore a nation-wide fear of communists in America spread throughout the country. This was known as the "Red Scare," a fear that America was being constantly watched and spied upon by sinister communist secret agents whose sole goal was to convert the United States into a socialist state.

Such fears and beliefs were often brought to the screen by the popular British film series *James Bond*, an English secret agent that always seemed to stop the evil doings of the communists and their spies. While this was fiction, extreme forms of espionage were a reality. The GRU, the Soviet military intelligence agency comparable to America's CIA, was an elite spy organization that frequently and stealthily penetrated the United States government, obtaining confidential information. Thus, the NSA was established to counter this espionage and ensure greater homeland security for the United States. Then the United States then realized that they needed to counter the Soviet espionage by doing the same effectively to the USSR itself.

Thus, the CIA was born to replace the older and less efficient OSS. The CIA sent hundreds of agents all over the world, primarily to Soviet states and spheres of influence. American spies began infiltrating the Soviet Union, obtaining confidential information to give to the United States. To defend itself against such infiltrations, the USSR strengthened its homeland security by reorganizing it and giving it a new name. The final product was the KGB, a Russian acronym for Soviet State Security/Secret Police. It sent its agents to all parts of the Union to scour for double agents or American spies. KGB agents even went abroad to investigate double agents and to find the identity of foreign spies. While the Americans were good at spying on the Russians, no one was better than the British. The English secret service program, known as MI6 (Military Intelligence 6), was by far the most advanced intelligence agency in the world. It obtained a far greater amount of information on the USSR than the CIA had been able to find. MI6 and the CIA often worked together, sharing responsibilities, duties, and information.

During the Cold War, new methods of espionage were used. U-2 spy planes, CIA jets that flew so close to outer space that the pilot needed to wear a space suit, soared over Soviet lands taking brilliant aerial photographs of USSR installations that could be directly or indirectly a threat to the United States. This method of spying was effective until the Soviet Union developed surface-to-air ballistic anti-aircraft missiles capable of reaching the altitudes that the U-2 flew at, and the result was the downing of Gary Powers. Powers was a pilot of a U-2 that was shot down over the USSR during a routine spy run. The result was hostile diplomacy between the USA and the USSR. However, whereas these planes could *almost* fly into space, both sides knew the next frontier for spying would be permanent satellites that flew above the earth.

Until recently the public was made to believe that American space station *Skylab* and Russian space station *Mir* were merely part of the development of both nation's space programs. However this was not entirely true. While this was indeed one of the reasons why the stations were developed, the greater reason was an attempt to spy on each other's nations.

Minutes from World War III

The quest to stop communism wasn't just fought halfway around the world. The nearby island of Cuba, located off the coast of Florida, had recently been taken over by the communists under leader Fidel Castro after he and his followers had revolted against the previous Cuban leader Batista. Fearing that communism might hop over to the nearby Americas, President Kennedy backed a CIA headed operation to try and spark a revolt in Cuba against Castro. This operation ultimately failed. This Bay of Pigs invasion saw both Americans and anti-communist

Cubans massacred when Castro easily overthrew the invading forces. Kennedy was humiliated and America lost a bit of its prestige.

Relations between the United States and Cuba were not very close, but the USSR found itself a new ally in the western hemisphere. In a letter to Fidel Castro, Soviet Union premier Khrushchev once wrote:

> "We were together with the Minister of Defense, Marshal Malinovsky, in Varna, Bulgaria. And we were walking on the beach of the Black Sea and Marshal Malinovsky told me, 'Look, over on the other side of the Black Sea, in Turkey, there are American nuclear missiles which can destroy in six minutes all cities in the south of the Soviet Union…'[and then Khrushchev asked Malinovsky], 'Why can't we do the same as the United States? Why couldn't we place arms, for example, on Cuba?'…Malinovsky answered that maybe it was a good idea."

Castro and Khrushchev began holding conferences between their two nations planning out the design to transport Soviet missiles to Cuba. The shipping of Soviet medium-and intermediate-range ballistic missiles began early in 1962. On October 14, 1962, a routine American U-2 spy plane noticed some ballistic missiles and nuclear warheads on the island. America was stricken with the fear of being a potential target of nuclear warfare, and thus President Kennedy was thrust into a whirlpool of diplomatic confrontations with the Soviet Union. Kennedy demanded that the USSR take back their missiles in hope of preventing a third world war, however the Soviets refused.

All over America people prepared for a nuclear war. In schools children were learning to duck and hide under their desks if a missile were to hit the premises, and some families were having underground bomb shelters built. For thirteen long days Kennedy met with his advisors trying to come up with a solution to the crisis. He feared that if the United States led a preemptive strike against Cuba that the USSR might retaliate by attacking West Germany thrusting the world into another world war. At last after thirteen tense days, an American quarantining of Cuba took place preventing Soviet ships from transporting anything to Castro's nation. Soon after Kennedy and Khrushchev came to a mutual agreement, America removes arms in Turkey if the USSR removes missiles in Cuba.

This face-off between the two nations almost pushed the world to nuclear war. America had prevailed and it would spend the next two decades again trying to stop the spread of communism.

Back to Dominos

Far from the United States in the Asian country of Vietnam a communist political leader had recently taken over the northern regions of the country. The
leader's name was Ho Chi Minh. The monarchy-ruled southern part of the country signaled for help to maintain the government and prevent Ho from uniting
the nation as a communist one. The United States was quick to answer the need
for assistance. As early as the 1950s the United States started giving economic
and medical aid to the south and to the French controlled parts of the region.

In August of 1964 some American navy ships were attacked in the Gulf of
Tonkin off the coast of Vietnam. Later, this attack was questioned for its legiti-
macy (See the chapter on Vietnam for more details). Regardless, President Lyndon B. Johnson received congressional approval through the Gulf of Tonkin
Resolution to go in and defeat the communist forces. This sinking became the
direct catalyst for the war that would take place between Ho Chi Minh and the
United States. Soon after American troops landed in Da Nang and began setting
up installations as bases for the upcoming war. The war lasted a decade, thousands of Americans were drafted and thousands died. Ultimately the Ameri-
can-South Vietnamese allied forces were defeated, and Vietnam was united under
the communist regime of Ho Chi Minh. Vietnam was the last major direct conflict between the capitalist and communist worlds, and though there were other
"hostilities" none were so great as this war.

The Coming of the End

With the incredible competition between the USSR and the USA, the Soviets
had an obligation to prevail over the United States to prove that communism was
dominant over capitalism. Both sides built up their military, space programs, and
industry to support the ongoing competition, however around the later years of
the Cold War the Soviet Union's structure had begun to deteriorate due to the
inability to successfully support itself and continue to compete with America.
The USSR's economy was in shambles and citizens were crying out for change.

In 1991 the last leader of the Union of Soviet Socialist Republics, Mikhail
Gorbachev, declared all states in the Soviet Union that were not Russian inde-
pendent. At the same time he let go of the Soviet influence on the nations in
Soviet Bloc, allowing them to govern themselves under their own form of govern-
ment. Gorbachev then declared Russia to be the Russian Federation, a republic.
He then stepped down. The USSR was no more, and Eastern Europe fell into a

depression. Communism had eaten into the former Soviet Union and Bloc states like an acid. East Germany was poverty-stricken, and upon re-admittance back into the greater part of Germany, its economic state drastically hurt the rest of Germany. Former Soviet-controlled states in the Balkans are still displaying the detrimental effects of the Soviet Union such as organized crime, revolts, poverty, and serious corruption. The breakup of the Soviet Union left Eastern Europe maimed.

The Cold War can easily be nicknamed as both the second Age of Exploration or the Third Industrial Revolution. With the vigorous competition between the superpowers, technology and industry flourished. The Soviet Union produced a great deal of cheap steal for export, domestic use, and military purposes. The United States did likewise to remain competitive. Much new technology came out of the Cold War that is still used today such as solar power, Velcro, and CD players. In addition, the boost in industry was a major liftoff in the space programs of both nations. New rockets were being built to accomplish new goals in the exploration of space. Space stations were concocted, and man even set foot on the moon. With the space race, the race between the USSR and the USA over who could dominate the space. If it were not for the space race, satellite TV would not exist. Imagine the consequences of only local TV? The inventions, exploration, and increase in industry directly affected technology, industry, and everyday life in the present.

Major Events of the Cold War

Date	Event
August 6, 1945	United States drops atomic bomb on Hiroshima.
March 5, 1946	Winston Churchill gives "Iron Curtain" speech
March 12, 1947	Truman Doctrine—Congress grants money to nations trying to overthrow revolution—Turkey and Greece granted $400 million
April 1, 1948	Soviet Union blockades incoming supplies to Berlin. Westen airlifts begin June 21
April 4, 1949	US led NATO established
August 1949	Soviet Union explodes an atomic bomb

Major Events of the Cold War (Continued)

June 25, 1950	North Korean troops cross 38th Parallel to invade South Korea
May 14, 1955	Soviet led Warsaw Pact established
January 5, 1957	Eisenhower Doctrine—Commit troops to Middle East to overthrow communism
October 4, 1957	Soviet Union launches Sputnik—space race begins
May 1, 1960	U-2 spy plane shot down over Soviet Union. Pilot Gary Powers held captive.
December 20, 1960	Ho Chi Minh declares he will overthrow US backed South Vietnamese government
April 17, 1961	Bay of Pigs attempt to liberate Cuba ends in disaster
October 23, 1962	Cuban Missile Crisis almost brings America into World War III
June 17, 1967	China explodes an atomic bomb
December 1968	535,000 troops in Vietnam
January 28, 1973	Vietnam War ends
March 23, 1983	Reagan proposes SDI "Star Wars" to intercept incoming missiles
March 13, 1985	Mikhail Gorbachev becomes Soviet General Secretary
November 21, 1985	Geneva Summit—Reagan and Gorbachev agree to 50% reduction in nuclear weapons
November 9, 1989	Berlin Wall opened
December 25, 1991	Gorbachev resigns. United States recognizes Armenia, Belorussia, Kazakhstan, Kirghizia, Russia, Ukraine as independent countries

▼

CHAPTER 21

THE PATH TO EQUALITY: THE CIVIL RIGHTS MOVEMENT

Anika Arya
Austin Radford

The Government Says Segregation is Legal

The main purpose of the Civil Rights Movement in the United States was to achieve equal rights and total racial equality for African-Americans. First, this movement called for an end to segregation, which separated blacks from whites. This separation gave whites the more respected role in society and therefore the power to control the blacks. During this movement for equality, individuals and organizations fought the cruel, unfair racial discriminatory practices through boycotts, protest marches, and education. The fight would take decades, and most would agree equality has yet to be reached. We'll be starting the discussion on the Civil Rights Movement by taking you back to the 1890s, in a case that set a horrible precedent that would last in America for over 60 years.

The Original Jim Crow
E. Riley

Old Jim Crow's come agin, as you must all know,
And ebery body say I cum to jump Jim Crow.

Wheel about and turn about, and do jis so,
Ebery time I weel about, I jump Jim Crow.

My name is Daddy Rice, as you berry well do know.
And none in de Nited States like me, can jump Jim Crow.

I was born in a cane brake, and cradled in a trough,
Swam de Mississippi, whar I cotch'd de hoopen coff.

To whip my weight in wild cats, eat an alligator,
And drink de Mississippi dry, I'm de very critter.

I went to de woods, heard a debil of a howl,
I look'd up a tree, and saw a great owl.

Old Jim Crow's come agin, as you must all know,
And ebery body say I cum to jump Jim Crow.

During the 1890s new laws were coming out called the Jim Crow laws. The name came from an old 1830 folk song popularized by Thomas Rice, a white man who performed at minstrel shows. In these minstrel shows, whites would paint their faces black with burnt cork and then act out stereotypical scenes where blacks behaved foolishly. These shows became very popular prior to the Civil War and helped create the stereotype of the lazy, ignorant, childlike black man.

After the Civil War and the freedom of slaves, many blacks hoped they would have an equal opportunity to share in the riches of America. However, white Southerners had a different idea. They quickly enacted "Black Codes" to keep the freed blacks in their place. By the 1890s these black codes became known as Jim Crow laws.

One such law was the Separate Cars Act. This act stated that it was legal for railroad companies to separate passengers due to race, as long as the sections on the train were equal. This law would be challenged at the highest court and the outcome would define race relations for the first half of the twentieth century.

The *Plessy vs. Ferguson* case all started with a thirty year old man named Homer Adolph Plessy from New Orleans, Louisiana. This man was only one-eighth black because he had an African American great-grandmother. Other than that, his family passed as being white in almost every state except for Louisiana. Louisiana considered him to be a black man. In 1892, the Citizens Committee, which is a political group made up of African Americans and Creoles (those of mixed ethnicity) asked Plessy to help them fight the Separate Car Act. This act divided blacks from whites in railroad cars. The act also provided a penalty of twenty days or a fine of twenty-five dollars for anyone who disobeyed it.

Plessy agreed to help the committee out. He took a ride on a train to Covington, Louisiana. He sat down in the white section of the train. When a conductor walked by, Plessy told him that he was one-eighth black and that he would not move to the colored section of the train. Plessy was then arrested by the police and put in jail for refusing to move. After one night in jail, he was taken out on bond. Plessy got an attorney named Albion W. Tourgee, who had previous experience working on civil rights cases. After one month, his case went to trial. During the trial, Tourgee insisted that Plessy's civil rights had been violated under the thirteenth and fourteenth amendments. However, Judge John Ferguson said that the state had a right to lie out segregation laws inside its own borders. If Plessy had taken a train out of the state, that would be a different matter altogether.

The *Plessy vs. Ferguson* case then went to the Supreme Court in 1896. There was an eight-person majority that ruled against Plessy. Justice John Harlan was the only person in favor of Plessy. This decision allowed the policy of separate but equal facilities for blacks and whites. In other words, blacks, just like whites, would have schools, public facilities, restaurants, theaters, and public transportation, but they would still be segregated from the whites and they could not use the other's facilities. Even though separate and equal don't usually go together, the Plessy doctrine granted legal protection for segregation for over fifty years.

Plessy vs. Ferguson Supreme Court Ruling
1896

The argument also assumes that social prejudice may be overcome by legislation, and that equal rights cannot be secured to the Negro except by an enforced commingling of the two races. We cannot accept this proposition. If the two races are to meet on terms of social equality wit must be the result of natural affinities, a mutual appreciation of each other's merits and a voluntary consent of individuals…. Legislation is powerless to eradicate racial instincts or to abolish distinctions based upon physical differences, and the attempt to do so can only result in accentuating the difficulties of the present situation.

How to Solve the Problem

In the years that followed *Plessy vs. Ferguson*, many blacks simply accepted their fate as simply just the next phase in oppression that had followed them throughout American history. Others tried to end the unfair treatment.

One such man, Booker T. Washington believed that before blacks could even consider social equality, they must first pave the road toward economic equality. In 1895, he gave his "Atlantic Compromise" speech in which he claimed, "The opportunity to earn a dollar in a factory just now is worth infinitely more than the opportunity to spend a dollar in an opera-house." He encouraged blacks to skill themselves in factory and agricultural labor, and asked for equality in other areas later. The white population embraced his ideology, but other black leaders disagreed strongly. Why should blacks have to work only at manual labor.

W.E.B. DuBois was the foremost hero of blacks at the turn of the century. He believed African-Americans should protest and struggle actively to obtain their Constitution dictated rights. DuBois organized the Niagara Movement in 1905, and the National Association for the Advancement of Colored People (NAACP) in 1909.

He was also the editor of the NAACP magazine, *The Crisis*. Along with the NAACP lawyers who strived for equality through legal channels, DuBois used *The Crisis* to strike back at white America and show them the inequity and absurdity of unfair race relations in a nation founded on the principle that "All men are created equal."

Liberty Abroad, Persecution at Home

Throughout the twentieth century, African-Americans never hesitated to support their nation in armed conflict. Even though during both World War I and World War II, blacks continued to be given inferior military postings, they continued to fight in order to free the oppressed around the world.

African-American Participation in America's Wars

War	Years	Numbers Involved
World War I	1917-1918	Over 200,000
World War II	1941-1945	Over 500,000
Korean War	1950-1953	195,000
Vietnam War	1961-1973	275,000

The World Wars had numerous effects on black life in America. Firstly, those African-Americans who didn't serve in the war filled in for the white soldiers at the factories and workplaces back home. Even though they proved their ability to perform any task a white man could perform, black laborers were still expected to give up their jobs when the white soldiers returned. Second, African-Americans who had fought to free people around the world had difficulty returning to a nation that appeared unwilling to accept them.

The years following wartime saw heightened conflict on the streets of America as both blacks and whites struggled to make sense of the changing social hierarchy. Each side wanted to ensure their freedom, though the whites essentially controlled the conflict.

During World War II, the number of blacks in the armed forces mirrored the percentage of blacks in the general population. However, many of them were only in support and non-combat jobs. Many blacks left Southern farms to join the forces in the East and West. Here racial discrimination was somewhat less. And with their higher incomes they settled down in the new states, from where they continued their fight against repression in the South. Blacks continued to fight discrimination at home during the war. The membership of the NAACP grew considerably from 50,000 to 500,000 people.

The blacks used the war to fight fascism in Europe and racism in America since both were forms of discrimination. Also many whites observed the bravery and patriotism of the blacks during the war, and supported the end of discrimination against persons they had fought along side during the war.

When the war was over, the black soldiers returned and continued their struggle. Finally in 1948, President Truman ordered the end of discrimination in the armed force. Blacks would no longer be forced into jobs such as cooking, cleaning up, or other domestic chores. He also proposed civil rights policy, calling for equal voting and employment opportunities, but the US congress did not approve his proposals.

Say Goodbye to the Party of Lincoln

The quest for Civil Rights started to change as the demographic make-up of America changed. During the First World War, some southern blacks migrated north to find job opportunities instead of joining the army. In just two years, 1916-1917, hundreds of thousands of blacks from the south made their way north looking for jobs left vacant by soldiers leaving for war. Throughout the twentieth century, blacks across America became urbanized as a result of this migration. In 1890, 85% of the southern blacks were living in rural areas but that number decreased to 42% in 1960. At the same time, 95% of blacks in the North were in urban areas. As black communities became more urbanized, they gained a strong political influence and were able to organize more readily for protest. With their continuous pressure on local political leaders, they were able to elect politicians who believed in civil rights. Using money and their newly acquired political influence, northern black communities were able to help the southern black communities.

Aside from war, the social and economic conditions of the 1930s brought the black community closer to their goal of equality. As the Great Depression devastated the US economy, protests against discrimination increased, especially in the Northern states and cities. Blacks wanted to change society. They wanted to have equality in the job market and they encouraged the government to help them out.

During this time, slogans such as "Don't buy where you can't work" became campaigns for the blacks, as they tried to persuade others to boycott businesses, which refused to hire people of color. Not only were there boycotts of stores and commercial businesses, but school boycotts were organized as well. Blacks boycotted the schools, mainly in Northern cities, in order to protest the unfair treatment of their children. The communities of blacks and whites were far from unified in the 1930s. The Great Depression did not help the situation, as more people were unemployed and became more desperate. Treatment of blacks was prejudiced as they were refused work and unjustly treated even in schools.

A second goal of the protests in the 1930s was to encourage government regulation of the economy and social freedoms. Since the Civil War, the blacks believed Lincoln's Republican Party best spoke on their behalf. However, blacks finally shifted their allegiance when the Democrat Franklin D. Roosevelt took office. Fortunately, during the administration of Roosevelt, federal programs were created in order to guarantee the welfare of all individual citizens. Many of these programs are still used today, an example being Social Security.

Although the President was not an open advocate of black rights in America, his wife was. Eleanor Roosevelt became an open supporter for black rights and she encouraged other leaders of the administration to join her. In response to the protests, the Roosevelt Administration opened federal jobs to blacks. The federal judges were no longer concerned with solely protecting the free business corporations but they were now protecting individual rights, or those of minorities. Roosevelt also worked to choose judges that favored black rights. With the employment of Hugo Black in the US Supreme Court in 1937, the courts began to show new attitudes toward black rights. In 1938, the Supreme Court ruled that Missouri was now required to offer public law school for blacks, as they did for whites. Due to the Roosevelt administration and the government action taken during the late 1930s, blacks began to realize that the government might be able to help them gain the rights they deserved.

And Say Goodbye to Plessy vs. Ferguson

After World War II, the NAACP continued to use legal means to fight for civil rights. They concentrated on desegregation in schools, the bringing together of blacks and whites to be taught in the same classroom. The Supreme Court listened to five cases that disputed elementary and secondary school segregation. However, the most noteworthy case was *Brown vs. Board of Education.*

The case dealt with Linda Brown, a black third grader from Topeka, Kansas, who had to walk a mile each day to arrive at her black school. This was quite a long, unnecessary walk for her, considering that there was a white school just seven blocks away from her house. Oliver Brown, her father, tried to put her into the white school, but the principal of the school did not accept her. Brown was furious and he sought help from McKinley Burnett, who was the head of the Topeka, Kansas branch of the NAACP. The NAACP willingly offered to assist

Brown because it had wanted to challenge segregation in schools for many years. Many other black parents also supported Brown.

The U.S District Court on the 25th and 26th of June, 1951 heard browns case. During the trial, the NAACP said that segregated schools made black children believe that they were inferior to white children—so schools were therefore unequal. However, the Board of Education argued against the NAACP, saying that segregated schools were not harmful to the black children, it just prepared them for the segregation that they would have to face later in life.

Brown and the NAACP took their case to the Supreme Court on October 1st, 1951. The Court heard the case on December 9th, 1952, but did not come to a decision. The case was heard again from December 7th to the 8th, 1953. The court had to make its decision by finding out whether or not the Fourteenth Amendment applied to the segregation of schools. When the ruling came out, Linda Brown won!

The ruling established that forcing blacks to go to only colored schools deprived them of the equal protection of the laws assured by the Fourteenth Amendment. It was also concluded that the separate but equal doctrine would not apply to public education. Therefore the Supreme Court took away the separate but equal doctrine for public education. It also established the desegregation of schools all over the U.S.

While this was a great victory for the African Americans, the white Southerners did everything possible to prevent it from becoming reality. Whites were persuaded not to comply, and continued to segregate white students from black. Practically no schools actually followed the Supreme Court ruling in the initial years after it was passed. However, gradual progress was eventually made.

The Man Named King

If *Brown vs. Board of Education* brought racial equality to the surface of American political debate, the actions of Dr. Martin Luther King Jr. and the black citizens of Montgomery sent the nation into the Civil Rights Movement. By 1955, the black community in Montgomery was extremely angry with the segregated bus system in their city. They were treated badly and abused by bus drivers and the local white community. On December 1st, 1955, Rosa Parks, an African-American lady, decided that she would not allow this kind of treatment. When a white passenger demanded her to move from the white section on the bus so that he could sit down, she refused.

Rosa Parks was a member of the Montgomery, Alabama branch of the NAACP, led by Edgar D. Nixon. Aware of the built-up anger in the community, Nixon saw the possibility of a rally against segregated buses. It took only one night to organize a bus boycott after Parks' arrest because the issue had been discussed for months. Fifty thousand African Americans supported the boycott, which lasted for almost one year. They walked. They carpooled. They wiped out the earnings of the Montgomery Public Transportation system. The Montgomery Boycott proved the determination of the blacks to stop segregation. In November 1956, a federal court ruled that bus segregation was illegal, thus ending the boycott.

The success of the boycott can be credited to the Montgomery Improvement Association. A new Baptist minister named Martin Luther King Jr., became famous after the boycott. At the time, he was the president of the Montgomery Improvement Association. He constantly made moving and powerful speeches about Christian and American values. The speeches affected people all across the nation, giving him the respect of many followers. In 1957, the Southern Christian Leadership Conference (SCLC) was created with Martin Luther King Jr. chosen as president. The SCLC encouraged non-violence in politics in order to have a strong impact. They showed their approval of the NAACP's legal strategies by continuing their peaceful boycotts and protests. The white community did not react in such a peaceful manner and often reacted violently. The federal government had no choice but to investigate the issues in the south dealing with segregation and racism.

Martin Luther King Jr. had the support and dedication of thousands of blacks. Liberal Northerners agreed with his views and with their help he began to have an influence on the national public opinion. He also sparked an interest in peace groups who protested violence. The American Jewish community became affiliated with him giving him their full support. The wealthy and important Protestants of the north also decided to follow. King was able to earn money for the SCLC by frequently preaching for these various congregations.

Segregation protests continued in the 1960's at the North Carolina A&T University. On February 1st of that year, four black college students began protests against racial segregation in restaurants by sitting at the designated "white-only" lunch tables. This form of protest was not new, however the response to these 'sit-ins' was. The impact of the sit-ins spread quickly throughout North Carolina within days and within weeks sit-ins were taking place in cities all across the south. Due to the sit-in movement many restaurants were desegregated and it demonstrated to the county that many young blacks were determined to openly oppose segregation.

Passive Resistance

During the Civil Rights Movement, Martin Luther King supported protests and disobedience that would increase the nation's awareness of social injustices.

In April of 1960 the Student Nonviolent Coordinating Committee (SNCC) was created to organize and direct the student sit-in movement. Although King encouraged SNCC's founding, Ella Baker was the adviser to the students. Baker, who had worked for both the NAACP and SCLC, believed that the SNCC should be a separate organization from the SCLC, and an independent student run organization. Baker also felt that civil rights activities should be based in black communities and the SNCC quickly adopted this approach. They began focusing on making changes in the local black communities before striving for national change. This goal, of the SNCC, was different from King's SCLC, which worked to change laws on a national level. Due to the different methods between the SCLC and the SNCC tension between the organizations rose occasionally during the Civil Rights Movement.

In 1961, after the sit-ins, some members of the SNCC participated in Freedom Rides, which were organized by CORE. The Freedom Riders were blacks and whites that traveled around the South in buses, in an attempt to test the effectiveness of the Supreme Courts 1960 decision, that declared segregation in bus stations illegal. The Freedom Rides began in DC and the early part of the trip was relatively peaceful, except for some violence in South Carolina. However, once they reached Alabama, violence broke out. In Anniston, a bus was burned and the freedom riders were beaten. Similarly in Birmingham, the riders were attacked by a mob upon exiting the bus. Even more severe cases of violence and beatings were seen in Montgomery, Alabama.

National attention was only given to the Freedom Riders after the violence erupted. Alabama officials were harshly condemned for allowing the outbreaks of violence. The Kennedy administration intervened when it became evident that the Alabama state officials would not comply with travel segregation. The Freedom Riders were not stopped. They continued to Jackson, Mississippi where they were then arrested and imprisoned, ending the protest. Nonetheless, the work of the Freedom Riders did result in the desegregation of some bus stations and it also demonstrated to the public how far civil rights workers were willing to go in order to achieve their goal of equality.

Congress passed the Civil Rights Act in 1964. It forbade segregation in public places. It also stopped discrimination in educational places and in the workplace. It gave the executive branch of government the authority to enforce the act's necessities and requirements. Social injustices were starting to become illegal.

Finally the Right to Vote

One of the most important elements of the Civil Rights Movement was the registering of blacks to vote. Though the century old Fifteenth Amendment guaranteed blacks the right to vote, a series of ridiculous literacy tests and poll taxes kept blacks from actually voting. Both the SLCC and the SNCC understood that the

African-American voice could only be heard once blacks started voting for leaders to represent their needs.

Beginning in 1961, voter registration campaigns were organized by the SNCC and CORE. These campaigns focused on the dense black and rural areas of Mississippi, Alabama, and Georgia. The SNCC was more focused on voter registration with the belief that voting was the way to bring blacks to power with the ability to then make some change to the racist policies of the South. SNCC taught blacks essential skills such as reading and writing as a means to register blacks to vote. They were also taught the right answers to the voter registration application. Violence seemed to follow these people who fought for Civil Rights. In 1963, NAACP field secretary Medgar Evers paid the ultimate price for equality when he was killed in front of his home.

Later, in 1965, the SCLC used its "direct action" techniques of marching to bring recognition to the problem of voter injustice. The SNCC in Selma, Alabama started this protest. The protests at the local courthouse were not successful, so protestors began a march to Montgomery. The police beat up these protestors as they were trying to leave Selma. This day became known as Bloody Sunday. Watched on TV, these acts shocked Americans and they were so furious that they decided to continue the Selma March. Martin Luther King and SCLC then led hundreds of marchers on a five-day march to Montgomery. The march established broad national support for the creation of a law to protect Southern Blacks right to vote. Congress then passed the Voting Rights Act of 1965. This act prohibited the use of voter qualification tests. Three years after the enactment, approximately a million more blacks from the South were registered to vote. Black voters were having a substantial effect on Southern politics by 1968, and by the 1970s blacks were winning offices in electoral districts that had a black majority.

The Leader is Killed

After the Voting Rights Act passed in 1965, the focus of the Civil Rights Movement shifted. Martin Luther King Jr. devoted his time to poverty and racial discrimination in the North. He led protests against school discrimination in Chicago, led marches against housing discrimination, and voiced concern for the increasing poverty of his people. In 1967, he planned the Poor People's Campaign where another march on Washington D.C. would force lawmakers to face the issue of violence and poverty.

King wanted equality for everyone and he would not rest until blacks and whites sat down together as equals. Nowhere were his views better expressed than his famous, "I Have a Dream" speech given on the footsteps of the Lincoln Memorial.

Excerpt from "I Have a Dream" Martin Luther King, Jr.—August 28, 1963

I have a dream that one day the state of Alabama, whose governor's lips are presently dripping with the words of interposition and nullification, will be transformed into a situation where little black boys and black girls will be able to join hands with little white boys and white girls and walk together as sisters and brothers. I have a dream today. I have a dream that one day every valley shall be exalted, every hill and mountain shall be made low, the rough places will be made plain, and the crooked places will be made straight, and the glory of the Lord shall be revealed, and all flesh shall see it together. This is our hope. This is the faith with which I return to the South. With this faith we will be able to hew out of the mountain of despair a stone of hope. With this faith we will be able to transform the jangling discords of our nation into a beautiful symphony of brotherhood. With this faith we will be able to work together, to pray together, to struggle together, to go to jail together, to stand up for freedom together, knowing that we will be free one day.

This will be the day when all of God's children will be able to sing with a new meaning, "My country, 'tis of thee, sweet land of liberty, of thee I sing. Land where my fathers died, land of the pilgrim's pride, from every mountainside, let freedom ring." And if America is to be a great nation, this must become true. So let freedom ring from the prodigious hilltops of New Hampshire. Let freedom ring from the mighty mountains of New York. Let freedom ring from the heightening Alleghenies of Pennsylvania! Let freedom ring from the snowcapped Rockies of Colorado! Let freedom ring from the curvaceous peaks of California! But not only that; let freedom ring from Stone Mountain of Georgia! Let freedom ring from Lookout Mountain of

Tennessee! Let freedom ring from every hill and every molehill of Mississippi. From every mountainside, let freedom ring.

When we let freedom ring, when we let it ring from every village and every hamlet, from every state and every city, we will be able to speed up that day when all of God's children, black men and white men, Jews and Gentiles, Protestants and Catholics, will be able to join hands and sing in the words of the old Negro spiritual, "Free at last! Free at last! Thank God Almighty, we are free at last!"

Like Booker T. Washington and W.E.B. Du Bois before, not all African-American leaders agreed on how to best secure their black rights. Some believed King's plans were too moderate and played too much into the hands of white America.

Some wanted blacks to strike out for equality. Stokely Carmichael, a former member of the SNCC, invented the term Black Power and believed blacks should use violence if necessary to achieve a revolution.

Malcolm X, a minister of the Nation of Islam, also supported radical, and possibly violent protest. He brought the Nation of Islam from a small group numbering in the hundreds to a massive organization whose membership surpassed 10,000. Malcolm X disagreed strongly with King's passive resistance, instead championing Black Power and self respect. In 1965, Malcolm X was assassinated.

Tragically, Martin Luther King's vision died when he too was assassinated in 1968. From there, the Civil Rights Movement lost its spiritual and emotional leader and gradually slowed its push for reform. King never had a chance to see how far America could come, but his legacy can never be overestimated. If you think about it, aside from Abraham Lincoln and George Washington, he is the only man in the history of America to have a holiday named after him. He changed the face of America and his "I Have a Dream" speech set a goal for America that hopefully one day our nation will fulfill.

CHAPTER 22

▼

THE AGONY OF DEFEAT: THE VIETNAM WAR

Eric Williams

A Dent in the Armor

Following World War II, America was the biggest kid on the block. It was the richest country. It had the largest military. It had the best toys. It was the envy of the world and nothing seemed able to bring the mighty nation off its throne.

And then there was Vietnam.

In a conflict that lasted nearly thirty years, Vietnam proved to be a situation America wanted to control, but found they were totally unable to do so. How could Vietnam defeat the Americans? How could a third world nation with inferior weapons and limited resources defeat a nation that had defeated every enemy they'd faced across two centuries?

To answer these questions, you need some background information on Vietnam. Let's go back to before World War II. Like other European nations, France had attempted to spread its colonial empire around the globe. They controlled an area known as French Indochina, the region that today goes by the names Cambodia, Laos and Vietnam. With the coming of World War II, France lost control of Vietnam as German forces marched through Paris and the Japanese Empire spread across the Asian continent.

Throughout the war, Vietnamese groups struggled to kick out the Japanese invaders. One man proved to be the most successful, Ho Chi Minh. Ho Chi

Minh turned out to be one of the most important leaders of the twentieth century. Educated in America, England, France, Russia and China, Ho Chi Minh combined Confucian ideals with those of communism to create his unique ideology. He later created the Viet Minh, a communist group dedicated to an independent Vietnam.

America saw promise in this man, and supported Ho Chi Minh throughout World War II. Oddly enough, this same man who became America's greatest ally in Vietnam, became their feared enemy throughout the 1950s and 1960s.

Those Pesky French

When World War II ended, the Vietnamese believed independence was theirs. They were wrong. France reclaimed Vietnam as one of their colonial holdings. Ho Chi Minh changed his strategy. Now he was dedicated to destroying the French forces. Of course, the French underestimated their enemy and spent the 1950s trying to defeat Ho's forces.

It was here that America became a major player in Vietnamese politics. Whereas they helped Ho Chi Minh during World War II, America couldn't tolerate the communist spread after Japanese defeat. America wanted to "contain" communism, and the fear became if communism spread to Vietnam, all of Southeast Asia would fall. This prediction became known as the "domino theory," and it was used frequently to justify why America even cared about this tiny little country on the other side of the world.

Domino Theory Principle, Dwight D. Eisenhower, 1954
Public Papers of the Presidents Dwight D. Eisenhower,
1954, p. 381-390

First of all, you have the specific value of a locality in its production of materials that the world needs.

Then you have the possibility that many human beings pass under a dictatorship that is inimical to the free world.

Finally, you have broader considerations that might follow what you would call the "falling \cf2 domino\cf0" principle. You have a row of dominoes set

---

up, you knock over the first one, and what will happen to the last one is the certainty that it will go over very quickly. So you could have a beginning of a disintegration that would have the most profound influences.

Now, with respect to the first one, two of the items from this particular area that the world uses are tin and tungsten. They are very important. There are others, of course, the rubber plantations and so on.
Then with respect to more people passing under this domination, Asia, after all, has already lost some 450 million of its peoples to the Communist dictatorship, and we simply can't afford greater losses.
But when we come to the possible sequence of events, the loss of Indochina, of Burma, of Thailand, of the Peninsula, and Indonesia following, now you begin to talk about areas that not only multiply the disadvantages that you would suffer through loss of materials, sources of materials, but now you are talking really about millions and millions and millions of people.

Finally, the geographical position achieved thereby does many things. It turns the so-called island defensive chain of Japan, Formosa, of the Philippines and to the southward; it moves in to threaten Australia and New Zealand.

Because America believed that Vietnam was key to all of Southeast Asia, they threw a lot of money into France's war effort. At one point in the 1950s, they were responsible for 80% of the cost of the war. In addition to the tons of money and supplies being sent France's way, America also sent over some of its finest soldiers. However, because America wasn't technically at war with Vietnam, these soldiers weren't called soldiers but "advisors." Even though they carried guns, killed the enemy and were killed themselves, these men were not soldiers, just advisors.

America was less than pleased with France's handling of the war, but they had little choice but to continue supporting them. Because Ho Chi Minh kept embarrassing French forces, America knew that if it stopped aiding France, Vietnam would turn communist in a heartbeat.

France finally had enough after the battle at Dien Bien Phu. France thought it was going to totally annihilate the Viet Minh, but in reality, it was the Viet Minh that caused the most damage. This battle signaled the end for French occupation of Vietnam. Tired of being defeated for a chunk of muggy, jungle land half way around the world, France met the Viet Minh in Geneva and called off the fighting. Vietnam was then officially divided at the 17th parallel for two years, after which time there would be a nationwide election to reunify Vietnam and choose a leader.

Vietnam finally controlled their fate.

Or so they thought.

Still Not Technically at War

In a perfect world, Vietnam would have held elections and the Vietnamese people would have elected their leader. But no. Life can't ever be that easy.

At the Geneva convention, it was decided that Ngo Dinh Diem would be a great leader for South Vietnam for the next couple years. A Roman Catholic, he had spent a few years in America and had even met future President John F. Kennedy. America believed he would be the perfect little puppet leader that they could control. Unfortunately, the guy was a bit crazy, and had no idea how to make intelligent political decisions. He amazingly won 98.2% of his election (even though America suggested he might want to print 70% so it looked a bit more legit). Diem's greatest mistake, apart from treating the rural peasants like garbage, was punishing the Buddhists. His government was made up of mostly Catholics, even though less than 10% of the country was actually Catholic. He also refused to pass laws forbidding abuse of Buddhists. The Buddhists had had enough of this treatment and staged one of the most powerful demonstrations in the history of mankind. A monk named Thich Quang Due soaked his body in gasoline and sat down in the middle of a busy Saigon road and lit himself on fire.

The world was aghast. How bad must this guy Diem be if citizens were willing to set themselves on fire?

By 1963, America had enough of Diem. Over 15,000 "advisors" were in Vietnam trying to train the South Vietnamese to repel the Viet Minh, but it looked like the Communists were continuing to gain support from the masses. Not too tough when the Vietnamese president was an idiot.

How does America solve this problem? A nice little assassination. Then president John F. Kennedy ordered the CIA to take care of the problem. Amazingly, on November 1, 1963, Diem was overthrown and killed. America thought this would help solve the problem in Vietnam. They were wrong.

It only got worse.

The Creation of a Catalyst

Here's a question for you. If you were to go right up to some kid at your school, put your face right in front of his and then start screaming at the top of your lungs, while your arms waved wildly and spit flew from your blazing mouth, what would this kid do after a few minutes? Would he just sit there and smile and thank you for the refreshing bath? Doubtful.

You know the real answer, and so did the Americans back in 1964. America needed justification to go to war with Vietnam. Problem was it was a bit hard to justify going to war in a small country that no one could even locate on a map for a cause many didn't totally understand.

Kennedy's successor, Lyndon B. Johnson, had an idea. All of a sudden, World War II popped into his head and that wacky little raid over Hawaii. Even though in 1941 Americans were pretty hesitant to enter Europe's war, once those Japanese planes bombed Pearl Harbor, the war mood of the nation changed overnight. Then everyone wanted revenge, and they wanted it immediately.

All LBJ needed was the bombing of an American ship. It would work wonders. So, with his knowledge of Pearl Harbor and also of the previous spitting analogy, the American military went to work. America parked a few ships off the coast of North Vietnam in a chunk of water called the Gulf of Tonkin. Here, the ships tracked Viet Minh movements and told the South Vietnamese where and when to attack. One day in 1964, the North Vietnamese forces had enough of these Americans spying off their waters, so they sent some ships to investigate. A kid on the destroyer *Turner Joy*, saw some beeping lights on his radar and told his captain that torpedoes were locked in and coming fast. They fired back at North Vietnamese ships. The *Maddox* saw similar blips and also started firing.

Back in Washington D.C., Johnson had his catalyst. The Vietnamese attacked the Americans!!! Even though technically the Americans fired first (the "blips" were nothing more than bad weather), Johnson claimed that innocent little America was attacked by the big, bad Viet Minh.

LBJ claimed they were "attacked without a cause." With no confirmation, LBJ immediately ordered air strikes within a few hours, and decided to announce the incident to the public later. He then asked Congress for control of future military action; this meant control of the entire military. It passed easily with no negative votes in the House of Representatives and only two negative votes in the Senate. One of the senators who voted negative, Senator Wayne Morse debated that those powers belonged to the Congress. But what did he know? Sure it says in the

Constitution that only the Congress has the right to declare war, but who reads that long old document anyway?

Nevertheless, on August 7, Congress passed the Gulf of Tonkin Resolution giving control of the whole army to the president. The resolution gave the president the power "to take all necessary measures to repel any armed attack against the forces of the United States." This was a resolution that could be easily stretched out of proportion.

Hey, and then guess what? After all this power was given to the president, it was later proved that there was no attack on the US destroyers. Through the testimony of U.S officials from the destroyers and planes overhead, along with that of Vietnamese captured during the war, it was clear that there was no attack. Not only that, LBJ was taped stating that he doubted that there was even an attack. However he also joked, "it was like grandma's nightshirt—it covered everything."

If you want to know why people don't trust the government of America, look no further than the Gulf of Tonkin Resolution. Totally fabricated catalyst to fight a war.

Who's The Boss and What's the Plan?

In June 1964 General William Westmoreland became the senior military commander of the United States. He is most known for increasing the number of U.S soldiers fighting in the war. His strategy was to 'search and destroy' which was to find communists and then kill them. Success was no longer based on what land you were able to conquer, but body counts, enemy kills. This probably caused a lot of innocent deaths because of confusion. Soldiers said that it was hard to tell the difference between enemy and friend because they dressed and looked alike. Remember, they were both Vietnamese. However, can you really fault the Americans for any accidental deaths? Americans all heard stories or saw firsthand how fellow soldiers were killed by women or children carrying grenades or a Viet Cong soldier hiding in a villagers home. No war is fun, but America was totally unprepared for this type of fighting.

Three months after LBJ was elected as president, he put Operation Rolling Thunder into action. The point of Operation Rolling Thunder was to destroy North Vietnam's economy and stop them from sending help to troops in the South. America would use its supreme military advantage to bomb the North into oblivion. They'd have to surrender. The plan was originally made to last eight weeks but it ended up lasting three years.

And the communists just wouldn't surrender. Remember, they'd been fighting for decades to regain their nation. They weren't going to stop just because the Americans were the latest invaders. They would fight until there wasn't a single soldier left. Could America say the same thing?

You Can't Hit What You Can't Find

How can you fight an enemy you can't see? How can you fight an enemy willing to live underground in tunnels when most Americans couldn't even fit?

You can't.

The Vietnamese did just that.

They created a network of tunnels that stretched out all over the country connecting cities, and acted as hospitals, living areas, and military headquarters. The most well known tunnels were found at Cu Chi.

The Cu Chi area is outside Saigon and its tunnels extend over 150 miles. The tunnels ran deep into the ground several stories. Amazingly, the whole thing was dug with hand tools and even had such incredible inventions like vents and underwater trap doors. The Vietnamese people actually lived in the tunnels with underground towns, public places, hospitals, theaters and schools. It was an underground society where people stayed for years, rarely seeing daylight. It functioned as a town where you could play with friends or meet a new love. The tunnel was not only a social place used for shelter but also a way of transportation for the North Vietnamese. It was used to transport artillery around, and a place to retreat to take care of wounded or plan the next attack.

Follow the Ho Chi Minh Trail

Basically, the Ho Chi Minh Trail is a bunch of complicated paths used by the North Vietnamese. It extends from North Vietnam to South Vietnam going through the bordering countries of Laos and Cambodia. It was for transportation of supplies and men during the Vietnam War. The North Vietnamese was moving hundreds of tons of war supplies per day from North to South. This trail was very important! It served as a "vital gateway" that included over twelve thousands miles of roads and paths. The North Vietnamese fought to keep it open while the South and U.S tried to close it. Not only was it used for supplies, but also to transport troops to travel into South Vietnam. The Ho Chi Minh Trail also had set up camps in different parts of the trail so troops could rest and get the medical attention that was needed. During the war, there was as much as 20,000 communist soldiers coming down per month. Before the trail, it would take about six months for someone to travel from North Vietnam to Saigon. With the new and improved, speedy trail it took less as 6 weeks.

The United States Air Force, tried repeatedly to cut off the trail by air strikes. They tried…and failed. The communist Vietnamese just wouldn't quit. Even if bombarded the trail could either be diverted or simply rebuilt.

Make Up Your Mind

War has a way of making even the best presidents look fickle. Oftentimes your goals for how the war will proceed differ just a bit from the reality.

This was the case for Vietnam. It made a liar out of a few presidents, Johnson included.

In the 1964 presidential election campaign, Senator Barry Goldwater asked LBJ to send more American troops to Vietnam. The President did not agree with this and pledged that he would not send troops to Vietnam. He exclaimed, "We are not about to send American boys nine or ten thousand miles from home to do what Asian boys ought to be doing for themselves."

Of course, when his military advisors came to him and said they risked losing the war if he did not increase the number of troops, LBJ had to give in. He had a choice. Appear fickle or have the nation humiliated by a third world nation. He chose to appear fickle.

At the end of 1965 the number of troops in Vietnam raised to 185,000. After this, it raised to 400,00 in 1966.

So much for keeping American boys close to home.

This is Going to Hurt

Between 1965 and 1973, eight million tons of bombs were dropped on Vietnam. This was more than three times the amount of bombs in the whole Second World War. Statistically, this was 300 tons for every man, woman and child living it Vietnam. And personally speaking, that's way more than I can carry.

One of the developments that disgusted Americans was the use of new kinds of weapons, not meant to merely kill the enemy but to destroy his will to continue fighting. Some Americans believed the military was using the tactic of merely injuring the Vietnamese so that others would be forced to care for the them. That's an odd strategy to fight a war.

Weapons like napalm, pineapple bombs, Agent Orange, and Agent Blue became common during the Vietnam War. Napalm is a mixture of gasoline and chemical thinner that burned the skin, causing excruciating pain. Pineapple bombs were small and made of 250 metal or plastic pellets which would shoot out horizontally in all directions. Just drop a bomb and a bunch of little pellets exploded in all directions. Lovely. Agent Orange was sprayed to destroy Communist hiding places. In 1969 alone, it destroyed over a million acres of forestry. It didn't only destroy trees but also caused chromosomal damage to the people nearby. When those exposed eventually reproduced, their offspring were stricken with a variety of abnormalities. Agent Blue, on the other hand, was made just for destroying agricultural crops, with the thought being that with crops destroyed the troops would eventually starve to death. Unfortunately this affected innocent Vietnamese as well as the soldiers.

Though the Vietnamese paid in lost lives, Americans bared the brunt of the financial cost of the war. It was estimated that the Vietnamese suffered over $300 million in damages, whereas the American cost flowed into the billions.

Hey, Hey LBJ. How Many Kids Did You Kill Today?

As president this is not exactly the chant you want repeated in your honor.

As the war progressed, more and more Americans got fed up with it. Americans were suffering from taxes and by 1968 the war was costing $66 million a day. $66 MILLION A DAY! Johnson was losing the support of his people. With the casualty numbers (total of deaths+injured+missing in action) in Vietnam increasing fast, people had had about enough of this war. There was an increase in casualties from 2500 in 1965 to 33,000 in 1966.

At the beginning of 1964, protests were pretty much confined to colleges where students had a ton of ideas, and a ton of free time. In December 1964, it all changed. There was a 25,000 person march to Washington, the largest anti-war march in America's history. Later in the decade nearly a million protesters gathered in New York to challenge America's role in Vietnam.

Other forms of protest started popping up. In November 1965 Norman Morrison, like the Buddhist monk years before, publicly burnt himself to death. Two other men did the same in the following weeks. When drafting was announced, protests increased yet again. Men believed they should be able to control their fate, not their government. In 1965, David Miller burned his draft card and was sentenced to two and a half years in prison. He became an inspiration to hundreds of men who met and discussed massive draft card burnings. Between 1963 and 1973, 9,118 men were prosecuted for refusing to be drafted. This included the heavy weight champion, Muhammad Ali.

What was happening to America?

Two decades earlier, war had united a nation and brought it out of depression. Now it was tearing the nation apart.

Would Somebody Just End This Thing?

Americans wanted an end. But how? The moment Americans withdrew the Viet Cong would enter Saigon and turn the nation communist. America had to find a way to end the war without losing the a country to communism.

For a brief moment in 1967, Americans thought the war might be turning in their favor.

They were wrong.

General William Westmoreland reported that the war was being won and victory was near. Unfortunately, he forgot to tell this to the North Vietnamese.

On the 31st of January 1968, the North Vietnamese used 70,000 troops and deployed a surprise attack on a hundred cities in Vietnam. Americans and South Vietnamese were caught off guard due to the Tet holiday that celebrated a new lunar year. The Viet Cong attacked American military posts. This act served as a decoy and it pulled the troops from the cities.

General Westmoreland explained that it was a victory for America because 37,000 North Vietnamese were killed as opposed to 2,500 Americans. Although America won, it proved that the North Vietnamese had many men that would fight until death. Americans were informed about the destruction they caused and were then informed that the military would need 206,000 more troops. Not exactly the order you'd expect after a "victory."

In March 1968, President Johnson's Secretary of Defense explained that America could not win the war and suggested negotiations be held. Johnson agreed. He momentarily stopped bombing North Vietnam if they would agree to start negotiating a possible end to the war, a cease fire. Later that month, President Johnson announced restrictions on air strikes in North Vietnam and that he intended to start negotiations to end the war.

Johnson also said he wasn't running for president again.

He'd had enough. The next president could clean up the mess.

Not a Victory, and Looks A Lot Like a Defeat

In the election of 1968, Richard Nixon defeated Vice-president Hubert Humphrey by promising to end the war in Vietnam. He had a secret plan.

His plan: make better friends with China and the Soviet Union and then they would cut off aide to Vietnam. Not exactly the kind of war strategy the American people were expecting.

Plus, it would take a ton of time. In 1968, Nixon promised the end of the war. The final troops wouldn't be pulled out for another five years. Technically he ended the war, but some might question the time and the tactics.

One of Nixon's original ideas was to start blowing up the border areas in Laos and Cambodia. The Vietnamese kept retreating to the hills and into those countries to avoid direct combat with American troops. Bombings would hopefully cut off the Ho Chi Minh trail.

Nixon also started slowly pulling troops out of Vietnam. At the height of Johnson's escalation, over 500,000 troops were stationed in Vietnam. Nixon pulled this number back to 175,000 by the end of 1971.

Those troops still in Vietnam wondered what in the world was going on. Was America trying to win the war or not. Many troops started to protest in their own way. Some turned to drugs, others tried to avoid combat. Others even resorted to fragging (assassinating) their leader. They didn't care who won or lost. They just wanted to get home.

Throughout 1972, America continued to negotiate a peace settlement with the Vietnamese so that America could avoid losing as much face as possible. On January 31, 1975, the United States and Vietnam officially ended the war by both agreeing to the Paris Accords. These stated that America would pull out if American POWs were returned.

On March 29, 1973, the last American troops left Vietnam. However, America didn't totally pull out its involvement in Vietnam. It continued to bomb Cambodia, fly missions over North Vietnam and send a ton of aide to South Vietnam. In 1975, America stopped funding the South Vietnamese forces and on April 30th of that year, the South officially surrendered to the North.

After over three decades of involvement that saw 58,000 Americans killed and over $150 billion spent, Vietnam became communist anyway. Under all definitions of defeat, this was one. America lost and the nation would spend the rest of the century questioning the actions of their government.

Timeline of the Vietnam War

Date	Event
1950	Truman grants aid to the French to overthrow Viet Minh
1954	French withdraw from Vietnam following Geneva convention
1955	American aide to Vietnam tops $200 million a year
1959	Two American "advisors" killed. First soldiers killed in action.
1962	"Advisors" sent to train South Vietnamese army increased to 12,000
1965	*Maddox* and *Turner Joy* fired upon in Gulf of Tonkin. Johnson given full control.
1965	Rolling Thunder bombing of North Vietnam begins
1968	America heavily defends Khe Sanh, believing it is great North Vietnamese attack
1968	Surprise Tet Offensive shows how the Viet Cong will never surrender
1969	Draft lottery begins. College students can no longer get out of the draft.
1971	*New York Times* publishes Pentagon Papers showing government lied
1973	Cease fire announced and last ground troops leave Vietnam
1975	Saigon falls to communists
1976	Jimmy Carter pardons all draft dodgers
1982	Vietnam War Memorial opened commemorating 58,000 lives lost

CHAPTER 23

▼

CHILLIN' THROUGH SOME PHAT DECADES: POP CULTURE IN THE 20TH CENTURY

Jessica Fries
Fred Glander
Mercedes Moore

How You Like Me Now?

In the twentieth century, people didn't worry about surviving, but rather they worried about more important things like what's showing at the local movie house, or what Britney Spears is wearing in her new video. Popular Culture flourished in the twentieth century because of this newfound freedom, in a century that was faster than Taco Bell through my small intestine. Music diversified, mass media became king, and stories were brought to life on the big screen.

Hold on a second. Didn't we forget something? Oh yeah. What in the world is Pop Culture? You probably need to know that before we go any further. Well, every country has a culture. It's the food they eat, the clothes they wear, the art on their walls, the music in their ears, the books on their nightstand, and the words they use when talking to buddies. The term "Pop Culture" is a more recent, and more commonly used phrase. It has to do with what is *pop*ular for ordinary people, the masses.

Do You Have a Point?

America at the very beginning of the century was still growing trying to cope with all of the social and political issues of the time. It wasn't until the late 1910s and the early 1920s that America's Pop Culture started to really bloom. The 1920s was an age of economic growth, which saw the first appearances of the Model T car: the vehicle that allowed people to escape for the weekend. America's brand new wealth in the roaring twenties made it possible for the average Joe to go get a radio and enjoy the many shows in this vast new mass media. One of radios greatest contributions to society was that it gave news and information out to people almost instantaneously. But the radio has always been recognized for the music it plays, and in the 1920s nothing was hotter than Jazz.

Hey, That Sounds Pretty Jazzy

Jazz was not simply music: it was the expression of the generation in the 1920s. Jazz was what we would look at today as a really hot, sexy, controversial new sound. Okay maybe not when your comparing it to the stars on MTV, but for its time, Jazz was WILD. Jazz was a style of music that was brought to life by that rebel attitude of the people who listened to it, and it became a scapegoat for the conservative folks of the time. One unique trait was that both the white and African American communities loved it. This could be seen at night clubs that served both races, like the Cotton Club in New York City.

The essentials for this type of music combined African tribal music with European music to create a uniquely American sound. Many believed that Jazz originally began in New Orleans, or Dixieland as people usually referred to it as. Dixieland Jazz consisted of small bands that played instruments such as trumpets, clarinets, trombones, bass, guitar, drums and sometimes piano. Jazz became known for its improvisation. People would watch the top Jazz musicians and know that every night they'd be getting something just a little bit different.

This new sound soon spread to Los Angeles, New York and Kansas City where new types of Jazz were produced. One of these types was Progressive Jazz. Even though this music originated in New York, it became very popular on the West Coast during the 1940s and 1950s.

Blues was another new, all American sound that expressed the plight of the African American's daily life at the time. Created in the 1920s and 1930s, the Blues was not just a style of music, but a feeling that it gave people inside. Many great stars came out of the early days of blues, but there was none greater than Bessie Smith who was considered the Empress of Blues.

Radios and Movies and Stars, Oh My!

Radio wasn't just about music and news. Before television shows, there were radio shows, and during the 1930s the radio was pumping out some classics. Americans planned their weekly schedule around shows such as "The Shadow," "The Lone Ranger," and "The Green Hornet." Radio was so powerful, that people actually had difficulty distinguishing between reality and the radio world. One time, in 1938, after listening to "The War of the Worlds," Americans actually thought aliens were invading the earth. The show caused mass hysteria, but the audience kept coming back. By 1939, 80% of all households in America owned a radio.

Pop culture would have never been the same in the twentieth century if it weren't for the introduction of the motion picture, also known as a movie. The motion picture came out in the 1890s and continued to develop into the twentieth century. Everyone started looking to Hollywood to see what was cool. The expansion of film also gave birth to the first movie stars. The biggest star in the early days of movies had to be the English actor, Charlie Chaplin. He came to America on a traveling theater show and eventually cut a deal with Keystone Films in 1914. First appearing in movies that didn't have sound, Charlie Chaplin used action comedy to dazzle his audiences.

By the 1930s, the motion picture scene had changed a ton. For instance, Charlie Chaplin's first movie, *Making a Living,* only had a running time of fifteen minutes, which is about how long those movie previews and commercials last today! Movies resembled more of what they do today. They were bigger, better, and longer. The motion picture industry was entering what some people called the "Golden Age of Film." This was the era of the epic movies and the blonde bombshells. During this time, the motion picture industry made some of its best movies ever such as *Gone with the Wind*, the world's all-time most watched movie (yes…it even beats Titanic). *Gone with the Wind* premiered in 1939 and showed a graphic and romanticized Civil War story. It was nominated for twelve Academy Awards, and won seven, which included best picture, best actress, and best director.

1939 was also the year that Walt Disney introduced his first full-length animated film *Snow White*. Walt Disney included some of the best animation techniques of the time, and collected enough money from the movie to start his Grand Empire. There was no stopping Disney after that. Over the years that followed, the mouse empire spewed out *Fantasia*, *Dumbo*, and *Bambi*. Even when World War II started, Disney still had his hand in animation, making war films and having Donald Duck sell the new federal income tax.

TV Turns Golden

In the 1950s, another invention changed America forever, as the nation could now sit on their couch and the entertainment world would come to their family room.

Welcome to the world of television.

Television was invented in the 1920s but was popularized at the 1939 New York Worlds Fair. By the 1950s, television became America's new number one form of mass media. This Golden Age of Television, produced shows like *Lassie*, *The Honeymooners*, and the *Ed Sullivan Show*. These shows were more directed towards entertainment for the entire family, which kept the beatniks and the rebels without a cause off the airways.

There were situation comedies, also known as sitcoms, like *I Love Lucy,* which captured the comedy of everyday life. Then there were variety shows like *The Ed Sullivan Show*, and *American Bandstand*. These talent shows featured many of America's rising stars in the entertainment industry. Many who were coming from a new type of music called Rock 'n' Roll.

The King Shakes His Groove Thing

The music that really defined the term "generation gap" was Rock 'n' Roll. Many parents and "America's white establishment" hated this fresh style of music. They believed it to be too antisocial, rebellious, and sexual. What were they talking about? What could possibly be wrong with "Goodness Gracious Great Balls of Fire" or "Whole Lotta Shaking Going On?"

Rock 'n' Roll started in the mid 1950s. White, middle class teenagers were the biggest group to enjoy this style of music. The music was a mixture of rhythm and blues. Alan Freed, a disc jockey, actually coined the phrase "Rock 'n' Roll." Some musicians, such as Bill Haley and the Comets, adapted the work of many of the earlier African American artists to produce their sound.

Some of the biggest stars of Rock 'n' Roll were: Chuck Berry (who set the ground rules), Jerry Lee Lewis, and Little Richard. Of course the most famous of them all was Elvis Presley. Before Presley's successful career he was a truck driver from Tupelo, Mississippi. He took all the styles of Rock 'n' Roll from the country-western feel to rhythm and blues and created his own variety of Rock 'n' Roll. Presley's voice spanned two and a half octaves, which allowed him to do every style of Rock N' Roll imaginable. As most of you know, he became known as "The King."

The King

Elvis Presley's dance moves frightened parents all over the nation.

Elvis Presley was born in Mississippi on January 8, 1935. His twin brother was stillborn, so Elvis grew up as an only child. In 1948, his parents moved him to Memphis, Tennessee where he graduated High School in 1953. Many different genres of music influenced Elvis' style: gospel, country, blues, and the pop music of the era, all of which played an important part in the development of his music. He began his singing career in 1954 and became a worldwide phenomenon by 1956. His singing career was also highlighted by his unique gyrations on stage. Moms and Dads across the country got a bit nervous when Elvis started getting a bit funky on the Ed Sullivan Show. The show's creators even decided to just film him from the waist up. But that wasn't enough. The power of Elvis would transform an entire nation into lovers of Rock 'n' Roll.

Rock 'n' Roll changed the face of music and while it was changing music it was changing itself. For example, in the1960s Jimi Hendrix and Acid Rock changed the definition of Rock 'n' Roll. It was the perfect voice for the counter culture. The 1960s saw a lot of demonstrations against the Vietnam War in the lyrics of the songs. The 1960s also saw the coming of the great British invasion led by a rock band called The Beatles. The whole decade could have been summed up in a three day concert, in 1969, known as Woodstock, where the greatest artists of the decade got together for good music and for some (slightly illegal) fun.

Top Recording Artists of All Time

Artist	Millions of Albums Sold
The Beatles	164.5
Led Zeppelin	105
Garth Brooks	105
Elvis Presley	102
Eagles	86
Billy Joel	77
Pink Floyd	73.5
Barbara Streisand	68.5
Elton John	64.5
Aerosmith	63.5

Video Killed the Radio Star

In the very early 1980s, Michael Jackson and Madonna began their reign of pop music. The music video, still a novel idea to most, had buried prospective musicians who couldn't cut it on TV. However, there were two stars who grabbed the music video scene and redefined it. Not only did singers now have to be able to belt out a tune, but also they had to look visually appealing to their audience.

Michael Jackson had been in the spotlight since he was a little munchkin singing the ABCs with his brothers. In the 1980s, he used his magical dancing ability to awe the planet. His high voice, his dramatic physical performances, and his occasional trademark "Oowww!" while touching his lower stomach region made him the King of the Pop Hill, where he ruled supremely for most of the decade.

In fame, Madonna was the 80s female equivalent of Michael Jackson. At first she experimented with her own band called Emmy, then she tried out a bit of acting, and then she tried nude modeling. Eventually though, she was Madonna. The Madonna we know from the short blonde hair and thick eyeliner, to the longer blonde hair and less eyeliner. Her songs were in-your-face sex appeal. She performed strong, expressive music that appealed to women with attitude and an admiring male audience. Her videos were edgy and famous for their individuality and the odd elements she tried to incorporate.

Madonna and Michael were just two of the many artists that came on the music scene during the 1980s. This was a high-energy time with big dreams, heavy makeup, mass bodybuilding, passionate music, and an excited, urgent sense of direction. This energized momentum contrasted sharply against the following decade, where Nirvana and grunge music made us realize what music from the opposite end of the spectrum sounded like.

Enough About Music, What About Movies Again

As I'm writing this, I'm starting to realize that this could go on forever. What should be put in, what should be left out? Decisions, decisions. Well, let's just jump through the decades.

In the 1950s and 1960s people started getting excited about musicals and watching a nun sing about how the hills were "alive with the sound of music." Pop culture in the movie world always swung back and forth between this type of happy, the-world-is-wonderful theme, and exploring the darkest parts of humanity.

The 1970s were a perfect example. While America was involved in the Vietnam War, moviegoers went to see *The Godfather* or *Butch Cassidy and the Sundance Kid* or *Jaws*. By the end of the decade, a transformation would take place. America wanted to be entertained again, and now Hollywood had the special effects to take the viewer to different worlds. Lines formed around the block to see *Star Wars*, the first of a wave of science fiction movies that took an unlucky boy and made him a hero, while saving the world in the process.

The 1980s continued with the theme of science fiction, and then America started the historical fiction era. *Forrest Gump*, *Braveheart*, and *Titanic* all did well at the box office, even if they did skew the facts just a bit. The century ended with a wave of movies where the goal became how much could you gross out the audience without getting an X rating.

Best Selling Movies of All Time

Movie	Year	Adjusted Gross in Millions*
Gone With the Wind	1937	$1187.7
Star Wars	1977	$1026.7
Sound of Music	1965	$824.1
E.T.	1982	$815
The Ten Commandments	1956	$758.1
Titanic	1997	$747.4
Jaws	1975	$747.1
Dr. Zhivago	1965	$700.7
The Jungle Book	1967	$626.8
Snow White and the Seven Dwarfs	1937	$615.2

* Adjusted gross means how much the movie would have sold if all tickets cost $8. You can't punish *Gone With the Wind* because it cost 25 cents a ticket.

What Were People Wearing?

The story of pop culture in America is not merely about the music and the movies; it's also about what people put on their bodies. For the majority of humans throughout history, the goal of clothes had been warmth. The rich could care about style, but the masses cared about not freezing to death.

That changed in the 20th century as clothes could be mass-produced and copied. Each decade seemed to have a different fashion style. Some fashion styles even came back and became popular in the late 20th Century. Probably the biggest change in women's fashion was during the 1920s. Instead of wearing long dresses that covered their whole body, women started wearing skirts that rose to their knees and the waistline dropped from their waist to their hips. These skirts, known as flappers, showed off women's independence while still showing off a little skin. The men on the other hand wore pinstriped suits and trousers that fit tightly around their ankles. Hats were also in style, as many men started to wear them to compliment their suits.

During the 1930s, women started finding jobs and working, mainly due to the depressed economy. Their work attire was usually made up of a business looking shirt (similar to that of a man's), accompanied by a tight skirt with a slit along the back or the side. On top of the shirt was a jacket that contained shoulder pads.

In the 1940s America was involved in World War II. Women used the least amount of material they could to make their clothes so they could give the extra material to the war effort. This caused women's style to be somewhat plain and boring. Their dresses were made without buttons, collars or cuffs. The men who were not at war usually wore a pair of pants and a jacket. In my opinion, unlike the 1940's, the 1950's were a lot more stylish. Some girls wore pedal pushers (pants that cut off at the knee) with blouses. Their hair was puffed out and flipped in the fashionable styles of the decade. They wore sandals or white Keds sneakers. Alternatively, the boys had their own sense of style. Most of them wore tight Levis jeans, black or white shirts and leather jackets. If you don't know what I'm talking about just watch the movie *Grease*. The popular shoes during these years for boys were Converse or loafers. Their hair was greased back with either a curl in the middle or wing tips at the side. This was the famous look that James Dean had in his movie "A Rebel Without a Cause."

Throughout the 50s, boys and girls tended to dress differently, while during the 60s, boys and girls wore similar clothes. In the 60s they both wore Levis bell-bottoms that, as the name suggested, were wide from the knee down. On their jeans they placed decorations and patches. Combined with the bell-bottoms men wore leather vests with tee shirts and sometimes a bare chest. Along with jeans women wore cotton blouses, also known as "peasant blouses," but they also wore loose, flowery dresses sometimes.

The 1970s was known as the disco era. Men still wore bell-bottoms, but instead of vests they wore a jacket over a solid color shirt. Sometimes gold chains were added for a little more style. The women wore loose ruffled dresses that stopped at the knee. Lycra, acrylic and polyester were popular fabrics used to make these clothes. Not only did they look snazzy, but they were highly flammable too. Both men and women wore platform shoes. Nothing like adding a few inches to your height by standing on stilt shoes.

A new kind of clothing fashion became popular in the 80s. This new kind of clothing was like our present-day "exercise clothes." These outfits had bright colors, such as greens and pinks, and were made from spandex and Lycra material. Women's suits had been around for many years now, however, now they came in brighter colors like blues, pinks, and yellows. Shoulder pads in women's blouses and suits were fashionable. And finally, the 1990's, was a mixture of a variety of different styles. Platform shoes for girls returned and the classic color was black. The vests that were quite popular in the 1960s were not considered trendy in the 1990's. Men's pant legs became looser and the idea of men wearing bell-bottoms was out of the question.

THE 21st CENTURY: Y2K and Beyond

So, here we are in the 21st century, and what is now considered true Pop Culture Americana. On TV, America fell in love with *Survivor* and soon after, many reality based shows popped up. *The Simpsons* are still on air, and they've been cool since Reagan was president. Nothing like a cartoon that makes fun of America, but at the same time has a main character that is fat, chubby and has funny sounds come out of his body.

Music has started another change. After the Spice Girls and the boy bands slowly faded out of the scene, we have now witnessed the anti-band movement with Avril Lavigne, Norah Jones and Eminem leading the charge. "It's all about the music man."

Movies continue to get bigger and more expensive to make. *Harry Potter, The Lord of the Rings,* and *The Matrix Reloaded* rule the world, but we are always ready to watch whatever movies Hollywood throws at us.

In the area of clothing, the showing off of your underwear has finally passed, and just a few guys still feel the need to sag their pants. Everyone is getting things pierced and parents are getting worried as they're paying more money for clothes that have less and less fabric. Retro is in; wearing a 1970s shirt with "7-11" printed on it is cool, even though if you wore it in the 1980s you'd be beat up and thrown in the trash can.

The world of Pop Culture changes as quickly as we change our clothes, and nobody really knows what will be coming next. But if history ever taught us anything, we would know to just sit back and wait for the revolution of Pop Culture to continue. Meanwhile, the clothes in the closet would get cool again and the music from when you were a baby would someday raise the roof again. That's life for ya. Peace out!

CHAPTER 24

▼

OUR LEADERS
BEING NAUGHTY:
POLITICAL CORRUPTION

The Rich Get Richer

Corruption: where the leaders of our country, the people who we trust to take care of us and guide us through hardship, the men and women who are supposed to be the symbols of the nation, begin behaving badly. These people all knew right from wrong, but they chose to ignore their Mommies and listen to the bad voice inside their head that kept saying, "Don't worry about it. No one will ever find out."

Well, the authorities always find out. In a recent survey that polled over three people, it was found that people who do naughty things get caught 97 percent of the time. It's a statistical fact, but remember, 78.4 percent of all statistics are made up.

When you first think of corruption and leaders being naughty, you probably immediately think of Bill Clinton, a dress, and a college girl with funny hair. However, our former saxophone playing president wasn't the first guy to be mischievous. Nope, in fact, if you go back to the dawn of civilization, people in Mesopotamia were even breaking laws. That's where they came up with that whole idea of "An eye for an eye."

But I'm getting sidetracked. There's not enough paper in the world to write a book about all the men throughout world history who have been on Santa's bad list. So let's just focus on American leaders in the last couple centuries. You probably weren't alive for most of the other things mentioned in this chapter, so I will fill you in as much as possible. Although we do talk about Bill Clinton and his affair later in this chapter, we are going to start further back in time, when industry first started to boom: the era of the robber barons.

The Big, Bad Boss

There are bad people in the world. I know, I know. This destroys your view of humanity, but it's true. Even though most of the world is super nice, loving, and caring and would help you out in your time of need, there are bad people. In a recent survey conducted by the Students Who Want to Fabricate Data Committee (SWWFDC), it was found that 10 percent of humans are always bad, 10% of humans are always good, and the rest in the middle could go either way depending on the weather and what their buddy is doing.

What's my point? My point is that before I start making fun of presidents and governmental leaders, understand that I don't think they were the only ones being naughty. In fact, I would bet you $20 that you could find corruption in every profession, at every age, in every town, city and village in the world.

But let's focus for a minute on cities in America. Around the turn of the century, American cities were a combination of immigrants, natives, skilled and unskilled laborers. Some people called America a melting pot (when different cultures come together to become one), others called it a mixed salad. Sometimes these groups got along, sometimes they didn't.

But there was money to be made. Whenever you have taxes coming in, the government receives money. Here's what happens: political leaders believe that because the quantity of money coming in is so huge, no one would miss a small little percentage. Now, what if you could have money other than taxes coming in; say in the form of bribes or other types of suggestive donations? See where I'm getting at?

The symbol of this era was William Marcy Tweed. Also known as "Boss" Tweed, he was a political leader in the late nineteenth century in New York. Not only was Tweed a state senator and a federal representative, he controlled all aspects of the Democratic party during the post-Civil War era. During his reign, he stole anywhere between $30 million and $200 million.

All this money was made through a series of frauds, primarily by selling government contracts to people that supported him, with the expectation that he would receive a "kickback." Here's how it worked. A firehouse needed to be built. Boss Tweed would then have construction companies bid for how much it would cost to build it. Say a guy named Bob the Builder, comes in and says it will cost $500,000 to build the firehouse. Boss Tweed says he'll give Bob the contract and pay him $600,000 from the city treasury, the taxpayers' money. In fact, Bob could even keep $50,000 of the leftovers. Of course, he was also expected to give Tweed a bit of the "kickback" also.

This is not very nice, but it was a standard way in which political leaders, and the companies that get the contracts, made a ton of money. If you think this doesn't happen anymore, you are confused. Next time you have hours to spare, pull out your copy of the Department of Defense's budget for last year and look at some of the items. Here is a listing of some of the items used in Saudi Arabia and the United Arab Emirates in the fight against Saddam Hussein's regime in Iraq.

Necessary Expenditures?

Item	Cost to America
Cappuccino machine	$16,758
White beach sand	$4,638
Cowboy hats	$4,896
Decorative river rock	$18,980
Nacho cheese warmer	$1,039
Remote-control cars	$3,766
Sumo wrestling suit	$3,395
Love seat and armchair	$23,989
"The Intelligent Investor" software	$2,987
Genie lamp with Riyadh stone	$432
Corporate golf membership	$16,000
Golf-club set with bag	$1,478

Not My Cup of Teapot Dome

George Washington. Thomas Jefferson. Abraham Lincoln. Warren Harding. Which one of those names doesn't belong? Well, sorry Mr. Harding, but if you weren't in a textbook, nobody would even know your name, and the sad thing is you're only mentioned in connection with a scandal. That's why you're in this chapter.

Warren Harding made the mistake of hiring his buddies to be on his presidential cabinet. His cabinet was soon known as the "Ohio Gang." That's a great idea to hire your friends, if they're not scum. Well, one of his buddies, Albert B. Fall, became head of the Department of Interior, the department that overseas how America's land is used. Here's where he got into trouble.

Fall walked down the hall to the Secretary of the Navy's office and asked Mr. Secretary, Edwin Denby, if he could control all of the navy's oil reserves. Now, usually the navy controls these because they are on American land, but Mr. Fall decided this little fact wasn't that important. He then decided he'd let two guys lease this land from the government, for a nice little bribe of $400,000. These two guys were Harry F. Sinclair, the owner of the Mammoth Oil Company, and Edward L. Doheny, owner of Pan-American Petroleum and Transport Company.

Let's see if you're following along. Imagine if George Bush leased Niagra Falls to Coca Cola so that they could have fresh water for their soft drinks, and then Coca Cola gave George Bush a nice $3 million Christmas present. Now, I must tell you right now, this is an analogy. There is absolutely no proof that Coca Cola owns Niagra Falls.

Now, even though Harding was innocent, he took a lot of blame for this incident. The incident must have really burned inside him and possibly caused his death in office shortly after the incident was made public and the involved parties were punished.

The Granddaddy of Them All

It almost sounds pathetic to mention a scandal called Teapot Dome before mentioning the greatest scandal in the history of America: Watergate. This one is so bizarre that it almost sounds like it was created by Hollywood. But it's all true.

It all started back in 1969 when the press started finding out information from the government that should never have been leaked to them. Now, you might not know this, but the government doesn't tell you everything. In fact, they have a ton of things they keep secret. On, March 24, 2003, George Bush issued an executive order saying that he could keep government documents private for the sake of national security. Presidents like their privacy.

So did Nixon. Well, information was being leaked and Nixon wanted to find out who did it. He tried out different types of surveillance and in 1971 created the Special Investigations Unit, which became nicknamed the "plumbers." Plumbers. Get it. They plug leaks.

Their job was to find out dirt on Democrats that might be involved in the leaking and then publicize this information so that Republicans would do better in the coming elections.

Here's where things get weird.

G. Gordon Liddy walks into a planning room and discussed his ideas on how to make the Democrats look bad. Now, the conversation went something like this:

Liddy: Hey guys, I got this great idea. How about if we kidnap some people and blame it on the Democrats? Then we can rent a boat with some "high-priced" ladies and invite some Democrats along on the boat ride. Then we can take pictures. Then we can possibly do some blackmail. And I think I can deliver this to you all for the low, low price of $1 million.

Guys: Are you crazy?

Liddy: I see you're not totally sold on the idea. How about if we get rid of the kidnapping? That'll bring it down to $500,000.

Guys: Who let this guy in here?

Liddy: Fine, fine. Just the boat and some pictures. $300,000 and that's my final offer.

Guys: (Stare with mouths open at nutball in front of them.)

Liddy: Whatever. I see you're not the adventurous type. You guys are no fun at all. We might as well go with the boring plan. I'll just hire some guys to break into the Watergate Hotel and look through some of the Democrats files. That'll cost only $250,000.

Guys: (Looking at each other, wanting to find away to get this guy out of the room.) OK fine, go do what you have to Gordon.

Now, though this wasn't the exact conversation, it was pretty close. In fact Jeb Magruder said that they agreed to the idea just because they were reluctant to send Liddy away with nothing.

What great logic in deciding to bring down your entire presidency and the people's faith in the federal government? Anyway, the Plumbers did just exactly what Liddy said they'd do. They broke into the Watergate Hotel, the location of the Democratic national headquarters. Unfortunately, on June 17, 1972 five of the Plumbers were caught.

Over the next few months, reporters and police found out slowly that the plumbers were connected to some pretty important people in the White House. Eventually, it was traced all the way to Nixon. Now, one of Nixon's aides, Alexander Butterfield, testified that Nixon had a bunch of tapes of all the conversations he'd had in the Oval Office. Why? Why would you be so naughty and so stupid?

For a while, Nixon went back and forth with the Grand Jury saying he didn't have to give the tapes. Finally, under a ton of pressure, he gave the tapes to the grand jury, but they were amazingly missing 18 minutes. What happened to the 18 minutes? The world may never know.

But by now the damage was done. Nixon would have been impeached, asked to resign and maybe even put in jail (doubtful), so he did what any smart President would have done: he resigned, and Gerald Ford became President. And whatever trust America had left in their government went right out the window.

I Take the Fifth

After a few years without a scandal, Ronald Reagan felt it was time to spice things up a bit, so he got himself involved in the Iran-Contra Affair. Now, Reagan was naughty because he allowed/enabled/ordered people in the executive department to run little secret missions around the world without Congress knowing about it. That's not nice. And, it also happened to be illegal. Congress gets to declare war and Congress gets to decide how much money is spent, where it's spent, and how it is spent. Not the President. I think the President knew this, but he ignored it. That makes him naughty.

Here's basically what happened. There are two different events in two different parts of the world, but they are both related. First, the Contras. The Contras are a group of rebels who wanted to overthrow their government in Nicaragua. Back in the 1980s, America liked these rebels, but we didn't like the Sandinistas, the people running Nicaragua. So, what does America do when it doesn't like another country's government? That's right, they overthrow it.

Problem. It's illegal to overthrow a government, so you have to do it secretly. In fact, Congress even passed a law, the Boland Amendment, that clearly said, "You are not allowed to give money to the Contras." It was pretty clear. However, the President must have been confused by the wording, because a secret operation was funded to overthrow the Sandinistas by doing bad things like assassinating people and putting mines in the water.

Let's see if you see a problem here: America was giving money and help to the Contras. Congress made it illegal to give money to the Contras. See the problem? Where was the American government going to get the money? For this we turn to Iran.

Iran had for years wanted American weapons for their war against Iraq. Who wouldn't? If you haven't heard, America makes pretty good weapons. In 1985, the Iranians asked the Israelis to ask the Americans if they could buy some TOW (**T**ube launched, **O**ptically tracked and **W**ire guided) anti-tank missiles. This was a problem for a couple reasons. Again, Congress hadn't approved any sales. Second, Iran had been labeled a terrorist country by Reagan's very own Secretary of State. Subsequently, exports to Iran were heavily restricted.

Do you see the connection coming yet? America needs money to pay the Contra guerrilla rebels. Iran wants to purchase some expensive American missiles.

I almost forgot. One more thing. At this time, Lebanon has American hostages. Reagan has already publicly claimed that he will never negotiate with terrorists holding hostages. But, Lebanon and Iran are friends. Do you see what could be done?

America sold missiles to Iran, and then received money from Iran who also promised to work with the Lebanese to free the hostages. The money was then sent down to the Contras who had already been trained by Americans to overthrow the Sandinistas who ran Nicaragua. Everything was going fine. Guys played super spy and Congress was none the wiser. It wasn't until October 5, 1986, when a cargo plane was shot down and the one survivor was captured. This guy, Eugene Hasenfus, then proceeded to tell the whole story on TV.

America had a problem. There were a ton of Congressional hearings to find out what happened. These trials were on TV and cut into such great shows as *All My Children* and *Days of Our Lives*. Two guys, Oliver North and John Poindexter, seemed to always be on trial, and every other word out of their mouth was, "I take the fifth." This basically meant they were using their Fifth Amendment rights not to incriminate themselves. This worked pretty well since they were the only ones involved in the conversation. If neither one said anything, they'd both be in good shape.

North was eventually fired, and Poindexter resigned. However, just a few days ago I saw Oliver North on CNN talking about battle plans in Iraq. He's a soldier again back in the Middle East, so I guess he's doing OK.

President Reagan and VP George Bush claimed they knew nothing about it, and no connection was ever made. But, yet again, the American public was a bit skeptical.

You Should be Ashamed of Yourself

And now we come to Bill Clinton and Monica Lewinsky. Unfortunately, this is a PG rated book so I can't go into too much detail. A lot of the stuff is dirty and shouldn't be talked about in public. Bill Clinton was very naughty, and he got in trouble, big trouble.

Clinton's troubles started in 1998, when he was asked to testify in a hearing where Paula Jones accused him of sexually harassing her when he was governor of Arkansas. He of course denied the whole thing. During this trial, Jones' lawyers went interviewing every woman who ever knew Clinton to see if any of them had ever been harassed by Clinton. During the trial, Clinton was asked, "Have you ever had sexual relations with Monica Lewinsky?"

He said, "No."

That was his problem.

You see, having an affair isn't illegal, but lying under oath is. Lying under oath can put you in jail. Lewinsky had also said that she never had relations with Clinton. The problem was Lewinsky's oh-so-good friend Linda Tripp had tape recorded a conversation where Lewinsky admitted to having an affair with Clinton.

Attorney Kenneth Starr then got permission to go investigate further. Over the next few months, America learned way more than it ever needed to know about Clinton and Lewinsky. Every night on the news, something would come out about a cigar, or a dress, or what Clinton considers to be sexual relations. It was explicit and dirty. Yuck. It even came out that Clinton had asked his buddy Vernon Jordan to get Lewinsky a job in another state if she just shut up about the whole thing.

This stuff kept coming out all of 1998, and in December of 1998, Clinton was impeached by the House of Representatives. Impeached means he was just publicly told he was naughty for two reasons: 1) lying under oath 2) obstruction of justice by telling Mr. Jordan to get Lewinsky a job. Even though he was impeached, when the vote came to the Senate he was found innocent.

The nation was just glad to have this thing over. He eventually had to pay a couple fines and agree not to practice law for five years. Oddly enough, Linda

Tripp was taken to court for making an illegal wire tap. She too was a bit mischievous, and a bad friend, too.

And that, ladies and gentlemen, is the last presidential scandal in America, and I promise that never again will any president ever do anything naughty. Cross my heart, hope to die, stick a needle in my eye.

CHAPTER 25

▼

THE FIGHT FOR
THE HOLY LAND:
CONFLICT IN ISRAEL

Luc Nutter
Doug Fagan

The Source of Conflict

You might be wondering why an entire chapter is devoted to Israel. It's because you can't separate American politics and America's future from the incessant conflict in Israel. As America entered the 21st century, they were faced with growing tension with extremists in the Arab world who condemned and still condemn to this day American support of Israel. You can't have a talk about the Middle East, without bringing up Israel. And because we don't want you to look ignorant the next time your friends at a party start discussing current events, we want to catch you up to speed.

The conflict between Israel and Palestine goes way back. Hebrews (name given to those that are Jewish) entered Israel in 1300 B.C., and built the area up into a self-sufficient community. However, a series of foreign invasions forced the Jews to leave the land and Jews subsequently spread throughout the world. About seven centuries after their arrival in Israel, Nebuchadnezzar II, the leader of Babylon (what used to be called Mesopotamia), took the Jews into captivity and initiated a nearly 3,000 year pattern of Jewish persecution. Even after this initial capture by the Babylonians, many Jews remained in Israel and attempted to rebuild the community. Again, Jews faced total destruction in 70 C.E, when the Romans entered their region, murdering and kicking out any Jews that stood in their way. Some Jews remained, and again tried to rebuild their community. See a pattern here?

The coming of the prophet Muhammad again led to Jewish harassment while intensifying negative feelings between Arabs and Jews. In 622, Muhammad moved to Medina (a city housing many Jews) and forced them to either agree to his teachings or leave. By marrying politically valuable women and using his teaching strengths, Muhammad was able to spread Islam throughout the region. Upon his death, Islam continued to spread throughout the Arab world, uniting the people under a common language and religion. Later, this Arab Empire would evolve into the Ottoman Empire.

Timeline of Main Events

Date	Event
2344 B.C.E.	The Flood and Noah's Ark
1446 B.C.E.	Moses frees slaves from Egypt
1312 B.C.E.	Israel becomes a nation
586 B.C.E.	Nebuchadnezzar II captures Jews
4 B.C.E.	Jesus Christ is born
70 C.E.	Romans invade Israel and kick Jews out
622 C.E.	Muhammad leaved Mecca for Medina
1095-1291 C.E.	Christians fail in attempt to recapture Holy Land from Muslim control
1922	Following World War I, Great Britain receives Israel as a mandate

* Note: B.C.E. means before common era. It used to be called B.C., before Christ, but now that's not politically correct. Also, you don't say A.D. anymore, you say C.E., common era.

Muhammad's kingdom, was one of the strongest in the area. Throughout the time Europe called the Middle Ages, war was being fought across the Middle East, Africa and Europe to see who would control the region. After a countless number of bloody and gruesome battles, called the Crusades, the Ottoman Empire prevailed. Though I could go into the history of the battles and give you a plethora of information, all you have to really know is this: the Middle East is still predominantly Muslim to this day.

Here's a key factor you need to consider. When we use the word Muslim, we are talking about people who follow the religion of Islam. People don't say, "Oh we're Catholicism." They say "We're Catholic." Same thing here. You wouldn't say "We're Islam." You would say that you're Muslim.

Religion Guide

Religion	People	Prophet	Holy Book
Judaism	Jews	Moses	Torah
Islam	Muslims	Muhammad	Qu'ran
Christianity	Christians	Jesus Christ	Bible

The Zionist Movement

When I first heard the term Zionist I had no idea what it meant. It sounded like Zinc or Zodiac, something that we should be learning about in science class, not history. Then I thought of the movie, *The Matrix*. Weren't they looking for Zion?

The real Zionist Movement had one main purpose: return Israel to the Jews. To help you understand the Zionist Movement a little better, let's turn to our good friends at Dictionary.com! The root word of Zionist of course is Zion. So what is Zion? "An idealized, harmonious community; utopia." I'd like to live in Zion. Sounds like one big happy place. I have to say though, there's nothing easy about getting to this Zion.

Starting in 1880, Jews from around the world, but predominantly Britain and America, started putting pressure on Arab countries to allow Israel to be reclaimed for Jews. In World War I, this pressure hit a turning point when Britain tried to gather support from both the Arab world and the Jews. In 1917, British officials stated "His Majesty's Government view with favor the establishment in Palestine of a National Home for the Jewish People." The Jews took this Balfour Declaration as proof that the Allies favored the return of Palestine to the Jews. Oddly enough, at the same time, other British officials were making contradictory claims. General Maude and Commander Hogarth claimed they offered their support to the Arabs, as they wanted help in overthrowing the Ottoman Empire.

Unfortunately, only one group took these claims and used it to their advantage—the Jews. The Balfour Declaration became the cornerstone that allowed Zionist pressure to mount in the 1920s and 1930s. Britain gave in to the pressure, and slowly started permitting Jews to move into Palestine. In 1920, 60,000 Jews lived in Palestine. By 1948, the number had jumped to 600,000. The Jews were then a major threat that and had to be dealt with. During this same time, the Palestinians (the Arabs living in the area known as Israel) did pretty much nothing. They were unorganized and never took the Jewish threat seriously. They just couldn't imagine being kicked off land they considered their own.

Following World War II, the force of the Zionist Movement only intensified. Hitler's horrific attempt to exterminate the European Jewish population was publicized and there was a general outcry to help the Jews. Eventually, in 1947, the United Nations decided to divide Palestine into three parts: one Jewish, one Arab, and Jerusalem—an area that would be jointly run by the United Nations. To you, this should look quite similar to the plan for Germany after World War II: split it up into sections and have different groups govern different areas. This type of division doesn't always work. The Arabs rejected this plan so it was irrelevant.

The British had had enough and withdrew on May 14, 1948. Immediately, war broke out between Jews and Arabs. The Jews won easily. They had all the British weapons and war veterans fighting on their side, the Arabs were unorganized and militarily inferior. The Jews had their independent Israel.

More War and More Conflict

Israelis gradually spread out their region, conquering nearby lands and pushing the Palestinians out of the newly formed countries. In 1967, Egypt and Israel went to war over the area around the Suez Canal. Again, Israel easily won.

The Palestinians were just overmatched. There was no way they could fight the American and British supported Israeli Army. Their weapons and training far surpassed anything the bordering Arab nations could organize.

Here is where the Arabs entered their next phase of conflict. Terrorism. Not being able to fight equally on the battlefield, Muslim extremists resorted to bombings and suicide missions meant to drive terror into Israel with the hope of pushing the Jews out. Today, it is the Palestinians who desperately demand a homeland.

The Cycle of Terror

If you turn on CNN there's a good chance they'll be talking about violence in Israel. Palestinians have resorted to bombings of shopping malls, busses and other public places. In turn, the Israeli Army is pushing into Palestinian villages, destroying homes and killing civilians. This cycle of violence isn't any closer to being solved.

So where does America come in to this whole thing? The Muslim world sees America as the primary suppliers of Israel's military. Because of this, they have a distinct advantage over the area. Even though Israel is totally surrounded by Arab nations, those nations are seemingly powerless in relation to Israel. If they did fight the countries, not only would they face Israel's powerful force, they would run up against Israel's number one ally, the unbeatable Americans.

Recently, the Arab world has become extremely frustrated with America and their handling of Iraq. Even though America invaded Iraq to overthrow Saddam Hussein for his ignoring of UN Resolutions, the United States seems to allow Israel to laugh at and likewise ignore these same resolutions. This seemingly obvious hypocrisy frustrates and angers Arab nations. Not only has Israel ignored dozens of United Nations Resolutions, America has used its veto power to block thirty-two resolutions against Israel from ever reaching the public. You can probably see why nations were so frustrated when America was totally annoyed at France's threat to use their veto power to stop a resolution. Wasn't France just doing what America had done for years?

Sample of Resolutions Ignored by Israel as of 2002

Resolution	Year	Description
252	1968	Urgently calls upon Israel to rescind measures that change the legal status of Jerusalem, including the expropriation of land and properties thereon.
262	1968	Calls upon Israel to pay compensation to Lebanon for destruction of airliners at Beirut International Airport.
452	1979	Calls on the government of Israel to cease, on an urgent basis, the establishment, construction, and planning of settlements in the Arab territories, occupied since 1967, including Jerusalem.

Sample of Resolutions Ignored by Israel as of 2002
(Continued)

471	1980	Demands prosecution of those involved in assassination attempts of West Bank leaders and compensation for damages
487	1981	Calls upon Israel to place its nuclear facilities under the safeguard of the UN's International Atomic Energy Agency.
573	1985	Calls on Israel to pay compensation for human and material losses from its attack against Tunisia and to refrain from all such attacks or threats of attacks against other nations.
607	1986	Reiterates calls on Israel to abide by the Fourth Geneva Convention and to cease its practice of deportations from occupied Arab territories.
799	1992	"Reaffirms applicability of Fourth Geneva Convention...to all Palestinian territories occupied by Israel since 1967, including Jerusalem, and affirms that deportation of civilians constitutes a contravention of its obligations under the Convention."
1402	2002	Calls for Israel to withdraw from Palestinian cities
1435	2002	Calls on Israel to withdraw to positions of September 2000 and end its military activities in and around Ramallah, including the destruction of security and civilian infrastructure.

What will happen next is anyone's guess. The Arab world is mad at America, and extremists now not only want to regain Palestine's homeland, but they want to punish Americans for their support of Israel. Recently elected Palestinian Prime Minister Mahmoud Abbas has promised to work with Israeli Prime Minister Ariel Sharon and George Bush to complete a Roadmap to Peace. However, no one seems able to stop the terrorist attacks that inevitably plunge the region into a cycle of violence. Until this cycle stops, the hopes for a Palestinian state and peace in the area seem distant.

CHAPTER 26

▼

GET ME OUT OF
THE HOUSE:
THE WOMEN'S
RIGHTS MOVEMENT

Kelly Waterman
Angela Tsai

Something's Just Not Right

Imagine a world where women were not allowed to have a say in their own government, a world where women were "trapped" in their homes. A world where women were not allowed to go to the bank and open up a checking account unless their husbands accompanied them. This is how the United States was in the 19th century. This is exactly how Elizabeth Cady Stanton's life was on July 9, 1848 during afternoon tea with her friends. She and her friends discussed many of the issues that women were facing and they decided to make a change. They no longer wanted to be victims locked away in their homes. They wanted to stand up for something they believed in and truly felt passionate about. They wanted to open those bank accounts, they wanted to write those checks and they wanted to vote in the elections. They wanted to decide whether or not to use birth control, have an abortion and they wanted equality in society. On July 19th, the first Women's Rights Convention in American history was held in the Wesleyan Chapel of Seneca Falls, New York. Although this convention signaled the beginning of the Women's Rights Movement, work would continue into the next century and still does today.

The Seneca Falls Convention was a historic meeting. Throughout 1848, Stanton drafted the Declaration of Sentiments that closely followed the Declaration of Independence. The document began with the declaration that "all men and women are created equal." Following this was the eleven resolutions within the Declaration that drew great attention from the community. The resolutions demanded for the equal access to education, and most importantly the right to vote. This daring request drew criticism from all places. Many men and women still believed a woman's place was in the home and important decisions needed to be left to the men. The Declaration of Sentiments was to be presented in the convention at the Wesleyan Methodist Church in Seneca Falls organized by Stanton and Lucretia Mott on July 19. Inputs also came from Jane Hunt, Martha Coffin Wright and Mary Ann McClentock.

The convention lasted two days and more than three hundred people attended. The convention succeeded as one hundred participants signed the declaration, sixty-eight of which were women and thirty-two were men. However, this success was only temporary. As the media and the people started to attack and criticize the convention and the women, many of the women who had signed the Sentiment withdrew.

Let Us Vote!

The National Women's Suffrage Association (NWSA) was organized in 1869 by Elizabeth Cady Stanton and Susan B. Anthony. Their ambition throughout this organization was to state the obvious injustices that women faced. They also wanted to end discrimination in the workplace and gain equal pay. They were assisted by Frederick Douglass, a former slave who had argued for human rights and saw the importance of gaining suffrage. "Suffrage," he declared, "is the power to choose rulers and make laws, and the right by which all others are secured."

Another group was formed shortly after called The American Women's Suffrage Association (AWSA). This group was not as confrontational as the NWSA; they would not join in protests or riots. These two groups found it impractical for there to be two groups fighting for the same cause. In 1890, the two groups came together and formed the National American Women's Suffrage Association (NAWSA). Some of the leaders of this new group included Elizabeth Stanton, Susan B. Anthony, Frances Willard, and Anna Shaw.

As soon as the NAWSA announced their drive for voting rights, the women involved were subjected to ridicule, embarrassment, and misrepresentation. Many of the women were so publicly humiliated that they withdrew their names from the petition. Many of the horrendous articles that were written about the women, in turn, had a positive effect. Those who lived in isolated towns or cities were now informed about the severity of this issue. People from all over began to join in the movement. Women from all over were finally beginning to make a difference. From this moment on, Women's Rights Conventions were held regularly up until the beginning of the Civil War. Before their right to vote was granted, some states, such as Ohio and Kentucky, gave women the right to vote in school board elections. Then, in 1890, Wyoming was admitted to the United States and it became the first state with voting rights for women. In the two decades that followed, one by one, western states began to grant suffrage to women.

First States to Grant Women the Right to Vote

State	Year
Wyoming	1890
Colorado	1893
Utah	1896
Idaho	1896
Washington	1910
California	1911
Oregon	1912
Kansas	1912
Arizona	1912

Gaining suffrage at the state level was one thing; gaining it at the national level would prove far more difficult. National suffrage was finally granted to women with the ratification of the Nineteenth Amendment, the product of seventy-two years of persistent effort. All of this was made possible with determined efforts put into delivering speeches, marches, protests, and lobbying of government officials. Attempts for the ratification of this amendment were also made through parades and strikes. Some of the more extreme activities ended with the imprisonment of the suffragettes as well as physical abuse. Other more rational efforts were put into the granting of women's voting rights, through a state-by-state approach of spreading women suffrage.

The cause was also aided by women's efforts during war. After World War I, people began to see the foolishness in depriving women of their rights. The war helped them gain success, as women rushed to the workplace to fill the shoes of the men who went to war. "The services of women during the supreme crisis have been of the most signal usefulness and distinction," wrote Woodrow Wilson, the same president who years earlier believed voting rights for women should be restricted to the states.

The Nineteenth Amendment, which gave women the right to vote, was proposed on June 4, 1919 and was finally ratified on August 18, 1920.

However, the Women's Rights Movement was not over, it had only just begun. Alice Paul "understood that the quest for women's rights would be an ongoing struggle that was only advanced, not satisfied, by the vote."

Equality in the Workplace

Even after the Nineteenth Amendment granted women the right to vote, women were still not treated equally in their jobs, even though they proved time and again they were equal to men in performing tasks at the workplace. When the men again left the workplace for World War II, a generation of women went to the factories and produced the weapons and materials for the allies. This generation of "Rosie the Riveters" demonstrated that regardless of task, women were equal to men.

But still equality lagged behind reality. When the men returned from war, women went back to their homes and helped with the Baby Boom. Throughout the 1950s and 1960s the Women's Right's Movement stalled and mounting cases of inequality at the workplace resulted.

Realizing it would be a long journey before absolute equality would be achieved, women united together after their spirits were re-awakened in the 1960s. One activist of the time was Betty Friedan. After graduating from Smith College, she published *The Feminine Mystique* in 1963. With her accomplishments, she demonstrated how women could be something else. Women could achieve beyond just taking care of the family and doing domestic chores. Women were just as capable as men to realize their dreams. With her eagerness to get involved, Friedan established the National Organization for Women (NOW) in 1970, encouraging women to speak up for themselves.

The National Organization for Women (NOW) wanted to bring women into the "mainstream of American society…in fully equal partnership with men." One of the biggest issues that women are facing today is equality in the work place. Women have always been observed as the creator of human life and nothing more. Women are often considered as the "weaker sex" or inferior in strength or intelligence to men. The phrase, "a women's place is at home" was becoming far too common. In the United States, men used to own their wives and children as though they were personal possessions.

High positions were rarely within reach by women because businesses believed that most women would leave due to pregnancy. As a result businesses avoided promoting women even if they were as equally qualified as men. Women were also discouraged from pursuing professions like medicine and law. In 1970, women constituted only seven percent of physicians and three percent of lawyers. Yet, this was not the worst discrimination that was encountered by women. What was even more upsetting was the lack of recognition they received. Women with a degree similar to that of man were paid only half of the salary of men.

In the 1960's, many laws started to slowly change that perception and narrow the gap between the sexes. The Equal Pay Act, established in 1963, stated that women and men should have equal wages for equal work. Even though this act was in place, women were still receiving about 45 percent less pay than men with equal jobs. In 1964, the Civil Rights Act prohibited any forms of discrimination towards women. Even though these acts were in place the law was ignored and women still faced many challenges. Gradually women moved up the ranks, year-by-year, at companies, and more women were hired for jobs previously reserved for men. As more women moved to the workplace, the issue of raising a family while working became a difficult issue. This issue was addressed when the federal government responded to enacted "maternity leave" laws. By the 1990's, the federal government required that women be guaranteed a job when they return from maternity leave. The federal government also required business to pay these women when they were on maternity leave.

The Right to Choose

Regardless of any changes in the workplace, women would never be able to take an equal place in American society until they had a say in child rearing. The moment women could choose when they had children, they could choose how they wanted to live.

The first step was being able to use birth control devices. This desire hit a roadblock when the Comstock Law passed in 1873. This law was banned "obscene literature" and birth control devices. Information about abortion, birth control, and sexuality was also banned. The politicians did not want women to become educated in these areas and therefore laws were made. Those who participated in the distribution of birth control devices were persecuted. However, after decades of pressure, in 1938 Margaret Sanger was involved in a case which eventually lifted the ban on birth control. After this, women had the right to use birth control legally.

Abortion has always been another controversial issue. Whether or not it was the woman's right to choose was always the question. By 1965, abortion was banned by all fifty states with very few exceptions. The only time abortions were allowed were in cases where rape or incest was present. The only other time it was allowed was when the life of the mother was jeopardized or if the fetus was discovered to be deformed. This all changed with *Roe vs. Wade*, a case that granted women the right to choose to have an abortion. However, even though the right to have an abortion was granted, legal protests and violence popped up around America at health clinics that performed abortions.

Equality on the Sports Field

Like the workplace, the athletic scene has always been dominated by men. Only in the last thirty years have women had the opportunity to play sports. Before the 1970s, women were essentially locked out of the sports world. Almost all the money schools received went to boys' athletic programs, while the girls were expected to involve themselves in more domestic extracurricular activities. Boys were playing ball on the fields, and girls were learning how to put frosting on cakes.

That all changed in 1972 with the most important piece of legislation in sports history—Title IX. This law stated that females should be provided equal access to sports equipment, playing fields, locker rooms, financial aid, and sports publicity. It also stated that women should have sports available to them that specifically fit their interest and athletic ability. Basically this meant that at high schools, girls can have field hockey or touch rugby teams, even if the boys don't have them. This opportunity has allowed millions of girls the chance to play sports at the high school and collegiate level.

This fact is extremely important. There is a direct correlation between people who excel on the sports field and people who excel in business. Once women were granted the right to compete, the social playing field became fairer.

Then came the tennis match between Billie Jean King and Bobby Riggs. In 1973, Bobby Riggs was a 59 year old male chauvinist who claimed women would never be able to compete with men at sports. Women were inferior. They always were and they always would be. Billie Jean King disagreed. Later named *Time Magazine's Woman of the Year*, Billie Jean King was a strong advocate of women's rights and accepted a challenge to play Bobby Riggs in a nationally televised tennis match that would be called "The Battle of the Sexes."

The Battle of the Sexes

When the sexes squared off, Billie Jean King proved she had the bigger muscles.

On September 20, 1973, Bobby Riggs entered the Houston Astrodome in a carriage pulled by women, while Billie Jean King entered on the shoulders of male football players. Over fifty million people watched the match in which Billie Jean King easily defeated her male challenger in three sets 6-4, 6-3, 6-3. The precedent had been set. Women could compete with and against men. And this went way beyond the tennis court. Billie Jean King didn't just win the battle for the title to be the better tennis player, she showed the world that women were equal to and, in many cases, better than men.

America had to take notice. Women were demanding their rights and proving they rightfully deserved them.

Still a Ways to Go

The last 150 years have shown monumental gains for women both in the workplace and at home. Think about it. For thousands of years, women lived as lesser humans, unable to fully participate in a man's world. However, with the work of a dedicated group of women and a government willing to change, the rights of women gradually progressed. America still has a ways to go as sexual harassment and discrimination still exists. But if America has shown one thing over the years, the struggle for equality will not end until the goal has been achieved.

CHAPTER 27

▼

COOL STUFF: INVENTIONS AND GADGETS

Deepti Dhir

Check Out Our Fancy Toys

New inventions and technological advances in the 20th century changed the life-styles of Americans all over the country. The automobile gave people the freedom to move away from the crowded and industrialized cities. As companies created new models, more and more people wanted to own a car and other innovations of their own.

Innovations like the radio and television allowed for better communication and understanding of events in and outside America. They also gave Americans something fun to do on boring nights. Refrigeration helped with the storage of foods, and air-conditioning brought comfort to the home and workplace. America also invested money in space exploration, landing people on the moon. Furthermore, the evolution of the computer sped up calculations and became the cornerstone of the technological revolution. It's hard to even imagine life at the turn of the century, though I'm pretty sure it's even more enjoyable today.

Big Wheels Keep on Rolling

The automobile went through dramatic changes throughout the 20th century and by the year 2000, Americans were driving about 12,000 miles yearly. That's pretty impressive, considering in the year 1900, there were only 144 miles of paved roads. A car in 1900 looked like a box, almost like a carriage, totally exposed to rain and dust. The engine was be placed under your body with a hand crank used to start it up. Rubber tires made rides extremely bumpy, and every 10 or 20 miles punctures often resulted. In addition kerosene and acetylene lamps were installed to light the pathway. Only the rich could own these hand made automobiles, costing around $1,550 when the average wage was only $12.74 a week. Two men, Ransom E. Olds and Henry Ford helped to solve this problem. The answer lay in mass production. While producing the automobiles, Olds thought it best to have the workers take the car parts right to the car frame. This simple idea increased production in 1907 to 2500 when in previous years the annual output of automobiles was only 425. Henry Ford then used electricity to speed up the process even more. A conveyer belt allowed workers to stay in one place and concentrate on one particular job as the car frame was being brought to them. This was called the assembly line. By using this method, the Model T car was manufactured in just ninety-three minutes, when it previously used to take more than a day. Costs were reduced, and in 1916 a car only cost $400. And for those who couldn't even afford $400 a car, Ford used the installment plan, where you could pay a little up front, and then pay a small bit once a month until it was paid for. People no longer had to catch trains, ride horses or walk; the masses could now afford to own a car.

As the years passed, automobiles developed in style and design. Heaters, air conditioners, seat adjusters and windshield wipers were some of its new accessories. Makers started to manufacture new car models, catering to the needs of people who demanded comfort, speed and variety in product. One example was the popular Cadillac, which came in many different colors, and was equipped with large fenders plus a push button starter! Larger and heavier cars with better engine performance and brake reliability were brought to the market.

How then did the automobile change the lifestyle of the Americans all over the country? First of all, Americans no longer had to live next to where they worked. This led to the creation of the suburb, and that wonderful little thing called a "commute." Not only did the people start to move out to the suburbs, but so did the malls and factories. Secondly, a wave of industries blew up to accommodate the cars. Motels, road construction, fast food, even drive-in movies needed to be built to satisfy the needs of this mobile population. Thirdly, the idea of taking a vacation with the family was introduced, which led to generations of children fighting in the backseat of the car while spilling McDonalds all over the floor. The making of automobiles took over America and revolutionized the way people lived in the 20th century.

Can You Hear Me Now?

The radio was an effective device that totally transformed our ability to talk to a huge crowd. In 1844, when Samuel Morse sent a message from Washington to Baltimore saying, "What hath God wrought?" the nation started constructing a mass network of telegraph lines that would connect the nation.

By 1899, signals could travel across water with Guglielmo's invention of the wireless telegraph. A few years later, sound was added to the telegraph and America was on its way to what we today know as the radio. Finally, in 1915 people's voices were heard on the radio for the first time.

In the beginning, many did not use the radio, as it required a receiver and headsets for operation. It was kind of tough to sit back with your family, relax and enjoy the radio when you had only one huge headset that you had to pass around. Plus, there really wasn't that much to listen to if you did buy one of the original bulky machines. However, by the late 1920s the distances to which signals were sent increased and radio stations were developed around the country. Microphones and loud speakers improved the look and efficiency of the radio, and almost every single home in America owned one by the mid 1930s. People were now able to learn about the major events happening in America and other foreign countries, even President Roosevelt liked to sit down and give his little Fireside Chats.

If radio changed the way we heard the world, television changed the way Americans viewed it. Only twenty-three running television stations were seen in the early 1940s, and in 1948 only one out of every hundred families in the United States actually had a TV. Though the TV had been invented in the late 1920s, it wasn't until the post WWII period that the television became widespread. First of all, the price tag of $500 dollars made it a difficult purchase, when the average annual salary was $3000. As adjustments and improvements were made to it, the television became more affordable, and in 1950 a set cost only $200. In the 1970s the industry boomed and 95.5 % of households in America owned at least one. Furthermore, now people were able to witness events that took place domestically as well as in Europe. The television was not only used for entertainment, but also brought people closer to the riots, civil rights marches and the war taking place in Vietnam. It also allowed for the replaying of events. Sports broadcasts featuring the most exciting moments in a game could be seen numerous times until you were satisfied. The development of this machine also brought farmers and country dwellers out of isolation, as they were able to watch the same programs and shows seen by those living in the heart of the city. The television brought Americans closer to reality, and in addition provided them with entertainment that reduced the stress in their lives.

Comforts of Home

Having a radio and TV was great, but they were still hard to enjoy on a 105 degree day in the middle of July. Life was exceptionally painful in the factories and backrooms where America's industry lived. Where do you think they got the name "sweatshop?" Since the dawn of mankind, man has always been able to deal with the cold by building a fire or putting on more clothes. However, dealing with the heat was a different story. There are only so many clothes you can take off, and it's pretty difficult to have a steady stream of ice cubes delivered to your door. The air conditioner changed all that and improved comfort at home and in the workplace.

A man named Willis Haviland Carrier invented the air conditioner, which had the ability to melt 108,000 pounds of ice daily. Carrier said he was able to work out an effective way to control temperature and humidity while waiting for his train to arrive in Pittsburgh one foggy night.

These more comfortable conditions improved both production and output. Medical, textile, processed meat, scientific and computer companies were all to benefit from this invention. In the 1920s the air conditioner finally became a useful household appliance. The air conditioner also allowed people to live in buildings and homes that had no windows or porches. Stores started to realize the benefits of having air conditioning, as customers flocked to their cool stores in the painful heat of the summer. By the end of the 20th century, about 70% of the homes in America had one of their own.

More important than cooling your home is keeping your food cold. The refrigerator was another appliance that helped simplify people's lives. Before mechanical refrigerators came into the market in the years that just prior to WWI, ice was used to chill food items. People would wait anxiously by their door for the "ice man" to stop by. However, people were willing to put the "ice man" out of business, for the chance to have a stand-alone refrigerator. By 1931, a million refrigerators were being annually manufactured by America's factories. This machine made food storage and transportation a lot easier. Money was saved, as shopping lists were cut short and the items bought were preserved for longer.

Other smaller inventions helped industry flourish and made life more efficient. The Xerox machine enabled the fast copying of a book, letter or other document. Imagine not being able to have enough textbooks to provide for everyone in a classroom or not being able to mass-produce novels or other literary works for the general public. And who can imagine school without all those wonderful hand-outs that teachers pass out so regularly.

Similarly, plastic changed the lives of the people enormously. Not only did plastics replace wood and metal in the creation of tools, but they also made toys a lot more enjoyable.

Motor-operated clothes washers installed with hand cranks and foot pumps aided women in the mid 1920s. With washers came the first dryers, and hours did not have to be spent hand washing clothes anymore. The making of the electric toaster troubled engineers at first. The right heating element was hard to find, and only in 1905 was this problem solved when a man named Albert Marsh combined nickel and chromium to produce the metal Nichrome. With these inventions alone, people can now toss an Eggo waffle in the toaster, plop it down on their plastic Barney plate while watching TV as their clothes finish drying in the garage. (Sigh)…isn't life grand?

Beam Me Up

Think about what you would have seen if you were born in the year 1900 and were still alive today. As a child you would have seen horses pulling carriages through town and as an adult you would see men landing on the moon. Probably nothing seemed more impossible to humans back at the turn of the century than space travel. Space travel had always been merely an idea put forth by authors of fantasy stories, but America would make the fantasy become a reality.

Spurned on by huge competition with the Soviet Union to create satellites capable of spying on each other's country, as well as owning bragging rights for who had the smarter scientists, the 1950s and 1960s saw an unprecedented amount of money and resources spent on space exploration. Between $25 and $35 billion was spent trying to land the first human on the moon. Presidents wholeheartedly supported the venture, none so much as John F. Kennedy who challenged Congress and America to put a man on the moon.

President Kennedy's
Special Message to the Congress on
Urgent National Needs
May 25, 1961

First, I believe that this nation should commit itself to achieving the goal, before this decade is out, of landing a man on the Moon and returning him safely to the Earth. No single space project in this period will be more impressive to mankind, or more important for the long-range exploration of space; and none will be so difficult or expensive to accomplish. We propose to accelerate the development of the appropriate lunar space craft. We propose to develop alternate liquid and solid fuel boosters, much larger than any now being developed, until certain which is superior. We propose additional funds for other engine development and for unmanned explorations—explorations which are particularly important for one purpose which this nation will never overlook: the survival of the man who first makes this daring flight. But in a very real sense, it will not be one man going to the Moon—if we make this judgement affirmatively, it will be an entire nation. For all of us must work to put him there.

There was a lot to be gained from the expedition, as it would open up new industries and job opportunities for a large number of people. Finally on July 16, 1969, the Apollo 11 spacecraft with astronauts Neil Armstrong, Edwin E. Aldrin and Michael Collins set out for space. What was even more exciting about this trip was that the whole nation was watching! Four days after takeoff, on July 20, the first humans landed on the moon. More importantly, these first humans were Americans. This voyage opened a whole new door to the world of science and exploration. People now knew that the possibilities were endless and that the sky really wasn't the limit!

Cool Inventions

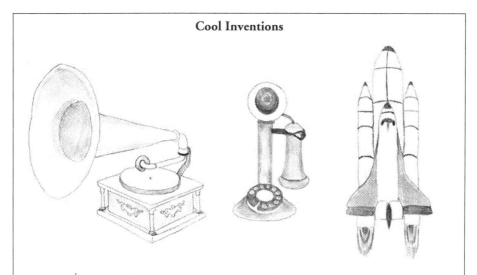

In the 20th century, the phonograph brought us closer to our entertainers, the phone brought us closer to our friends, and the spaceship brought us closer to other worlds.

The World Awaits Mice and Apples

You can't think of the 21st century without thinking of computers. They're everywhere: in our pockets, on our desks, in our cars, and on our telephones. Computers helped to reduce workload, which improved the efficiency in people's lives. Today people use them for typing papers, sending pictures to grandparents and playing video games where you get to blow people up. But the reason computers were invented had little to do with your desire to goof off by playing games for hours. It was something far more important than that.

Counting people.

United States Census officials, by the end of the 19th century, started to worry about how long it took to count the population. The constitution says that you must take a count every 10 years. However, in 1880, it took nine years to take the census. So, by the time you got the results, held a party celebrating the completion of the counting and then sent the results to Congress, you had to go out and start the whole process all over again. And your results were actually ten years old, which drastically affected how governments funded areas and where political representatives would be stationed. To make this process faster, Herman Hollerith came up with the electrically run tabulating machine. It now only took six weeks to take the population count. Go Herman!

The next wave of computer engineering came in 1944, when Howard Aiken created the Mark I. One could not call this invention a computer, as it did not make decisions. It was therefore classified as a very big, fancy, automatic calculator. Over five tons and fifty-one feet, the Mark I was huge in size and weight. In addition it was not very useful, as its 750,000 mechanical parts were difficult to assemble. Needless to say, no one really bought this gadget.

The computers of the first generation were the ABC and the ENIAC, made in the 1940s. The ABC, created by John Atanasoff and Clifford Berry, was the first electronic computer. It was powered by vacuum tubes and processed information through the binary number system of 1s and 0s. I'm sure this makes no sense to you, so just smile and nod.

A few years later the ENIAC was invented. It was supposed to work out the path artillery shells took during WWII. However, the machine was only completed after the war had come to an end. It was still useful though, as a problem that previously had taken three days for mathematicians to work out, was now answered in just twenty seconds! The disadvantage was that the ENIAC took up large amounts of space, and would probably occupy an average three-bedroom house! Moreover, it gave up so much heat that special fans needed to be put in place to cool it!

For the computers of the second generation, there was the transistor, which was invented in 1947. It was a small cylinder made of metal, which had two wires connected to a semi conductive material. The transistor could take the place of many vacuum tubes, decreasing the size of the computer, increasing its calculating speed, and making it more affordable. The third generation of computers introduced integrated circuits. These chips allowed for millions of calculations per second, and enough of a drop in the prices of computers that universities and hospitals could now afford them. The fourth generation brought about the microprocessor, which replaced some of the large parts that made up the computer. Through this invention, the microcomputer, which could fit on ones desktop, came about. It was as small as ones lunch box, but could be used for business and scientific tasks.

Now, unless you are a computer guru, you totally just skipped that last paragraph. Here's the only part that's probably interesting to you. In the 1970s, two guys, Steve Jobs and Steve Wozniak got together in the Jobs' family garage and got to work tinkering on a small computer. In 1975, Wozniak had created a working computer for the home, and took it to Hewlett Packard and Atari to see if they were interested. They both were impressed, but couldn't imagine people ever using "personal" computers. Wow, great thinking guys! I bet their boss was less than pleased when these two guys went on to start Apple Computers and create a technology boom, that in less than three decades has put computers in households and businesses around the world.

And of course, there's been a ton of other inventions in the last century, but I'll leave *that* research up to you.

Year	Inventions
1900–1905	Escalator, vacuum cleaner, air conditioner, windshield wipers, safety razor, tractor
1906–1910	Cornflakes, color photography, Instant coffee
1911–1915	Life Savers candy, crossword puzzle, zipper
1916–1920	Stainless steel, pop-up toaster, band aid
1921–1925	Lie detector, insulin, traffic signal, mechanical TV
1926–1930	Bubble gum, liquid fueled rockets, car radio
1931–1935	Parking meter, drive-in movie theater, Monopoly board game, nylon, canned beer
1936–1940	Ballpoint pen, freeze-dried coffee, helicopter
1941–1945	ABC computer, atomic bomb
1946–1950	Microwave oven, cake mix, credit card
1951–1955	Super glue, non-stick pan, McDonalds started
1956–1960	Hula Hoop, integrated circuit, Barbie Doll
1961–1965	Audio cassette, compact disk
1966–1970	Computer mouse, floppy disk
1971–1975	VCR, post-it note
1976–1980	Walkman, roller blades, hepatitis-B vaccine
1981–1985	CD-ROM, Windows program
1986–1990	Disposable camera, 3-D video game, World Wide Web

CHAPTER 28

▼

A WHOLE NEW WORLD: TERRORISM AND THE IRAQ WAR

Things Will Never Be the Same Again

Every generation has its signature moment. The moment when the whole world changes. The moment you'll always remember exactly where you were when you got the news. The 20th century had its share. Black Thursday. Pearl Harbor. Kennedy's assassination. Landing on the moon. Nixon's resignation. The OJ Simpson trial.

All of these events either united the nation or defined an era.

The 21st century started no differently.

Just as December 7, 1941 was a date that would "live in infamy," September 11, 2001 can never be forgotten. The horrific terrorist attacks on the World Trade Center and the Pentagon shocked Americans out of their security and forced America to rethink how it deals with rights of privacy, immigration and international politics.

This Can't Be Happening!

For those of us watching TV on September 11, 2001, the events unfolded like something out of a suspenseful blockbuster. CNN flashed on its screen that a plane had crashed into one of the World Trade Center towers. What could have happened? How could a plane not see the tower? How could this accident occur with today's technology?

What happened next proved that the first crash was no accident. Another plane entered the picture screen, and as if in slow motion, headed toward the second tower. It couldn't be real. Again, we all said to ourselves, "This can't be happening!"

But it was. The second plane smashed into the tower and black smoke started billowing into the sky. The CNN correspondents tried their best to make sense of the chaos, as more news came in that the Pentagon had just been struck by another plane. Soon, the news started reporting that yet another plane might be headed for Washington D.C.

We were under attack. The nation that had escaped foreign wars on its soil for over two centuries was under attack. How would it end? Where would the planes strike next? Who was responsible for this? How could they get past America's seemingly impenetrable military?

As the hours passed, each of these questions were slowly answered. But with the answers came many more doubts.

How Could This Happen?

As information came in, it became clearer what had actually happened. Between 7:45 and 8:10 four planes leaving East Coast cities were hijacked by terrorists yielding knives and demanding entrance to the cockpit. All of the hijackers were foreigners who had legally entered America using temporary visas, but a few of them had let their visas expire and remained in America illegally. The hijackers who would later pilot the planes had gained their training at American flight schools. The two pilots that flew their planes into the World Trade Center towers, Mohamed Atta and Marwan Al-Shehhi, gained their training at Florida flight schools.

Once hijacked, all but one of the planes hit their intended targets. At 8:46 a.m., American Airlines flight 11 crashed into the North tower of the World Trade Center. At 9:03, United Airlines flight 175 crashed into the South tower. At 9:43, the third plane, American Airlines flight 77 crashed into the Pentagon. And at 10:10 the fourth plane, United Airlines flight 93, after the passengers attempted to overthrow the terrorists, crashed into a field in Somerset County, Pennsylvania.

All passengers on the four airplanes died immediately upon impact. However, for hundreds of others, their deadly fate would take longer. After the initial explosion, employees in the floors below the impact ran down the smoke filled stairways to safety below. While the employees raced down, firemen raced up to aide in the evacuation. However, those above the site of impact had no option. They were cut off from the bottom. As temperatures rose and smoke filled the rooms, one can only imagine the fearful final moments before the towers collapsed.

At 10:05 A.M. the South Tower collapsed. At 10:28 A.M. the North Tower collapsed.

Now the search for survivors and rebuilding would have to begin.

United We Stand

Like the bombing of Pearl Harbor, the terrorist attacks united the nation. Everyone went to their televisions to watch the countless incidents of heroism. Policemen, firefighters, and locals risked their lives to help those in need. Businesses opened their doors to the volunteers and to those left homeless. Families rushed to Ground Zero to see if their loved ones had survived.

And across the country, Americans looked to each other for strength. Flags adorned car windows. Thousands donated money for the relief effort. The nation all came together and stood behind their leader. They all looked to President George W. Bush for guidance.

He would take the nation to the next level.

Revenge

In the weeks and months that followed the horrific terrorist attacks of September 11, Americans cried out for revenge. Something had to be done. Our peace of mind had been destroyed and we could not live like this.

However, here was Bush's problem. Unlike the bombing of Pearl Harbor, the sinking of the *Lusitania*, or even the attack on Fort Sumter, there was no clear enemy. What country would we attack? The men that flew the planes into the symbols of America claimed no country as their own. No one country was responsible.

And this is how America entered into an all new type of warfare. Not a war to defeat a nation, but a war to eradicate from the globe any company, peoples or nation that harbored or aided terrorists. If we couldn't destroy the terrorist network, we could destroy all of their resources so they would be virtually powerless.

Afghanistan became target #1. For years, Afghanistan had fallen under the rule of the Taliban, a group of fanatic Muslims who believed in a very extreme form of Islam. They took control of Afghanistan when the Soviets withdrew in the late 1980s and gradually installed their severe form of Islam—radically restricting the rights of women and even destroying centuries old Buddhist statues due to their alleged sacrilege. But this was not why America attacked Afghanistan, and more specifically the Taliban. America attacked Afghanistan because the Taliban allowed terrorists, specifically Osama bin Laden's Al Qaeda terrorist network.

On September 14, 2001, Congress, by an overwhelming majority (98-0 in the Senate and 420-1 in the House), gave President Bush all the power he would need to seek out and destroy those responsible for the attack. In October 2001, Bush launched Operation Anaconda to wipe out the Taliban while lending assistance to the Northern Alliance to gain control of the capital, Kabul, and eventually return control of the nation to the Afghan people. In November, troops entered Afghanistan to hunt down suspected terrorists, many of whom fled north to Pakistan.

By the new year, the Taliban and Al Qaeda had been pushed out of the major cities, though pockets of resistance still existed throughout the nation. Terrorist bases had been destroyed, but the capture or killing of Osama bin Laden never materialized.

America's Not Done Yet

Because bin Laden avoided capture by fleeing the country, many believe he is still residing somewhere in neighboring Pakistan, America knew the terrorist network had not been crushed.

And George Bush made it known that he would not tolerate any nation that posed a potential threat to the American people. In his State of the Union address on January 30, 2002, he clearly outlined where America was headed and put a target on the next countries on America's hit list, a group dubbed the "Axis of Evil."

The "Axis of Evil" Speech
The State of the Union—January 30, 2002

Our second goal is to prevent regimes that sponsor terror from threatening America or our friends and allies with weapons of mass destruction.

Some of these regimes have been pretty quiet since September 11th. But we know their true nature. North Korea is a regime arming with missiles and weapons of mass destruction, while starving its citizens.
Iran aggressively pursues these weapons and exports terror, while an unelected few repress the Iranian people's hope for freedom.

Iraq continues to flaunt its hostility toward America and to support terror. The Iraqi regime has plotted to develop anthrax, and nerve gas, and nuclear weapons for over a decade. This is a regime that has already used poison gas to murder thousands of its own citizens, leaving the bodies of mothers huddled over their dead children. This is a regime that agreed to international inspections, then kicked out the inspectors. This is a regime that has something to hide from the civilised world.

States like these, and their terrorist allies, constitute an axis of evil, arming to threaten the peace of the world. By seeking weapons of mass destruction, these regimes pose a grave and growing danger. They could provide these arms to terrorists, giving them the means to match their hatred. They could attack our allies or attempt to blackmail the United States. In any of these cases, the price of indifference would be catastrophic.

We will work closely with our coalition to deny terrorists and their state sponsors the materials, technology, and expertise to make and deliver weapons of mass destruction. We will develop and deploy effective missile defences to protect America and our allies from sudden attack. And all nations should know: America will do what is necessary to ensure our nation's security.

The rest of year 2002, America struggled with how to deal with each of these nations. By November, North Korea admitted it was ignoring a previous agreement to ban the research and production of nuclear weapons. The North Koreans proclaimed they would actively pursue the technology needed to make North Korea a nuclear power. America condemned this act, but could do little more. If North Korea had the weapons, could America risk an all out attack? How far was North Korea willing to take the threat? America continues to grapple with the issue, and at this point they have employed a diplomatic policy in which they will ask Japan, South Korea and China to help with negotiations.

Like North Korea, America believes Iran continues to pursue weapons of mass destruction, more specifically nuclear weapons. However, at this point, Iran's official stance is that the nuclear power plants they are constructing will be used solely for energy purposes.

And then there's Iraq.

Saddam Hussein: The Hitler of a Generation

Every generation has an evil monster to hate. We live in a world where there are two—Osama bin Laden and Saddam Hussein. Since the moment Saddam Hussein came into power as leader of Iraq, his reign has been filled with bloodshed, deceit and oppression.

Back in 1979, he made his move to take over the country. Taking a page right out of Hitler's book, *How To Take Over a Country in Three Easy Steps*, Hussein called a meeting to gather all the members of his Revolutionary Command Council. He then walked to the front of the room, and with his best, fake-sad face he started talking. He talked about how there were traitors in the room and something must be done. Right on cue, a man walked on to the stage and started confessing to a ton of treacherous sins against the country, and then he started naming names. Of course, Saddam forgot to mention that the man had been tortured into making a false confession. Facts can be so annoying sometimes when you're trying to take over a country.

As the man kept reading names, one by one people were taken from the room and then murdered a few weeks later.

And with this one aggressive move, Saddam had gained full control and also set the precedent for how he'd run the country. If you disagreed with him, he'd kill you. Plain and simple. If you're not for Saddam, you're dead. He would push Iraq into a decade long war against Iran, and even exterminate his own citizens while trying out new weapons.

This man was a demon. America could not let him survive as leader.

But what about Iraq? If Saddam was a demon, what about Iraq and the Iraqis? How could this seemingly insignificant country in the Middle East dominate America's foreign policy heading into the turn of the century?

Let's find out.

Just Another Nation After All

When a majority of Americans hear the word Iraq, they instantly associate it as "the enemy." This may be because in a little over a decade America has fought two wars against Iraqi President Saddam Hussein and his monopoly over power.

Iraq is located in the Middle East between Iran and Kuwait with a population of just over 16 million people. With the dominant religion being Muslim, 97 percent of the people refer to the country as Al Jumhuriyah al Iraqiyah.

Oh…and there's a ton of oil. In fact, next to Saudi Arabia, Iraq has the most oil in the world.

And Iraq is a monarchy which means all of the country's power and wealth fall into the hands of one man. Iraq claims to be a democracy. In fact, in his recent election Saddam won 100% of the votes. That's not too bad. Some might say there is a little bit of corruption involved, but that's totally unfair. Sure, it's pretty amazing that people who lived hundreds of miles away from any telephone were able to have their votes sent and counted within a few hours. Maybe he's just a really popular guy. I'm sure there were no threats whatsoever and no sneaky counting of ballots. In fact, he might even get 102% of the votes in the next election.

Enough of the Background Info, Let's Get to the War

Fresh off a hard fought victory against Iran, Saddam felt pretty cocky and wanted to take his army and stay on the offensive. The next target would be Kuwait. Kuwait had loaned Iraq a ton of money during the Iran-Iraq war and for some reason they wanted Iraq to pay them back. Plus, the Kuwait-Iraq border wasn't entirely clear and Saddam felt he needed to help "clarify" the land boundaries.

His decision. Invade Kuwait. He wouldn't have to pay back the loans, plus he'd be able to bring Kuwait and all its oil under Iraqi control. So, on August 2, 1990 Iraq invaded Kuwait.

America wouldn't stand for this invasion. They began gaining support from the international community. Eventually thirty-four countries allied with America.

By January, America had its coalition. Troops, ships, and planes were in the Persian Gulf and ready to strike. Saddam was given one last warning. Leave Kuwait by January 15, 1991, or face the full wrath of the American military.

He ignored America.

He paid the price. Starting January 16, America let loose a military force unseen in modern warfare. Day and night, airplanes and missiles flew through the sky, destroying Iraq's ability to communicate and use the skies. Huge bombs from the skies wiped out entire divisions of the Iraqi military. Thousands were killed before the Iraqis ever saw an American soldier.

And then the ground war began. On February 25, George Bush sent in the Marines. 100 hours later, the war would be over. Iraq tried to fight back, but many troops either surrendered or were killed by America's superior technology. At one point, Iraq tried to turn the war against Israel, by firing SCUD missiles into the capital city. Iraq hoped they could get Israel to fight back, which would then unite all the neighboring Muslim countries in a war against Jewish Israel.

However, Americans watched live on CNN how these bombs exploded harmlessly in the desert.

Saddam Hussein realized he had no way of winning. America also decided to not keep pushing forward. Had America overthrown Saddam, stability in the Middle East could have been endangered. Having a strong Iraq kept the surrounding nations from getting any wise ideas about invading each other. Plus, a lot of the members of the coalition signed on just to kick Iraq out of Kuwait. Many of these would back out if America pushed to overthrow Saddam.

So, both signed a cease-fire treaty that ended Operation Desert Storm. With this treaty, America agreed to stop blowing up Iraq, if Saddam agreed to destroy all of his chemical and biological weapons and let United Nations weapons inspectors into the country to make sure he was keeping his side of the bargain.

The final death count was one of the most skewed in military history. With just under 250 deaths on the American side, the troops inflicted over 30,000 Iraqi deaths and casualties.

With their awesome display of force and a comprehensive cease-fire agreement in place, America thought they had solved the Iraq problem.

They were mistaken.

Soldiers Bring War Back Home

Like all wars, the Persian Gulf War left soldiers physically and psychologically injured. As the months and years passed, soldiers found they shared certain symptoms since returning from the Persian Gulf. The symptoms included nausea, cramps, rashes, short-term memory loss, fatigue, difficulty in breathing, headaches, joint and muscle pain, and sometimes resulted in birth defects in their offspring. Some doctors dismissed the complaints as merely psychological. However, because of the numerous, similar claims, the military started to take these illnesses seriously. These illnesses became known as Gulf War Syndrome, and the causes still aren't known. Doctors and scientists have thrown out a series of possible causes from paint to drugs to chemical weapons. But none of these show conclusive proof.

Aside from Gulf War Syndrome, other diseases attacked the soldiers. One such disease, Leishmaniasis was parasitic and spread by sand flies. The disease affected white blood cells and could lead to fever, anemia, and discoloration of the skin.

Saddam Breaks His Word—Surprise, Surprise

Some of the terms and conditions Iraq had to comply with are as follows: Iraq *must* accept liability for damages, Iraq *must* destroy all chemical and biological weapons, and Iraq *must* accept weapons inspectors to search the country searching for remaining weapons of mass destruction. The agreement stated that if Iraq accepted the terms, the international community would lift the sanctions previously put on the country. However Iraq did not agree and claimed that withdrawing from Kuwait was a good enough sacrifice on their part. Due to the failure of Iraq to comply, the United Nations held the "no-fly" zones into effect and prevented supplies from reaching Iraq. The Iraqi people began to suffer because a limit was also put onto the amount of oil, food, and medicine that was allowed to be sold in the country. Saddam Hussein continued to break the UN agreement and frequently intervened in the work of weapons inspectors.

There's a Fox in the Desert

Seeing that Saddam was openly ignoring the cease-fire agreements, America was forced to react militarily again in 1998, with an aerial attack named Operation Desert Fox. The purpose of the attacks was to punish Iraq for not following the UN inspection regulations. United States and British jets attacked several sites that were producing chemical and nuclear weapons. Targets that were hit were airfields, military command centers, suspected missile factories and oil refineries.

Saddam's base for his military planning was also hit and he declared that Iraq would no longer follow the United Nations no fly zones.

And the weapons inspectors left.

So What Does This Have to Do With September 11

And here is where there the events of September 11 come into play. Following the terrorist bombings of New York City and Washington D.C., America's policy was to wipe out all governments responsible for helping terrorists. Saddam Hussein's history made him a prime target. His government has allowed terrorists to train in his country. His government continued to make weapons of mass destruction after the 1991 Persian Gulf cease-fire.

As long as Saddam was allowed to survive, terrorism could still thrive. George Bush spent most of 2002 trying to convince Americans and the world that the only logical step was to oust Saddam Hussein. He had lied once he would lie again. He had already proved that he was a sick man when he used mustard gas and nerve agents on Iraqi Kurds in northern Iraq. Something had to be done.

But unlike 1991, the nations of the world didn't jump up to help America. At the United Nations, the U.S. ambassador was finally able to secure a compromise from the members of the U.N. Security Council. Inspectors would go back into Iraq and look for weapons. From December 2002 to March 2003, the world sat and waited for reports from these inspectors. Would they find any weapons? They didn't find weapons and the world began to protest what they thought was American imperialism.

But the inspectors kept looking. And they kept finding nothing.

Finally, America pushed the United Nations to authorize a military strike. France and Russia threatened to use their veto rights and defeat any resolution created to authorize force.

America would have to go it alone with their good friends, the British. On March 17th 2003 George Bush delivered his ultimatum to Saddam Hussein giving him 48 hours to leave Iraq. As was expected, Saddam did not leave and America entered war on March 20, 2003. In the ultimatum George Bush also warned international journalists and news spokesmen to leave Iraq immediately. He warned the American people that another terrorist attack may be on the way due to the belief that Saddam Hussein has connections with terrorist organizations.

The first attack of the war occurred on Thursday morning Iraq time. It was named "operation decapitation" and was aimed for Saddam. Three ships gathered in the Red Sea sent three separate missiles all intended for the same building in which Saddam was said to be residing. However, three hours after the attack, Saddam Hussein appeared on television to deliver his message to Iraqi people. He depicted George Bush as the antagonist of the situation. He said that Iraq must unite and fight the evil forces of the western world.

This would be their fight. And they would fight to the death.

Baghdad Bob Looks a Bit Confused

As much as Iraq tried to look tough, they were no match for the Americans. Because of the no-fly zones implemented after the Persian Gulf War, Iraq couldn't fly over their own country, yet American ships flew over the country regularly. America owned the skies before the war even started.

Saddam's Fall

Saddam's reign of terror came tumbling down along with his statue.

When America entered Iraq they took a page from Hitler's blitzkrieg of World War II. Strike hard, strike fast, and then head straight for the capital and demand surrender. That's what America did. For weeks, tanks, trucks and helicopters raced across the highways of Iraq toward the capital city of Baghdad. By the beginning of April, American forces had captured Saddam Airport and began entering the city. They met limited resistance and took over the nation with relative ease.

The entire war was being filmed live, 24 hours a day. CNN, Fox News, and local networks fought to put out the most up to date information. The Internet became a new tool of war, as Americans checked their computers regularly for updates and even started looking at non-traditional American news sites like Al-Jazeera. One of the funniest members of this war was the Iraqi Minister of Information, Mohammed Saeed al-Sahaf, or Baghdad Bob as some Americans started calling him.

Baghdad Bob gave a lesson in ineffective propaganda. No matter how bad the news got for Iraq, Baghdad Bob always had a fresh way of looking at the world. Sure, it looked like he was insane when he claimed America didn't control Saddam Airport, while CNN was showing live footage of American planes landing on the runways. But the point is, he tried. No matter how bad his team was losing, he tried.

Baghdad Bob*isms*

March 22, 2003
Speaking on the American March to Baghdad
"Maybe they will enter Umm Qasr and Basra, but how will they enter Baghdad? It will be a big oven for them. They can penetrate our borders but they cannot reach Baghdad. They will try to pull our army and troops out but we are well aware of their plans and they will fail."

March 23, 2003
CNN shows American military speeding toward capital
"In Umm Qasr, the fighting is fierce and we have inflicted many damages. The stupid enemy, the Americans and British, failed completely. They're not making any penetration."

April 5, 2003
American Forces take Airport
"We butchered the force present at the airport. We have retaken the airport! There are no Americans there!"

American Forces enter Baghdad
"Nobody came here. Those America losers, I think their repeated frequent lies are bringing them down very rapidly.... Baghdad is secure, is safe."

American Forces shown walking through the streets of Baghdad
"They are not near Baghdad. Don't believe them.... They said they entered with...tanks in the middle of the capital. They claim that they—I tell you, I...that this speech is too far from the reality. It is a part of this sickness of their plan. There is no an...—no any existence to the American troops or for the troops in Baghdad at all."

April 7, 2003
CNN shows American soldiers bathing in Saddam's palace
"We have killed most of the [coalition] infidels, and I think we will finish off the rest soon."

Essentially all Iraqi forces have surrendered
"This invasion will end in failure."

A Long Road Ahead

With the surrender of almost the entire Iraqi force and the fleeing of all major leaders, George Bush flew to the aircraft carrier USS Abraham Lincoln to declare the war over.

Though the war might have officially ended, the battle for Iraq is far from settled. With Saddam's firm control over the nation gone, riots broke out all over Baghdad. At first, the American military let the looting continue. For weeks, images flashed across the TV screen showing men, women and children stealing from government buildings and private stores. Chaos reigned. Eventually, the American forces had to use force to put down the riots.

Yet still the city lay in ruins. After a month of bombings, hundreds of thousands were without work and without electricity. Leaders of various Iraqi factions struggled to gain control in the new Iraq, while America flew in its own leaders to make sure the rebuilding process moved forward.

And as for Saddam? Nobody knows. Some say he escaped to Syria, others say he died in a residential bombing. Along with Saddam, many other key leaders fled the city rather than surrender. The American military printed up a special deck of playing cards, with leading Iraqi officials on each card. Saddam Hussein was the ace of spades.

His card has yet to be pulled from the deck.

CHAPTER 29

▼

UNCERTAIN FUTURE:
AFTERWORD

Well, if the start of the 21st century is a sign of things to come, we're in for a rocky next few decades.

North Korea might have a nuclear bomb, and if they do we've got a serious problem. How do you negotiate with a country that has nothing to lose?

An epidemic called SARS has spread to thousands, with no known cure. Pneumonia killed millions at the beginning of the 20th century. Could SARS be this generations great plague?

Terrorism continues. On May 13, 2003 nine suicide bombers blew up buildings simultaneously in Saudi Arabia's capital city of Riyadh. A few days later, they bombed Casablanca. Al Qaeda is alive and kicking and Osama bin Laden is probably still calling the shots.

America's economy is in the dumps. The Internet and technology boom of the 1990s came to a crashing halt and billions of dollars was lost. The stock market has been stuck in a hole for years.

The Gilded Age looks like it's coming back. One of the richest companies in the world, Enron, was found to be built on lies. While executives built mansions, workers lost their life savings. Was the stock market just another basket of fraud?

Race relations are still a heated issue. Black coaches aren't getting hired for major positions. White students are protesting that they are being kept out of colleges because of the color of their skin. And the income gap between the races gets wider and wider. The Hispanic population is growing at a huge pace, and will soon be a huge voting block in the Southwest.

Women continue to struggle for equality. Female golfer Annika Sorenstam squared off against the men amid complaints from male competitors who said she should stay in her own league.

Sports salaries are spiraling out of control as spectators wonder how much of the ball players salaries is being spent on muscle enhancing drugs. Athletes get bigger and bigger as records seem to fall almost daily.

States can't afford to pay for teachers. Oregon had to cut school early because they ran out of money. American students are falling further behind grade level expectations, while the price of colleges continues to grow.

Americans are now some of the fattest people on the planet as the drive-thru window has replaced the sit-down dinner at home. But even if you're fat, you can still sue. Some knuckleheads even sued McDonald's because they didn't realize the food was fattening.

Divorce rates are climbing. Kids are being raised by MTV. Eminem is considered this generation's Elvis Presley. Reality TV shows with such catchy titles as *Survivor*, *Am I Hot?*, and *Fear Factor* compete for advertising dollars as they lower the bar on what we consider quality entertainment.

But with all its problems, America is still the number one country in the world. No, it's not perfect. But I challenge you to find a better nation.

America were the originators of the claim to "life, liberty and pursuit of happiness" and there has yet to be a nation created that can beat us at our own promise.

Yep, there's still work to be done, but if America has proven one thing, it's that it keeps moving forward. It took a couple centuries to become the #1 country in the world.

Who knows what the next couple centuries will bring? Maybe a utopia is possible after all.

Primary Sources

MAYFLOWER COMPACT

1620
New Plymouth

IN THE NAME OF GOD, AMEN. We, whose names are underwritten, the Loyal Subjects of our dread Sovereign Lord King *James*, by the Grace of God, of *Great Britain*, *France*, and *Ireland*, King, *Defender of the Faith*, &c. Having undertaken for the Glory of God, and Advancement of the Christian Faith, and the Honour of our King and Country, a Voyage to plant the first Colony in the northern Parts of *Virginia*; Do by these Presents, solemnly and mutually, in the Presence of God and one another, covenant and combine ourselves together into a civil Body Politick, for our better Ordering and Preservation, and Furtherance of the Ends aforesaid: And by Virtue hereof do enact, constitute, and frame, such just and equal Laws, Ordinances, Acts, Constitutions, and Officers, from time to time, as shall be thought most meet and convenient for the general Good of the Colony; unto which we promise all due Submission and Obedience. IN WITNESS whereof we have hereunto subscribed our names at *Cape-Cod* the eleventh of November, in the Reign of our Sovereign Lord King *James*, of *England*, *France*, and *Ireland*, the eighteenth, and of *Scotland* the fifty-fourth, *Anno Domini*; 1620.

DECLARATION OF INDEPENDENCE

July 4, 1776

When in the course of human events, it becomes necessary for one people to dissolve the political bands which have connected them with another, and to assume among the powers of the earth, the separate and equal station to which the laws of nature and of nature's God entitle them, a decent respect to the opinions of mankind requires that they should declare the causes which impel them to the separation.

We hold these truths to be self-evident: That all men are created equal; that they are endowed by their Creator with certain unalienable rights; that among these are life, liberty, and the pursuit of happiness; that, to secure these rights, governments are instituted among men, deriving their just powers from the consent of the governed; that whenever any form of government becomes destructive of these ends, it is the right of the people to alter or to abolish it, and to institute new government, laying its foundation on such principles, and organizing its powers in such form, as to them shall seem most likely to effect their safety and happiness. Prudence, indeed, will dictate that governments long established should not be changed for light and transient causes; and accordingly all experience hath shown that mankind are more disposed to suffer, while evils are sufferable than to right themselves by abolishing the forms to which they are accustomed. But when a long train of abuses and usurpations, pursuing invariably the same object, evinces a design to reduce them under absolute despotism, it is their right, it is their duty, to throw off such government, and to provide new guards for their future security. Such has been the patient sufferance of these colonies; and such is now the necessity which constrains them to alter their former systems of government. The history of the present King of Great Britain is a history of repeated injuries and usurpations, all having in direct object the establishment of an absolute tyranny over these states. To prove this, let facts be submitted to a candid world.

- He has refused his assent to laws, the most wholesome and necessary for the public good.

- He has forbidden his governors to pass laws of immediate and pressing importance, unless suspended in their operation till his assent should be obtained; and, when so suspended, he has utterly neglected to attend to them.

- He has refused to pass other laws for the accommodation of large districts of people, unless those people would relinquish the right of representation in the legislature, a right inestimable to them, and formidable to tyrants only.

- He has called together legislative bodies at places unusual uncomfortable, and distant from the depository of their public records, for the sole purpose of fatiguing them into compliance with his measures.

- He has dissolved representative houses repeatedly, for opposing, with manly firmness, his invasions on the rights of the people.

- He has refused for a long time, after such dissolutions, to cause others to be elected; whereby the legislative powers, incapable of annihilation, have returned to the people at large for their exercise; the state remaining, in the mean time, exposed to all the dangers of invasions from without and convulsions within.

- He has endeavored to prevent the population of these states; for that purpose obstructing the laws for naturalization of foreigners; refusing to pass others to encourage their migration hither, and raising the conditions of new appropriations of lands.

- He has obstructed the administration of justice, by refusing his assent to laws for establishing judiciary powers.

- He has made judges dependent on his will alone, for the tenure of their offices, and the amount and payment of their salaries.

- He has erected a multitude of new offices, and sent hither swarms of officers to harass our people and eat out their substance.

- He has kept among us, in times of peace, standing armies, without the consent of our legislatures.

- He has affected to render the military independent of, and superior to, the civil power.

- He has combined with others to subject us to a jurisdiction foreign to our Constitution and unacknowledged by our laws, giving his assent to their acts of pretended legislation:

- For quartering large bodies of armed troops among us;

- For protecting them, by a mock trial, from punishment for any murders which they should commit on the inhabitants of these states;

- For cutting off our trade with all parts of the world;

- For imposing taxes on us without our consent;

- For depriving us, in many cases, of the benefits of trial by jury;

- For transporting us beyond seas, to be tried for pretended offenses;

- For abolishing the free system of English laws in a neighboring province, establishing therein an arbitrary government, and enlarging its boundaries, so as to render it at once an example and fit instrument for introducing the same absolute rule into these colonies;

- For taking away our charters, abolishing our most valuable laws, and altering fundamentally the forms of our governments;

- For suspending our own legislatures, and declaring themselves invested with power to legislate for us in all cases whatsoever.

- He has abdicated government here, by declaring us out of his protection and waging war against us.

- He has plundered our seas, ravaged our coasts, burned our towns, and destroyed the lives of our people.

- He is at this time transporting large armies of foreign mercenaries to complete the works of death, desolation, and tyranny already begun with circumstances of cruelty and perfidy scarcely paralleled in the most barbarous ages, and totally unworthy the head of a civilized nation.

- He has constrained our fellow-citizens, taken captive on the high seas, to bear arms against their country, to become the executioners of their friends and brethren, or to fall themselves by their hands.

- He has excited domestic insurrection among us, and has endeavored to bring on the inhabitants of our frontiers the merciless Indian savages, whose known rule of warfare is an undistinguished destruction of all ages, sexes, and conditions.

In every stage of these oppressions we have petitioned for redress in the most humble terms; our repeated petitions have been answered only by repeated injury. A prince, whose character is thus marked by every act which may define a tyrant, is unfit to be the ruler of a free people.

Nor have we been wanting in our attentions to our British brethren. We have warned them, from time to time, of attempts by their legislature to extend an unwarrantable jurisdiction over us. We have reminded them of the circumstances of our emigration and settlement here. We have appealed to their native justice and magnanimity; and we have conjured them, by the ties of our common kindred, to disavow these usurpations which would inevitably interrupt our connections and correspondence. They too, have been deaf to the voice of justice and of consanguinity. We must, therefore, acquiesce in the necessity which denounces our separation, and hold them as we hold the rest of mankind, enemies in war, in peace friends.

We, therefore, the representatives of the United States of America, in General Congress assembled, appealing to the Supreme Judge of the world for the rectitude of our intentions, do, in the name and by the authority of the good people of these colonies solemnly publish and declare, That these United Colonies are, and of right ought to be, FREE AND INDEPENDENT STATES; that they are absolved from all allegiance to the British crown and that all political connection between them and the state of Great Britain is, and ought to be, totally dissolved; and that, as free and independent states, they have full power to levy war, conclude peace, contract alliances, establish commerce, and do all other acts and things which independent states may of right do. And for the support of this declaration, with a firm reliance on the protection of Divine Providence, we mutually pledge to each other our lives, our fortunes, and our sacred honor.

THE ARTICLES OF CONFEDERATION

Ratified 1781

Articles of Confederation and perpetual Union between the states of New Hampshire, Massachusetts-bay Rhode Island and Providence Plantations, Connecticut, New York, New Jersey, Pennsylvania, Delaware, Maryland, Virginia, North Carolina, South Carolina and Georgia.

I. The Stile of this Confederacy shall be "The United States of America".

II. Each state retains its sovereignty, freedom, and independence, and every power, jurisdiction, and right, which is not by this Confederation expressly delegated to the United States, in Congress assembled.

III. The said States hereby severally enter into a firm league of friendship with each other, for their common defense, the security of their liberties, and their mutual and general welfare, binding themselves to assist each other, against all force offered to, or attacks made upon them, or any of them, on account of religion, sovereignty, trade, or any other pretense whatever.

IV. The better to secure and perpetuate mutual friendship and intercourse among the people of the different States in this Union, the free inhabitants of each of these States, paupers, vagabonds, and fugitives from justice excepted, shall be entitled to all privileges and immunities of free citizens in the several States; and the people of each State shall free ingress and regress to and from any other State, and shall enjoy therein all the privileges of trade and commerce, subject to the same duties, impositions, and restrictions as the inhabitants thereof respectively, provided that such restrictions shall not extend so far as to prevent the removal of property imported into any State, to any other State, of which the owner is an inhabitant; provided also that no imposition, duties or restriction shall be laid by any State, on the property of the United States, or either of them.

If any person guilty of, or charged with, treason, felony, or other high misdemeanor in any State, shall flee from justice, and be found in any of the United States, he shall, upon demand of the Governor or executive power of the State from which he fled, be delivered up and removed to the State having jurisdiction of his offense.

Full faith and credit shall be given in each of these States to the records, acts, and judicial proceedings of the courts and magistrates of every other State.

V. For the most convenient management of the general interests of the United States, delegates shall be annually appointed in such manner as the legislatures of each State shall direct, to meet in Congress on the first Monday in November, in every year, with a powerreserved to each State to recall its delegates, or any of them, at any time within the year, and to send others in their stead for the remainder of the year.

No State shall be represented in Congress by less than two, nor more than seven members; and no person shall be capable of being a delegate for more than three years in any term of six years; nor shall any person, being a delegate, be capable of holding any office under the United States, for which he, or another for his benefit, receives any salary, fees or emolument of any kind.

Each State shall maintain its own delegates in a meeting of the States, and while they act as members of the committee of the States.

In determining questions in the United States in Congress assembled, each State shall have one vote.

Freedom of speech and debate in Congress shall not be impeached or questioned in any court or place out of Congress, and the members of Congress shall be protected in their persons from arrests or imprisonments, during the time of their going to and from, and attendence on Congress, except for treason, felony, or breach of the peace.

VI. No State, without the consent of the United States in Congress assembled, shall send any embassy to, or receive any embassy from, or enter into any conference, agreement, alliance or treaty with any King, Prince or State; nor shall any person holding any office of profit or trust under the United States, or any of them, accept any present, emolument, office or title of any kind whatever from any King, Prince or foreign State; nor shall the United States in Congress assembled, or any of them, grant any title of nobility.

No two or more States shall enter into any treaty, confederation or alliance whatever between them, without the consent of the United States in Congress assembled, specifying accurately the purposes for which the same is to be entered into, and how long it shall continue.

No State shall lay any imposts or duties, which may interfere with any stipulations in treaties, entered into by the United States in Congress assembled, with any King, Prince or State, in pursuance of any treaties already proposed by Congress, to the courts of France and Spain.

No vessel of war shall be kept up in time of peace by any State, except such number only, as shall be deemed necessary by the United States in Congress assembled, for the defense of such State, or its trade; nor shall any body of forces be kept up by any State in time of peace, except such number only, as in the judgement of the United States in Congress assembled, shall be deemed requisite to garrison the forts necessary for the defense of such State; but every State shall always keep up a well-regulated and disciplined militia, sufficiently armed and accoutered, and shall provide and constantly have ready for use, in public stores, a due number of filed pieces and tents, and a proper quantity of arms, ammunition and camp equipage.

No State shall engage in any war without the consent of the United States in Congress assembled, unless such State be actually invaded by enemies, or shall have received certain advice of a resolution being formed by some nation of Indians to invade such State, and the danger is so imminent as not to admit of a delay till the United States in Congress assembled can be consulted; nor shall any State grant commissions to any ships or vessels of war, nor letters of marque or reprisal, except it be after a declaration of war by the United States in Congress assembled, and then only against the Kingdom or State and the subjects thereof, against which war has been so declared, and under such regulations as shall be established by the United States in Congress assembled, unless such State be infested by pirates, in which case vessels of war may be fitted out for that occasion, and kept so long as the danger shall continue, or until the United States in Congress assembled shall determine otherwise.

VII. When land forces are raised by any State for the common defense, all officers of or under the rank of colonel, shall be appointed by the legislature of each State respectively, by whom such forces shall be raised, or in such manner as such State shall direct, and all vacancies shall be filled up by the State which first made the appointment.

VIII. All charges of war, and all other expenses that shall be incurred for the common defense or general welfare, and allowed by the United States in Congress assembled, shall be defrayed out of a common treasury, which shall be supplied by the several States in proportion to the value of all land within each State, granted or surveyed for any person, as such land and the buildings and improvements thereon shall be estimated according to such mode as the United States in Congress assembled, shall from time to time direct and appoint.

The taxes for paying that proportion shall be laid and levied by the authority and direction of the legislatures of the several States within the time agreed upon by the United States in Congress assembled.

IX. The United States in Congress assembled, shall have the sole and exclusive right and power of determining on peace and war, except in the cases mentioned in the sixth article—of sending and receiving ambassadors—entering into treaties and alliances, provided that no treaty of commerce shall be made whereby the legislative power of the respective States shall be restrained from imposing such imposts and duties on foreigners, as their own people are subjected to, or from prohibiting the exportation or importation of any species of goods or commodities whatsoever—of establishing rules for deciding in all cases, what captures on land or water shall be legal, and in what manner prizes taken by land or naval forces in the service of the United States shall be divided or appropriated—of granting letters of marque and reprisal in times of peace—appointing courts for the trial of piracies and felonies commited on the high seas and establishing courts for receiving and determining finally appeals in all cases of captures, provided that no member of Congress shall be appointed a judge of any of the said courts.

The United States in Congress assembled shall also be the last resort on appeal in all disputes and differences now subsisting or that hereafter may arise between two or more States concerning boundary, jurisdiction or any other causes whatever; which authority shall always be exercised in the manner following. Whenever the legislative or executive authority or lawful agent of any State in controversy with another shall present a petition to Congress stating the matter in question and praying for a hearing, notice thereof shall be given by order of Congress to the legislative or executive authority of the other State in controversy, and a day assigned for the appearance of the parties by their lawful agents, who shall then be directed to appoint by joint consent, commissioners or judges to constitute a court for hearing and determining the matter in question: but if they cannot agree, Congress shall name three persons out of each of the United States, and from the list of such persons each party shall alternately strike out one, the petitioners beginning, until the number shall be reduced to thirteen; and from that number not less than seven, nor more than nine names as Congress shall direct, shall in the presence of Congress be drawn out by lot, and the persons whose names shall be so drawn or any five of them, shall be commissioners or judges, to hear and finally determine the controversy, so always as a major part of the judges who shall hear the cause shall agree in the determination: and if either party shall neglect to attend at the day appointed, without showing reasons, which Congress shall judge sufficient, or being present shall refuse to strike, the Congress shall proceed to nominate three persons out of each State, and the secretary of Congress shall strike in behalf of such party absent or refusing; and the judgement and sentence of the court to be appointed, in the manner before prescribed, shall be final and conclusive; and if any of the parties shall refuse to submit to the authority of such court, or to appear or defend their claim or cause, the court shall nevertheless proceed to pronounce sentence, or judgement, which shall in like manner be final and decisive, the judgement or sentence and other proceedings being in either case transmitted to Congress, and lodged among the acts of Congress for the security of the parties concerned: provided that every commissioner, before he sits in judgement, shall take an oath to be administered by one of the judges of the supreme or superior court of the State, where the cause shall be tried, 'well and truly to hear and determine the matter in question, according to the best of his judgement, without favor, affection or hope of reward': provided also, that no State shall be deprived of territory for the benefit of the United States.

All controversies concerning the private right of soil claimed under different grants of two or more States, whose jurisdictions as they may respect such lands, and the States which passed such grants are adjusted, the said grants or either of them being at the same time claimed to have originated antecedent to such settlement of jurisdiction, shall on the petition of either party to the Congress of the United States, be finally determined as near as may be in the same manner as is before presecribed for deciding disputes respecting territorial jurisdiction between different States.

The United States in Congress assembled shall also have the sole and exclusive right and power of regulating the alloy and value of coin struck by their own authority, or by that of the respective States—fixing the standards of weights and measures throughout the United States—regulating the trade and managing all affairs with the Indians, not members of any of the States, provided that the legislative right of any State within its own limits be not infringed or violated—establishing or regulating post offices from one State to another, throughout all the United States, and exacting such postage on the papers passing through the same as may be requisite to defray the expenses of the said office—appointing all officers of the land forces, in the service of the United States, excepting regimental officers—appointing all the officers of the naval forces, and commissioning all officers whatever in the service of the United States—making rules for the government and regulation of the said land and naval forces, and directing their operations.

The United States in Congress assembled shall have authority to appoint a committee, to sit in the recess of Congress, to be denominated 'A Committee of the States', and to consist of one delegate from each State; and to appoint such other committees and civil officers as may be necessary for managing the general affairs of the United States under their direction—to appoint one of their members to preside, provided that no person be allowed to serve in the office of president more than one year in any term of three years; to ascertain the necessary sums of money to be raised for the service of the United States, and to appropriate and apply the same for defraying the public expenses—to borrow money, or emit bills on the credit of the United States, transmitting every half-year to the respective States an account of the sums of money so borrowed or emitted—to build and equip a navy—to agree upon the number of land forces, and to make requisitions from each State for its quota, in proportion to the number of white inhabitants in such State; which requisition shall be binding, and thereupon the legislature of each State shall appoint the regimental officers, raise the men and cloath, arm and equip them in a solid-like manner, at the expense of the United States; and the officers and men so cloathed, armed and equipped shall march to the place appointed, and within the time agreed on by the United States in Congress assembled. But if the United States in Congress assembled shall, on consideration of circumstances judge proper that any State should not raise men, or should raise a smaller number of men than the quota thereof, such extra number shall be raised, officered, cloathed, armed and equipped in the same manner as the quota of each State, unless the legislature of such State shall judge that such extra number cannot be safely spread out in the same, in which case they shall raise, officer, cloath, arm and equip as many of such extra number as they judeg can be safely spared. And the officers and men so cloathed, armed, and equipped, shall march to the place appointed, and within the time agreed on by the United States in Congress assembled.

The United States in Congress assembled shall never engage in a war, nor grant letters of marque or reprisal in time of peace, nor enter into any treaties or alliances, nor coin money, nor regulate the value thereof, nor ascertain the sums and expenses necessary for the defense and welfare of the United States, or any of them, nor emit bills, nor borrow money on the credit of the United States, nor appropriate money, nor agree upon the number of vessels of war, to be built or purchased, or the number of land or sea forces to be raised, nor appoint a commander in chief of the army or navy, unless nine States assent to the same: nor shall a question on any other point, except for adjourning from day to day be determined, unless by the votes of the majority of the United States in Congress assembled.

The Congress of the United States shall have power to adjourn to any time within the year, and to any place within the United States, so that no period of adjournment be for a longer duration than the space of six months, and shall publish the journal of their proceedings monthly, except such parts thereof relating to treaties, alliances or military operations, as in their judgement require secrecy; and the yeas and nays of the delegates of each State on any question shall be entered on the journal, when it is desired by any delegates of a State, or any of them, at his or their request shall be furnished with a transcript of the said journal, except such parts as are above excepted, to lay before the legislatures of the several States.

X. The Committee of the States, or any nine of them, shall be authorized to execute, in the recess of Congress, such of the powers of Congress as the United States in Congress assembled, by the consent of the nine States, shall from time to time think expedient to vest them with; provided that no power be delegated to the said Committee, for the exercise of which, by the Articles of Confederation, the voice of nine States in the Congress of the United States assembled be requisite.

XI. Canada acceding to this confederation, and adjoining in the measures of the United States, shall be admitted into, and entitled to all the advantages of this Union; but no other colony shall be admitted into the same, unless such admission be agreed to by nine States.

XII. All bills of credit emitted, monies borrowed, and debts contracted by, or under the authority of Congress, before the assembling of the United States, in pursuance of the present confederation, shall be deemed and considered as a charge against the United States, for payment and satisfaction whereof the said United States, and the public faith are hereby solemnly pledged.

XIII. Every State shall abide by the determination of the United States in Congress assembled, on all questions which by this confederation are submitted to them. And the Articles of this Confederation shall be inviolably observed by every State, and the Union shall be perpetual; nor shall any alteration at any time hereafter be made in any of them; unless such alteration be agreed to in a Congress of the United States, and be afterwards confirmed by the legislatures of every State.

And Whereas it hath pleased the Great Governor of the World to incline the hearts of the legislatures we respectively represent in Congress, to approve of, and to authorize us to ratify the said Articles of Confederation and perpetual Union. Know Ye that we the undersigned delegates, by virtue of the power and authority to us given for that purpose, do by these presents, in the name and in behalf of our respective constituents, fully and entirely ratify and confirm each and every of the said Articles of Confederation and perpetual Union, and all and singular the matters and things therein contained: And we do further solemnly plight and engage the faith of our respective constituents, that they shall abide by the determinations of the United States in Congress assembled, on all questions, which by the said Confederation are submitted to them. And that the Articles thereof shall be inviolably observed by the States we respectively represent, and that the Union shall be perpetual.

In Witness whereof we have hereunto set our hands in Congress. Done at Philadelphia in the State of Pennsylvania the ninth day of July in the Year of our Lord One Thousand Seven Hundred and Seventy-Eight, and in the Third Year of the independence of America.

THE UNITED STATES CONSTITUTION

1787

We the People of the United States, in Order to form a more perfect Union, establish Justice, insure domestic Tranquility, provide for the common defence, promote the general Welfare, and secure the Blessings of Liberty to ourselves and our Posterity, do ordain and establish this Constitution for the United States of America.

Article. I.

Section 1.

All legislative Powers herein granted shall be vested in a Congress of the United States, which shall consist of a Senate and House of Representatives.

Section. 2.

Clause 1: The House of Representatives shall be composed of Members chosen every second Year by the People of the several States, and the Electors in each State shall have the Qualifications requisite for Electors of the most numerous Branch of the State Legislature.

Clause 2: No Person shall be a Representative who shall not have attained to the Age of twenty five Years, and been seven Years a Citizen of the United States, and who shall not, when elected, be an Inhabitant of that State in which he shall be chosen.

Clause 3: Representatives and direct Taxes shall be apportioned among the several States which may be included within this Union, according to their respective Numbers, which shall be determined by adding to the whole Number of free Persons, including those bound to Service for a Term of Years, and excluding Indians not taxed, three fifths of all other Persons. The actual Enumeration shall be made within three Years after the first Meeting of the Congress of the United States, and within every subsequent Term of ten Years, in such Manner as they shall by Law direct. The Number of Representatives shall not exceed one for every thirty Thousand, but each State shall have at Least one Representative; and until such enumeration shall be made, the State of New Hampshire shall be entitled to chuse three, Massachusetts eight, Rhode-Island and Providence Plantations one, Connecticut five, New-York six, New Jersey four, Pennsylvania eight, Delaware one, Maryland six, Virginia ten, North Carolina five, South Carolina five, and Georgia three.

Clause 4: When vacancies happen in the Representation from any State, the Executive Authority thereof shall issue Writs of Election to fill such Vacancies.

Clause 5: The House of Representatives shall chuse their Speaker and other Officers; and shall have the sole Power of Impeachment.

Section. 3.

Clause 1: The Senate of the United States shall be composed of two Senators from each State, chosen by the Legislature thereof, for six Years; and each Senator shall have one Vote.

Clause 2: Immediately after they shall be assembled in Consequence of the first Election, they shall be divided as equally as may be into three Classes. The Seats of the Senators of the first Class shall be vacated at the Expiration of the second Year, of the second Class at the Expiration of the fourth Year, and of the third Class at the Expiration of the sixth Year, so that one third may be chosen every second Year; and if Vacancies happen by Resignation, or otherwise, during the Recess of the Legislature of any State, the Executive thereof may make temporary Appointments until the next Meeting of the Legislature, which shall then fill such Vacancies.

Clause 3: No Person shall be a Senator who shall not have attained to the Age of thirty Years, and been nine Years a Citizen of the United States, and who shall not, when elected, be an Inhabitant of that State for which he shall be chosen.

Clause 4: The Vice President of the United States shall be President of the Senate, but shall have no Vote, unless they be equally divided.

Clause 5: The Senate shall chuse their other Officers, and also a President pro tempore, in the Absence of the Vice President, or when he shall exercise the Office of President of the United States.

Clause 6: The Senate shall have the sole Power to try all Impeachments. When sitting for that Purpose, they shall be on Oath or Affirmation. When the President of the United States is tried, the Chief Justice shall preside: And no Person shall be convicted without the Concurrence of two thirds of the Members present.

Clause 7: Judgment in Cases of Impeachment shall not extend further than to removal from Office, and disqualification to hold and enjoy any Office of honor, Trust or Profit under the United States: but the Party convicted shall nevertheless be liable and subject to Indictment, Trial, Judgment and Punishment, according to Law.

Section. 4.

Clause 1: The Times, Places and Manner of holding Elections for Senators and Representatives, shall be prescribed in each State by the Legislature thereof; but the Congress may at any time by Law make or alter such Regulations, except as to the Places of chusing Senators.

Clause 2: The Congress shall assemble at least once in every Year, and such Meeting shall be on the first Monday in December, unless they shall by Law appoint a different Day.

Section. 5.

Clause 1: Each House shall be the Judge of the Elections, Returns and Qualifications of its own Members, and a Majority of each shall constitute a Quorum to do Business; but a smaller Number may adjourn from day to day, and may be authorized to compel the Attendance of absent Members, in such Manner, and under such Penalties as each House may provide.

Clause 2: Each House may determine the Rules of its Proceedings, punish its Members for disorderly Behaviour, and, with the Concurrence of two thirds, expel a Member.

Clause 3: Each House shall keep a Journal of its Proceedings, and from time to time publish the same, excepting such Parts as may in their Judgment require Secrecy; and the Yeas and Nays of the Members of either House on any question shall, at the Desire of one fifth of those Present, be entered on the Journal.

Clause 4: Neither House, during the Session of Congress, shall, without the Consent of the other, adjourn for more than three days, nor to any other Place than that in which the two Houses shall be sitting.

Section. 6.

Clause 1: The Senators and Representatives shall receive a Compensation for their Services, to be ascertained by Law, and paid out of the Treasury of the United States. They shall in all Cases, except Treason, Felony and Breach of the Peace, beprivileged from Arrest during their Attendance at the Session of their respective Houses, and in going to and returning from the same; and for any Speech or Debate in either House, they shall not be questioned in any other Place.

Clause 2: No Senator or Representative shall, during the Time for which he was elected, be appointed to any civil Office under the Authority of the United States, which shall have been created, or the Emoluments whereof shall have been encreased during such time; and no Person holding any Office under the United States, shall be a Member of either House during his Continuance in Office.

Section. 7.

Clause 1: All Bills for raising Revenue shall originate in the House of Representatives; but the Senate may propose or concur with Amendments as on other Bills.

Clause 2: Every Bill which shall have passed the House of Representatives and the Senate, shall, before it become a Law, be presented to the President of the United States; If he approve he shall sign it, but if not he shall return it, with his Objections to that House in which it shall have originated, who shall enter the Objections at large on their Journal, and proceed to reconsider it. If after such Reconsideration two thirds of that House shall agree to pass the Bill, it shall be sent, together with the Objections, to the other House, by which it shall likewise be reconsidered, and if approved by two thirds of that House, it shall become a Law. But in all such Cases the Votes of both Houses shall be determined by yeas and Nays, and the Names of the Persons voting for and against the Bill shall be entered on the Journal of each House respectively. If any Bill shall not be returned by the President within ten Days (Sundays excepted) after it shall have been presented to him, the Same shall be a Law, in like Manner as if he had signed it, unless the Congress by their Adjournment prevent its Return, in which Case it shall not be a Law.

Clause 3: Every Order, Resolution, or Vote to which the Concurrence of the Senate and House of Representatives may be necessary (except on a question of Adjournment) shall be presented to the President of the United States; and before the Same shall take Effect, shall be approved by him, or being disapproved by him, shall be repassed by two thirds of the Senate and House of Representatives, according to the Rules and Limitations prescribed in the Case of a Bill.

Section. 8.

Clause 1: The Congress shall have Power To lay and collect Taxes, Duties, Imposts and Excises, to pay the Debts and provide for the common Defence and general Welfare of the United States; but all Duties, Imposts and Excises shall be uniform throughout the United States;

Clause 2: To borrow Money on the credit of the United States;

Clause 3: To regulate Commerce with foreign Nations, and among the several States, and with the Indian Tribes;

Clause 4: To establish an uniform Rule of Naturalization, and uniform Laws on the subject of Bankruptcies throughout the United States;

Clause 5: To coin Money, regulate the Value thereof, and of foreign Coin, and fix the Standard of Weights and Measures;

Clause 6: To provide for the Punishment of counterfeiting the Securities and current Coin of the United States;

Clause 7: To establish Post Offices and post Roads;

Clause 8: To promote the Progress of Science and useful Arts, by securing for limited Times to Authors and Inventors the exclusive Right to their respective Writings and Discoveries;

Clause 9: To constitute Tribunals inferior to the supreme Court;

Clause 10: To define and punish Piracies and Felonies committed on the high Seas, and Offences against the Law of Nations;

Clause 11: To declare War, grant Letters of Marque and Reprisal, and make Rules concerning Captures on Land and Water;

Clause 12: To raise and support Armies, but no Appropriation of Money to that Use shall be for a longer Term than two Years;

Clause 13: To provide and maintain a Navy;

Clause 14: To make Rules for the Government and Regulation of the land and naval Forces;

Clause 15: To provide for calling forth the Militia to execute the Laws of the Union, suppress Insurrections and repel Invasions;

Clause 16: To provide for organizing, arming, and disciplining, the Militia, and for governing such Part of them as may be employed in the Service of the United States, reserving to the States respectively, the Appointment of the Officers, and the Authority of training the Militia according to the discipline prescribed by Congress;

Clause 17: To exercise exclusive Legislation in all Cases whatsoever, over such District (not exceeding ten Miles square) as may, byCession of particular States, and the Acceptance of Congress, become the Seat of the Government of the United States, and to exercise like Authority over all Places purchased by the Consent of the Legislature of the State in which the Same shall be, for the Erection of Forts, Magazines, Arsenals, dock-Yards, and other needful Buildings;—And

Clause 18: To make all Laws which shall be necessary and proper for carrying into Execution the foregoing Powers, and all other Powers vested by this Constitution in the Government of the United States, or in any Department or Officer thereof.

Section. 9.

Clause 1: The Migration or Importation of such Persons as any of the States now existing shall think proper to admit, shall not be prohibited by the Congress prior to the Year one thousand eight hundred and eight, but a Tax or duty may be imposed on such Importation, not exceeding ten dollars for each Person.

Clause 2: The Privilege of the Writ of Habeas Corpus shall not be suspended, unless when in Cases of Rebellion or Invasion the public Safety may require it.

Clause 3: No Bill of Attainder or ex post facto Law shall be passed.

Clause 4: No Capitation, or other direct, Tax shall be laid, unless in Proportion to the Census or Enumeration herein before directed to be taken.

Clause 5: No Tax or Duty shall be laid on Articles exported from any State.

Clause 6: No Preference shall be given by any Regulation of Commerce or Revenue to the Ports of one State over those of another: nor shall Vessels bound to, or from, one State, be obliged to enter, clear, or pay Duties in another.

Clause 7: No Money shall be drawn from the Treasury, but in Consequence of Appropriations made by Law; and a regular Statement and Account of the Receipts and Expenditures of all public Money shall be published from time to time.

Clause 8: No Title of Nobility shall be granted by the United States: And no Person holding any Office of Profit or Trust under them, shall, without the Consent of the Congress, accept of any present, Emolument, Office, or Title, of any kind whatever, from any King, Prince, or foreign State.

Section. 10.

Clause 1: No State shall enter into any Treaty, Alliance, or Confederation; grant Letters of Marque and Reprisal; coin Money; emit Bills of Credit; make any Thing but gold and silver Coin a Tender in Payment of Debts; pass any Bill of Attainder, ex post facto Law, or Law impairing the Obligation of Contracts, or grant any Title of Nobility.

Clause 2: No State shall, without the Consent of the Congress, lay any Imposts or Duties on Imports or Exports, except what may be absolutely necessary for executing it's inspection Laws: and the net Produce of all Duties and Imposts, laid by any State on Imports or Exports, shall be for the Use of the Treasury of the United States; and all such Laws shall be subject to the Revision and Controul of the Congress.

Clause 3: No State shall, without the Consent of Congress, lay any Duty of Tonnage, keep Troops, or Ships of War in time of Peace, enter into any Agreement or Compact with another State, or with a foreign Power, or engage in War, unless actually invaded, or in such imminent Danger as will not admit of delay.

Article. II.

Section. 1.

Clause 1: The executive Power shall be vested in a President of the United States of America. He shall hold his Office during the Term of four Years, and, together with the Vice President, chosen for the same Term, be elected, as follows

Clause 2: Each State shall appoint, in such Manner as the Legislature thereof may direct, a Number of Electors, equal to the whole Number of Senators and Representatives to which the State may be entitled in the Congress: but no Senator or Representative, or Person holding an Office of Trust or Profit under the United States, shall be appointed an Elector.

Clause 3: The Electors shall meet in their respective States, and vote by Ballot for two Persons, of whom one at least shall not be an Inhabitant of the same State with themselves. And they shall make a List of all the Persons voted for, and of the Number of Votes for each; which List they shall sign and certify, and transmit sealed to the Seat of the Government of the United States, directed to the President of the Senate. The President of the Senate shall, in the Presence of the Senate and House of Representatives, open all the Certificates, and the Votes shall then be counted. The Person having the greatest Number of Votes shall be the President, if such Number be a Majority of the whole Number of Electors appointed; and if there be more than one who have such Majority, and have an equal Number of Votes, then the House of Representatives shall immediately chuse by Ballot one of them for President; and if no Person have a Majority, then from the five highest on the List the said House shall in like Manner chuse the President. But in chusing the President, the Votes shall be taken by States, the Representation from each State having one Vote; A quorum for this Purpose shall consist of a Member or Members from two thirds of the States, and a Majority of all the States shall be necessary to a Choice. In every Case, after the Choice of the President, the Person having the greatest Number of Votes of the Electors shall be the Vice President. But if there should remain two or more who have equal Votes, the Senate shall chuse from them by Ballot the Vice President.

Clause 4: The Congress may determine the Time of chusing the Electors, and the Day on which they shall give their Votes; which Day shall be the same throughout the United States.

Clause 5: No Person except a natural born Citizen, or a Citizen of the United States, at the time of the Adoption of this Constitution, shall be eligible to the Office of President; neither shall any Person be eligible to that Office who shall not have attained to the Age of thirty five Years, and been fourteen Years a Resident within the United States.

Clause 6: In Case of the Removal of the President from Office, or of his Death, Resignation, or Inability to discharge the Powers and Duties of the said Office,) the Same shall devolve on the VicePresident, and the Congress may by Law provide for the Case of Removal, Death, Resignation or Inability, both of the President and Vice President, declaring what Officer shall then act as President, and such Officer shall act accordingly, until the Disability be removed, or a President shall be elected.

Clause 7: The President shall, at stated Times, receive for his Services, a Compensation, which shall neither be encreased nor diminished during the Period for which he shall have been elected, and he shall not receive within that Period any other Emolument from the United States, or any of them.

Clause 8: Before he enter on the Execution of his Office, he shall take the following Oath or Affirmation:—"I do solemnly swear (or affirm) that I will faithfully execute the Office of President of the United States, and will to the best of my Ability, preserve, protect and defend the Constitution of the United States."

Section. 2.

Clause 1: The President shall be Commander in Chief of the Army and Navy of the United States, and of the Militia of the several States, when called into the actual Service of the United States; he may require the Opinion, in writing, of the principal Officer in each of the executive Departments, upon any Subject relating to the Duties of their respective Offices, and he shall have Power to grant Reprieves and Pardons for Offences against the United States, except in Cases of Impeachment.

Clause 2: He shall have Power, by and with the Advice and Consent of the Senate, to make Treaties, provided two thirds of the Senators present concur; and he shall nominate, and by and with the Advice and Consent of the Senate, shall appoint Ambassadors, other public Ministers and Consuls, Judges of the supreme Court, and all other Officers of the United States, whose Appointments are not herein otherwise provided for, and which shall be established by Law: but the Congress may by Law vest the Appointment of such inferior Officers, as they think proper, in the President alone, in the Courts of Law, or in the Heads of Departments.

Clause 3: The President shall have Power to fill up all Vacancies that may happen during the Recess of the Senate, by granting Commissions which shall expire at the End of their next Session.

Section. 3.

He shall from time to time give to the Congress Information of the State of the Union, and recommend to their Consideration such Measures as he shall judge necessary and expedient; he may, on extraordinary Occasions, convene both Houses, or either of them, and in Case of Disagreement between them, with Respect to the Time of Adjournment, he may adjourn them to such Time as he shall think proper; he shall receive Ambassadors and other public Ministers; he shall take Care that the Laws be faithfully executed, and shall Commission all the Officers of the United States.

Section. 4.

The President, Vice President and all civil Officers of the United States, shall be removed from Office on Impeachment for, and Conviction of, Treason, Bribery, or other high Crimes and Misdemeanors.

Article. III.

Section. 1.

The judicial Power of the United States, shall be vested in one supreme Court, and in such inferior Courts as the Congress may from time to time ordain and establish. The Judges, both of the supreme and inferior Courts, shall hold their Offices during good Behaviour, and shall, at stated Times, receive for their Services, a Compensation, which shall not be diminished during their Continuance in Office.

Section. 2.

Clause 1: The judicial Power shall extend to all Cases, in Law and Equity, arising under this Constitution, the Laws of the United States, and Treaties made, or which shall be made, under their Authority;—to all Cases affecting Ambassadors, other public Ministers and Consuls;—to all Cases of admiralty and maritime Jurisdiction;—to Controversies to which the United States shall be a Party;—to Controversies between two or more States;—between a State and Citizens of another State; between Citizens of different States,—between Citizens of the same State claiming Lands under Grants of different States, and between a State, or the Citizens thereof, and foreign States, Citizens or Subjects.

Clause 2: In all Cases affecting Ambassadors, other public Ministers and Consuls, and those in which a State shall be Party, the supreme Court shall have original Jurisdiction. In all the other Cases before mentioned, the supreme Court shall have appellate Jurisdiction, both as to Law and Fact, with such Exceptions, and under such Regulations as the Congress shall make.

Clause 3: The Trial of all Crimes, except in Cases of Impeachment, shall be by Jury; and such Trial shall be held in the State where the said Crimes shall have been committed; but when not committed within any State, the Trial shall be at such Place or Places as the Congress may by Law have directed.

Section. 3.

Clause 1: Treason against the United States, shall consist only in levying War against them, or in adhering to their Enemies, giving them Aid and Comfort. No Person shall be convicted of Treason unless on the Testimony of two Witnesses to the same overt Act, or on Confession in open Court.

Clause 2: The Congress shall have Power to declare the Punishment of Treason, but no Attainder of Treason shall work Corruption of Blood, or Forfeiture except during the Life of the Person attainted.

Article. IV.

Section. 1.

Full Faith and Credit shall be given in each State to the public Acts, Records, and judicial Proceedings of every other State. And the Congress may by general Laws prescribe the Manner in which such Acts, Records and Proceedings shall be proved, and the Effect thereof.

Section. 2.

Clause 1: The Citizens of each State shall be entitled to all Privileges and Immunities of Citizens in the several States.

Clause 2: A Person charged in any State with Treason, Felony, or other Crime, who shall flee from Justice, and be found in another State, shall on Demand of the executive Authority of the State from which he fled, be delivered up, to be removed to the State having Jurisdiction of the Crime.

Clause 3: No Person held to Service or Labour in one State, under the Laws thereof, escaping into another, shall, in Consequence of any Law or Regulation therein, be discharged from such Service or Labour, but shall be delivered up on Claim of the Party to whom such Service or Labour may be due.

Section. 3.

Clause 1: New States may be admitted by the Congress into this Union; but no new State shall be formed or erected within the Jurisdiction of any other State; nor any State be formed by the Junction of two or more States, or Parts of States, without the Consent of the Legislatures of the States concerned as well as of the Congress.

Clause 2: The Congress shall have Power to dispose of and make all needful Rules and Regulations respecting the Territory or other Property belonging to the United States; and nothing in this Constitution shall be so construed as to Prejudice any Claims of the United States, or of any particular State.

Section. 4.

The United States shall guarantee to every State in this Union a Republican Form of Government, and shall protect each of them against Invasion; and on Application of the Legislature, or of the Executive (when the Legislature cannot be convened) against domestic Violence.

Article. V.

The Congress, whenever two thirds of both Houses shall deem it necessary, shall propose Amendments to this Constitution, or, on the Application of the Legislatures of two thirds of the several States, shall call a Convention for proposing Amendments, which, in either Case, shall be valid to all Intents and Purposes, as Part of this Constitution, when ratified by the Legislatures of three fourths of the several States, or by Conventions in three fourths thereof, as the one or the other Mode of Ratification may be proposed by the Congress; Provided that no Amendment which may be made prior to the Year One thousand eight hundred and eight shall in any Manner affect the first and fourth Clauses in the Ninth Section of the first Article; and that no State, without its Consent, shall be deprived of its equal Suffrage in the Senate.

Article. VI.

Clause 1: All Debts contracted and Engagements entered into, before the Adoption of this Constitution, shall be as valid against the United States under this Constitution, as under the Confederation.

Clause 2: This Constitution, and the Laws of the United States which shall be made in Pursuance thereof; and all Treaties made, or which shall be made, under the Authority of the United States, shall be the supreme Law of the Land; and the

Judges in every State shall be bound thereby, any Thing in the Constitution or Laws of any State to the Contrary notwithstanding.

Clause 3: The Senators and Representatives before mentioned, and the Members of the several State Legislatures, and all executive and judicial Officers, both of the United States and of the several States, shall be bound by Oath or Affirmation, to support this Constitution; but no religious Test shall ever be required as a Qualification to any Office or public Trust under the United States.

Article. VII.

The Ratification of the Conventions of nine States, shall be sufficient for the Establishment of this Constitution between the States so ratifying the Same.

LOUISIANA PURCHASE TREATY

April 30, 1803

The President of the United States of America and the First Consul of the French Republic in the name of the French People desiring to remove all Source of misunderstanding relative to objects of discussion mentioned in the Second and fifth articles of the Convention of the 8th Vendémiaire on 9/30 September 1800 relative to the rights claimed by the United States in virtue of the Treaty concluded at Madrid the 27 of October 1795, between His Catholic Majesty & the Said United States, & willing to Strengthen the union and friendship which at the time of the Said Convention was happily reestablished between the two nations have respectively named their Plenipotentiaries to wit The President of the United States, by and with the advice and consent of the Senate of the Said States; Robert R. Livingston Minister Plenipotentiary of the United States and James Monroe Minister Plenipotentiary and Envoy extraordinary of the Said States near the Government of the French Republic; And the First Consul in the name of the French people, Citizen Francis Barbé Marbois Minister of the public treasury who after having respectively exchanged their full powers have agreed to the following Articles.

Article I

Whereas by the Article the third of the Treaty concluded at St Ildefonso the 9th Vendémiaire on 1st October 1800 between the First Consul of the French Republic and his Catholic Majesty it was agreed as follows.

> "His Catholic Majesty promises and engages on his part to cede to the French Republic six months after the full and entire execution of the conditions and Stipulations herein relative to his Royal Highness the Duke of Parma, the Colony or Province of Louisiana with the Same extent that it now has in the hand of Spain, & that it had when France possessed it; and Such as it Should be after the Treaties subsequently entered into between Spain and other States."

And whereas in pursuance of the Treaty and particularly of the third article the French Republic has an incontestible title to the domain and to the possession of the said Territory—The First Consul of the French Republic desiring to give to the United States a strong proof of his friendship doth hereby cede to the United

States in the name of the French Republic for ever and in full Sovereignty the said territory with all its rights and appurtenances as fully and in the Same manner as they have been acquired by the French Republic in virtue of the above mentioned Treaty concluded with his Catholic Majesty.

Article II

In the cession made by the preceeding article are included the adjacent Islands belonging to Louisiana all public lots and Squares, vacant lands and all public buildings, fortifications, barracks and other edifices which are not private property.—The Archives, papers & documents relative to the domain and Sovereignty of Louisiana and its dependances will be left in the possession of the Commissaries of the United States, and copies will be afterwards given in due form to the Magistrates and Municipal officers of such of the said papers and documents as may be necessary to them.

Article III

The inhabitants of the ceded territory shall be incorporated in the Union of the United States and admitted as soon as possible according to the principles of the federal Constitution to the enjoyment of all these rights, advantages and immunities of citizens of the United States, and in the mean time they shall be maintained and protected in the free enjoyment of their liberty, property and the Religion which they profess.

Article IV

There Shall be Sent by the Government of France a Commissary to Louisiana to the end that he do every act necessary as well to receive from the Officers of his Catholic Majesty the Said country and its dependances in the name of the French Republic if it has not been already done as to transmit it in the name of the French Republic to the Commissary or agent of the United States.

Article V

Immediately after the ratification of the present Treaty by the President of the United States and in case that of the first Consul's shall have been previously obtained, the commissary of the French Republic shall remit all military posts of New Orleans and other parts of the ceded territory to the Commissary or Commissaries named by the President to take possession—the troops whether of France or Spain who may be there shall cease to occupy any military post from the time of taking possession and shall be embarked as soon as possible in the course of three months after the ratification of this treaty.

Article VI

The United States promise to execute Such treaties and articles as may have been agreed between Spain and the tribes and nations of Indians until by mutual consent of the United States and the said tribes or nations other Suitable articles Shall have been agreed upon.

Article VII

As it is reciprocally advantageous to the commerce of France and the United States to encourage the communication of both nations for a limited time in the country ceded by the present treaty until general arrangements relative to commerce of both nat ions may be agreed on; it has been agreed between the contracting parties that the French Ships coming directly from France or any of her colonies loaded only with the produce and manufactures of France or her Said Colonies; and the Ships of Spain coming directly from Spain or any of her colonies loaded only with the produce or manufactures of Spain or her Colonies shall be admitted during the Space of twelve years in the Port of New-Orleans and in all other legal ports-of-entry within the ceded territory in the Same manner as the Ships of the United States coming directly from France or Spain or any of their Colonies without being Subject to any other or greater duty on merchandize or other or greater tonnage than that paid by the citizens of the United. States.

During that Space of time above mentioned no other nation Shall have a right to the Same privileges in the Ports of the ceded territory—the twelve years Shall commence three months after the exchange of ratifications if it Shall take place in France or three months after it Shall have been notified at Paris to the French Government if it Shall take place in the United States; It is however well understood that the object of the above article is to favour the manufactures, Commerce, freight and navigation of France and of Spain So far as relates to the importations that the French and Spanish Shall make into the Said Ports of the United States without in any Sort affecting the regulations that the United States may make concerning the exportation of t he produce and merchandize of the United States, or any right they may have to make Such regulations.

Article VIII

In future and for ever after the expiration of the twelve years, the Ships of France shall be treated upon the footing of the most favoured nations in the ports above mentioned.

Article IX

The particular Convention Signed this day by the respective Ministers, having for its object to provide for the payment of debts due to the Citizens of the United States by the French Republic prior to the 30th Sept. 1800 (8th Vendé miaire an 9) is approved and to have its execution in the Same manner as if it had been inserted in this present treaty, and it Shall be ratified in the same form and in the Same time So that the one Shall not be ratified distinct from the other.

Another particular Convention Signed at the Same date as the present treaty relative to a definitive rule between the contracting parties is in the like manner approved and will be ratified in the Same form, and in the Same time and jointly.

Article X

The present treaty Shall be ratified in good and due form and the ratifications Shall be exchanged in the Space of Six months after the date of the Signature by the Ministers Plenipotentiary or Sooner if possible.

In faith whereof the respective Plenipotentiaries have Signed these articles in the French and English languages; declaring nevertheless that the present Treaty was originally agreed to in the French language; and have thereunto affixed their Seals.
Done at Paris the tenth day of Floreal in the eleventh year of the French Republic; and the 30th of April 1803.

THE STAR-SPANGLED BANNER

Written by Francis Scott Key on September 14th, 1814

Oh, say, can you see, by the dawn's early light,
What so proudly we hailed at the twilight's last gleaming?
Whose broad stripes and bright stars, thro' the perilous fight'
O'er the ramparts we watched, were so gallantly streaming.
And the rockets red glare, the bombs bursting in air,
Gave proof through the night that our flag was still there.
Oh, say, does that star-spangled banner yet wave
O'er the land of the free and the home of the brave?

On the shore dimly seen, thro' the mists of the deep,
Where the foe's haughty host in dread silence reposes,
What is that which the breeze, o'er the towering steep,
As it fitfully blows, half conceals, half discloses?
Now it catches the gleam of the morning's first beam,
In full glory reflected, now shines on the stream;
'Tis the star-spangled banner: oh, long may it wave
O'er the land of the free and the home of the brave.

And where is that band who so vauntingly swore
That the havoc of war and the battle's confusion
A home and a country should leave us no more?
Their blood has wash'd out their foul footstep's pollution.
No refuge could save the hireling and slave
From the terror of flight or the gloom of the grave,
And the star-spangled banner in triumph doth wave
O'er the land of the free and the home of the brave.

Oh, thus be it ever when free men shall stand,
Between their loved homes and the war's desolation;
Blest with vict'ry and peace, may the heav'n-rescued land
Praise the Power that has made and preserved us as a nation.

Then conquer we must, when our cause is just,
  And this be our motto: "In God is our trust";
And the star-spangled banner in triumph shall wave
O'er the land of the free and the home of the brave.

MONROE DOCTRINE

James Monroe
December 2, 1823

At the proposal of the Russian Imperial Government, made through the minister of the Emperor residing here, a full power and instructions have been transmitted to the minister of the United States at St. Petersburg to arrange by amicable negotiation the respective rights and interests of the two nations on the northwest coast of this continent. A similar proposal has been made by His Imperial Majesty to the Government of Great Britain, which has likewise been acceded to. The Government of the United States has been desirous by this friendly proceeding of manifesting the great value which they have invariably attached to the friendship of the Emperor and their solicitude to cultivate the best understanding with his Government. In the discussions to which this interest has given rise and in the arrangements by which they may terminate the occasion has been judged proper for asserting, as a principle in which the rights and interests of the United States are involved, that the American continents, by the free and independent condition which they have assumed and maintain, are henceforth not to be considered as subjects for future colonization by any European powers...

It was stated at the commencement of the last session that a great effort was then making in Spain and Portugal to improve the condition of the people of those countries, and that it appeared to be conducted with extraordinary moderation. It need scarcely be remarked that the results have been so far very different from what was then anticipated. Of events in that quarter of the globe, with which we have so much intercourse and from which we derive our origin, we have always been anxious and interested spectators. The citizens of the United States cherish sentiments the most friendly in favor of the liberty and happiness of their fellow-men on that side of the Atlantic. In the wars of the European powers in matters relating to themselves we have never taken any part, nor does it comport with our policy to do so. It is only when our rights are invaded or seriously menaced that we resent injuries or make preparation for our defense. With the movements in this hemisphere we are of necessity more immediately connected, and by causes which must be obvious to all enlightened and impartial observers. The political system of the allied powers is essentially different in this respect from that of America. This difference proceeds from that which exists in their respective Governments; and to the defense of our own, which has been achieved by the loss of so much blood and treasure, and matured by the wisdom of their most enlightened citizens, and under which we have enjoyed unexampled felicity, this whole nation is devoted. We owe it, therefore, to candor and to the amicable relations existing between the United States and those powers to declare that we should consider any attempt on their part to extend their system to any portion of this hemisphere as dangerous to our peace and safety. With the existing colonies or dependencies of any European power we have not interfered and shall not interfere. But with the Governments who have declared their independence and maintain it, and whose independence we have, on great consideration and on just principles, acknowledged, we could not view any interposition for the purpose of oppressing them, or controlling in any other manner their destiny, by any European power in any other light than as the manifestation of an unfriendly disposition toward the United States. In the war between those new Governments and Spain we declared our neutrality at the time of their recognition, and to this we have adhered, and shall continue to adhere, provided no change shall occur which, in the judgement of the competent authorities of this Government, shall make a corresponding change on the part of the United States indispensable to their security.

The late events in Spain and Portugal shew that Europe is still unsettled. Of this important fact no stronger proof can be adduced than that the allied powers should have thought it proper, on any principle satisfactory to themselves, to have interposed by force in the internal concerns of Spain. To what extent such interposition may be carried, on the same principle, is a question in which all independent powers whose governments differ from theirs are interested, even those most remote, and surely none of them more so than the United States. Our policy in regard to Europe, which was adopted at an early stage of the wars which have so long agitated that quarter of the globe, nevertheless remains the same, which is, not to interfere in the internal concerns of any of its powers; to consider the government de facto as the legitimate government for us; to cultivate friendly relations with it, and to preserve those relations by a frank, firm, and manly policy, meeting in all instances the just claims of every power, submitting to injuries from none. But in regard to those continents circumstances are eminently and conspicuously different.

It is impossible that the allied powers should extend their political system to any portion of either continent without endangering our peace and happiness; nor can anyone believe that our southern brethren, if left to themselves, would adopt it of their own accord. It is equally impossible, therefore, that we should behold such interposition in any form with indifference. If we look to the comparative strength and resources of Spain and those new Governments, and their distance from each other, it must be obvious that she can never subdue them. It is still the true policy of the United States to leave the parties to themselves, in hope that other powers will pursue the same course.

EMANCIPATION PROCLAMATION

Abraham Lincoln
January 1, 1863

Whereas, on the twenty-second day of September, in the year of our Lord one thousand eight hundred and sixty-two, a proclamation was issued by the President of the United States, containing, among other things, the following, to wit:

"That on the first day of January, in the year of our Lord one thousand eight hundred and sixty-three, all persons held as slaves within any State or designated part of a State, the people whereof shall then be in rebellion against the United States, shall be then, thenceforward, and forever free; and the Executive Government of the United States, including the military and naval authority thereof, will recognize and maintain the freedom of such persons, and will do no act or acts to repress such persons, or any of them, in any efforts they may make for their actual freedom.

"That the Executive will, on the first day of January aforesaid, by proclamation, designate the States and parts of States, if any, in which the people thereof, respectively, shall then be in rebellion against the United States; and the fact that any State, or the people thereof, shall on that day be, in good faith, represented in the Congress of the United States by members chosen thereto at elections wherein a majority of the qualified voters of such State shall have participated, shall, in the absence of strong countervailing testimony, be deemed conclusive evidence that such State, and the people thereof, are not then in rebellion against the United States."

Now, therefore I, Abraham Lincoln, President of the United States, by virtue of the power in me vested as Commander-in-Chief, of the Army and Navy of the United States in time of actual armed rebellion against the authority and government of the United States, and as a fit and necessary war measure for suppressing said rebellion, do, on this first day of January, in the year of our Lord one thousand eight hundred and sixty-three, and in accordance with my purpose so to do publicly proclaimed for the full period of one hundred days, from the day first above mentioned, order and designate as the States and parts of States wherein the people thereof respectively, are this day in rebellion against the United States, the following, to wit:

Arkansas, Texas, Louisiana, (except the Parishes of St. Bernard, Plaquemines, Jefferson, St. John, St. Charles, St. James Ascension, Assumption, Terrebonne, Lafourche, St. Mary, St. Martin, and Orleans, including the City of New Orleans) Mississippi, Alabama, Florida, Georgia, South Carolina, North Carolina, and Virginia, (except the forty-eight counties designated as West Virginia, and also the counties of Berkley, Accomac, Northampton, Elizabeth City, York, Princess Ann, and Norfolk, including the cities of Norfolk and Portsmouth[)], and which excepted parts, are for the present, left precisely as if this proclamation were not issued.

And by virtue of the power, and for the purpose aforesaid, I do order and declare that all persons held as slaves within said designated States, and parts of States, are, and henceforward shall be free; and that the Executive government of the United States, including the military and naval authorities thereof, will recognize and maintain the freedom of said persons.

And I hereby enjoin upon the people so declared to be free to abstain from all violence, unless in necessary self-defence; and I recommend to them that, in all cases when allowed, they labor faithfully for reasonable wages.

And I further declare and make known, that such persons of suitable condition, will be received into the armed service of the United States to garrison forts, positions, stations, and other places, and to man vessels of all sorts in said service.

And upon this act, sincerely believed to be an act of justice, warranted by the Constitution, upon military necessity, I invoke the considerate judgment of mankind, and the gracious favor of Almighty God.

In witness whereof, I have hereunto set my hand and caused the seal of the United States to be affixed.

Done at the City of Washington, this first day of
January, in the year of our Lord one thousand eight
hundred and sixty three, and of the Independence of the
United States of America the eighty-seventh.

GETTYSBURG ADDRESS

Abraham Lincoln
November 19, 1863

Fourscore and seven years ago our fathers brought forth on this continent a new nation, conceived in liberty and dedicated to the proposition that all men are created equal. Now we are engaged in a great civil war, testing whether that nation or any nation so conceived and so dedicated can long endure. We are met on a great battlefield of that war. We have come to dedicate a portion of that field as a final resting-place for those who here gave their lives that that nation might live. It is altogether fitting and proper that we should do this. But in a larger sense, we cannot dedicate, we cannot consecrate, we cannot hallow this ground. The brave men, living and dead who struggled here have consecrated it far above our poor power to add or detract. The world will little note nor long remember what we say here, but it can never forget what they did here. It is for us the living rather to be dedicated here to the unfinished work which they who fought here have thus far so nobly advanced. It is rather for us to be here dedicated to the great task remaining before us—that from these honored dead we take increased devotion to that cause for which they gave the last full measure of devotion—that we here highly resolve that these dead shall not have died in vain, that this nation under God shall have a new birth of freedom, and that government of the people, by the people, for the people shall not perish from the earth.

NOTHING TO FEAR BUT FEAR ITSELF

Franklin D. Roosevelt
Inaugural Address
March 4, 1933

I am certain that my fellow Americans expect that on my induction into the Presidency I will address them with a candor and a decision which the present situation of our Nation impels. This is preeminently the time to speak the truth, the whole truth, frankly and boldly. Nor need we shrink from honestly facing conditions in our country today. This great Nation will endure as it has endured, will revive and will prosper. So, first of all, let me assert my firm belief that the only thing we have to fear is fear itself—nameless, unreasoning, unjustified terror which paralyzes needed efforts to convert retreat into advance. In every dark hour of our national life a leadership of frankness and vigor has met with that understanding and support of the people themselves which is essential to victory. I am convinced that you will again give that support to leadership in these critical days.

In such a spirit on my part and on yours we face our common difficulties. They concern, thank God, only material things. Values have shrunken to fantastic levels; taxes have risen; our ability to pay has fallen; government of all kinds is faced by serious curtailment of income; the means of exchange are frozen in the currents of trade; the withered leaves of industrial enterprise lie on every side; farmers find no markets for their produce; the savings of many years in thousands of families are gone.

More important, a host of unemployed citizens face the grim problem of existence, and an equally great number toil with little return. Only a foolish optimist can deny the dark realities of the moment.

Yet our distress comes from no failure of substance. We are stricken by no plague of locusts. Compared with the perils which our forefathers conquered because they believed and were not afraid, we have still much to be thankful for. Nature still offers her bounty and human efforts have multiplied it. Plenty is at our doorstep, but a generous use of it languishes in the very sight of the supply. Primarily this is because the rulers of the exchange of mankind's goods have failed, through their own stubbornness and their own incompetence, have admitted their failure, and abdicated. Practices of the unscrupulous money changers stand indicted in the court of public opinion, rejected by the hearts and minds of men.

True they have tried, but their efforts have been cast in the pattern of an outworn tradition. Faced by failure of credit they have proposed only the lending of more money. Stripped of the lure of profit by which to induce our people to follow their false leadership, they have resorted to exhortations, pleading tearfully for restored confidence. They know only the rules of a generation of self-seekers. They have no vision, and when there is no vision the people perish.

The money changers have fled from their high seats in the temple of our civilization. We may now restore that temple to the ancient truths. The measure of the restoration lies in the extent to which we apply social values more noble than mere monetary profit.

Happiness lies not in the mere possession of money; it lies in the joy of achievement, in the thrill of creative effort. The joy and moral stimulation of work no longer must be forgotten in the mad chase of evanescent profits. These dark days will be worth all they cost us if they teach us that our true destiny is not to be ministered unto but to minister to ourselves and to our fellow men.

Recognition of the falsity of material wealth as the standard of success goes hand in hand with the abandonment of the false belief that public office and high political position are to be valued only by the standards of pride of place and personal profit; and there must be an end to a conduct in banking and in business which too often has given to a sacred trust the likeness of callous and selfish wrongdoing. Small wonder that confidence languishes, for it thrives only on honesty, on honor, on the sacredness of obligations, on faithful protection, on unselfish performance; without them it cannot live.

Restoration calls, however, not for changes in ethics alone. This Nation asks for action, and action now.

Our greatest primary task is to put people to work. This is no unsolvable problem if we face it wisely and courageously. It can be accomplished in part by direct recruiting by the Government itself, treating the task as we would treat the emergency of a war, but at the same time, through this employment, accomplishing greatly needed projects to stimulate and reorganize the use of our natural resources.

Hand in hand with this we must frankly recognize the overbalance of population in our industrial centers and, by engaging on a national scale in a redistribution, endeavor to provide a better use of the land for those best fitted for the land. The task can be helped by definite efforts to raise the values of agricultural products and with this the power to purchase the output of our cities. It can be helped by preventing realistically the tragedy of the growing loss through foreclosure of our small homes and our farms. It can be helped by insistence that the Federal, State, and local governments act forthwith on the demand that their cost be drastically reduced. It can be helped by the unifying of relief activities which today are often scattered, uneconomical, and unequal. It can be helped by national planning for and supervision of all forms of transportation and of communications and other utilities which have a definitely public character. There are many ways in which it can be helped, but it can never be helped merely by talking about it. We must act and act quickly.

Finally, in our progress toward a resumption of work we require two safeguards against a return of the evils of the old order; there must be a strict supervision of all banking and credits and investments; there must be an end to speculation with other people's money, and there must be provision for an adequate but sound currency.

There are the lines of attack. I shall presently urge upon a new Congress in special session detailed measures for their fulfillment, and I shall seek the immediate assistance of the several States.

Through this program of action we address ourselves to putting our own national house in order and making income balance outgo. Our international trade relations, though vastly important, are in point of time and necessity secondary to the establishment of a sound national economy. I favor as a practical policy the putting of first things first. I shall spare no effort to restore world trade by international economic readjustment, but the emergency at home cannot wait on that accomplishment.

The basic thought that guides these specific means of national recovery is not narrowly nationalistic. It is the insistence, as a first consideration, upon the interdependence of the various elements in all parts of the United States—a recognition of the old and permanently important manifestation of the American spirit of the pioneer. It is the way to recovery. It is the immediate way. It is the strongest assurance that the recovery will endure.

In the field of world policy I would dedicate this Nation to the policy of the good neighbor—the neighbor who resolutely respects himself and, because he does so, respects the rights of others—the neighbor who respects his obligations and respects the sanctity of his agreements in and with a world of neighbors.

If I read the temper of our people correctly, we now realize as we have never realized before our interdependence on each other; that we can not merely take but we must give as well; that if we are to go forward, we must move as a trained and loyal army willing to sacrifice for the good of a common discipline, because without such discipline no progress is made, no leadership becomes effective. We are, I know, ready and willing to submit our lives and property to such discipline, because it makes possible a leadership which aims at a larger good. This I propose to offer, pledging that the larger purposes will bind upon us all as a sacred obligation with a unity of duty hitherto evoked only in time of armed strife.

With this pledge taken, I assume unhesitatingly the leadership of this great army of our people dedicated to a disciplined attack upon our common problems.

Action in this image and to this end is feasible under the form of government which we have inherited from our ancestors. Our Constitution is so simple and practical that it is possible always to meet extraordinary needs by changes in emphasis and arrangement without loss of essential form. That is why our constitutional system has proved itself the most superbly enduring political mechanism the modern world has produced. It has met every stress of vast expansion of territory, of foreign wars, of bitter internal strife, of world relations.

It is to be hoped that the normal balance of executive and legislative authority may be wholly adequate to meet the unprecedented task before us. But it may be that an unprecedented demand and need for undelayed action may call for temporary departure from that normal balance of public procedure.

I am prepared under my constitutional duty to recommend the measures that a stricken nation in the midst of a stricken world may require. These measures, or such other measures as the Congress may build out of its experience and wisdom, I shall seek, within my constitutional authority, to bring to speedy adoption.

But in the event that the Congress shall fail to take one of these two courses, and in the event that the national emergency is still critical, I shall not evade the clear course of duty that will then confront me. I shall ask the Congress for the one remaining instrument to meet the crisis—broad Executive power to wage a war against the emergency, as great as the power that would be given to me if we were in fact invaded by a foreign foe.

For the trust reposed in me I will return the courage and the devotion that befit the time. I can do no less.

We face the arduous days that lie before us in the warm courage of the national unity; with the clear consciousness of seeking old and precious moral values; with the clean satisfaction that comes from the stem performance of duty by old and young alike. We aim at the assurance of a rounded and permanent national life.

We do not distrust the future of essential democracy. The people of the United States have not failed. In their need they have registered a mandate that they want direct, vigorous action. They have asked for discipline and direction under leadership. They have made me the present instrument of their wishes. In the spirit of the gift I take it.

In this dedication of a Nation we humbly ask the blessing of God. May He protect each and every one of us. May He guide me in the days to come.

PEARL HARBOR SPEECH

Franklin D. Roosevelt
December 8, 1941

To the Congress of the United States:

Yesterday, Dec. 7, 1941—a date which will live in infamy—the United States of America was suddenly and deliberately attacked by naval and air forces of the Empire of Japan.
The United States was at peace with that nation and, at the solicitation of Japan, was still in conversation with the government and its emperor looking toward the maintenance of peace in the Pacific.

Indeed, one hour after Japanese air squadrons had commenced bombing in Oahu, the Japanese ambassador to the United States and his colleagues delivered to the Secretary of State a formal reply to a recent American message. While this reply stated that it seemed useless to continue the existing diplomatic negotiations, it contained no threat or hint of war or armed attack.

It will be recorded that the distance of Hawaii from Japan makes it obvious that the attack was deliberately planned many days or even weeks ago. During the intervening time, the Japanese government has deliberately sought to deceive the United States by false statements and expressions of hope for continued peace.

The attack yesterday on the Hawaiian islands has caused severe damage to American naval and military forces. Very many American lives have been lost. In addition, American ships have been reported torpedoed on the high seas between San Francisco and Honolulu.

Yesterday, the Japanese government also launched an attack against Malaya.
Last night, Japanese forces attacked Hong Kong.
Last night, Japanese forces attacked Guam.
Last night, Japanese forces attacked the Philippine Islands.
Last night, the Japanese attacked Wake Island.
This morning, the Japanese attacked Midway Island.

Japan has, therefore, undertaken a surprise offensive extending throughout the Pacific area. The facts of yesterday speak for themselves. The people of the United States have already formed their opinions and well understand the implications to the very life and safety of our nation.

As commander in chief of the Army and Navy, I have directed that all measures be taken for our defense.

Always will we remember the character of the onslaught against us.

No matter how long it may take us to overcome this premeditated invasion, the American people in their righteous might will win through to absolute victory.

I believe I interpret the will of the Congress and of the people when I assert that we will not only defend ourselves to the uttermost, but will make very certain that this form of treachery shall never endanger us again.

Hostilities exist. There is no blinking at the fact that that our people, our territory and our interests are in grave danger.

With confidence in our armed forces—with the unbounding determination of our people—we will gain the inevitable triumph—so help us God.
I ask that the Congress declare that since the unprovoked and dastardly attack by Japan on Sunday, Dec. 7, a state of war has existed between the United States and the Japanese empire.

I Have a Dream

Martin Luther King, Jr.
August 28, 1963

Five score years ago, a great American, in whose symbolic shadow we stand signed the Emancipation Proclamation. This momentous decree came as a great beacon light of hope to millions of Negro slaves who had been seared in the flames of withering injustice. It came as a joyous daybreak to end the long night of captivity. But one hundred years later, we must face the tragic fact that the Negro is still not free.

One hundred years later, the life of the Negro is still sadly crippled by the manacles of segregation and the chains of discrimination. One hundred years later, the Negro lives on a lonely island of poverty in the midst of a vast ocean of material prosperity. One hundred years later, the Negro is still languishing in the corners of American society and finds himself an exile in his own land.

So we have come here today to dramatize an appalling condition. In a sense we have come to our nation's capital to cash a check. When the architects of our republic wrote the magnificent words of the Constitution and the Declaration of Independence, they were signing a promissory note to which every American was to fall heir.
This note was a promise that all men would be guaranteed the inalienable rights of life, liberty, and the pursuit of happiness. It is obvious today that America has defaulted on this promissory note insofar as her citizens of color are concerned. Instead of honoring this sacred obligation, America has given the Negro people a bad check which has come back marked "insufficient funds." But we refuse to believe that the bank of justice is bankrupt. We refuse to believe that there are insufficient funds in the great vaults of opportunity of this nation.

So we have come to cash this check—a check that will give us upon demand the riches of freedom and the security of justice. We have also come to this hallowed spot to remind America of the fierce urgency of now. This is no time to engage in the luxury of cooling off or to take the tranquilizing drug of gradualism. Now is the time to rise from the dark and desolate valley of segregation to the sunlit path of racial justice. Now is the time to open the doors of opportunity to all of God's children. Now is the time to lift our nation from the quicksands of racial injustice to the solid rock of brotherhood.

It would be fatal for the nation to overlook the urgency of the moment and to underestimate the determination of the Negro. This sweltering summer of the Negro's legitimate discontent will not pass until there is an invigorating autumn of freedom and equality. Nineteen sixty-three is not an end, but a beginning. Those who hope that the Negro needed to blow off steam and will now be content will have a rude awakening if the nation returns to business as usual. There will be neither rest nor tranquility in America until the Negro is granted his citizenship rights.

The whirlwinds of revolt will continue to shake the foundations of our nation until the bright day of justice emerges. But there is something that I must say to my people who stand on the warm threshold which leads into the palace of justice. In the process of gaining our rightful place we must not be guilty of wrongful deeds. Let us not seek to satisfy our thirst for freedom by drinking from the cup of bitterness and hatred.

We must forever conduct our struggle on the high plane of dignity and discipline. we must not allow our creative protest to degenerate into physical violence. Again and again we must rise to the majestic heights of meeting physical force with soul force.

The marvelous new militancy which has engulfed the Negro community must not lead us to distrust of all white people, for many of our white brothers, as evidenced by their presence here today, have come to realize that their destiny is tied up with our destiny and their freedom is inextricably bound to our freedom.

We cannot walk alone. And as we walk, we must make the pledge that we shall march ahead. We cannot turn back. There are those who are asking the devotees of civil rights, "When will you be satisfied?" we can never be satisfied as long as our bodies, heavy with the fatigue of travel, cannot gain lodging in the motels of the highways and the hotels of the cities. We cannot be satisfied as long as the Negro's basic mobility is from a smaller ghetto to a larger one. We can never be satisfied as long as a Negro in Mississippi cannot vote and a Negro in New York believes he has nothing for which to vote. No, no, we are not satisfied, and we will not be satisfied until justice rolls down like waters and righteousness like a mighty stream.

I am not unmindful that some of you have come here out of great trials and tribulations. Some of you have come fresh from narrow cells. Some of you have come from areas where your quest for freedom left you battered by the storms of persecution and staggered by the winds of police brutality. You have been the veterans of creative suffering. Continue to work with the faith that unearned suffering is redemptive.

Go back to Mississippi, go back to Alabama, go back to Georgia, go back to Louisiana, go back to the slums and ghettos of our northern cities, knowing that somehow this situation can and will be changed. Let us not wallow in the valley of despair. I say to you today, my friends, that in spite of the difficulties and frustrations of the moment, I still have a dream. It is a dream deeply rooted in the American dream.

I have a dream that one day this nation will rise up and live out the true meaning of its creed: "We hold these truths to be self-evident: that all men are created equal." I have a dream that one day on the red hills of Georgia the sons of former slaves and the sons of former slaveowners will be able to sit down together at a table of brotherhood. I have a dream that one day even the state of Mississippi, a desert state, sweltering with the heat of injustice and oppression, will be transformed into an oasis of freedom and justice. I have a dream that my four children will one day live in a nation where they will not be judged by the color of their skin but by the content of their character. I have a dream today.

I have a dream that one day the state of Alabama, whose governor's lips are presently dripping with the words of interposition and nullification, will be transformed into a situation where little black boys and black girls will be able to join hands with little white boys and white girls and walk together as sisters and brothers. I have a dream today. I have a dream that one day every valley shall be exalted, every hill and mountain shall be made low, the rough places will be made plain, and the crooked places will be made straight, and the glory of the Lord shall be revealed, and all flesh shall see it together. This is our hope. This is the faith with which I return to the South. With this faith we will be able to hew out of the mountain of despair a stone of hope. With this faith we will be able to transform the jangling discords of our nation into a beautiful symphony of brotherhood. With this faith we will be able to work together, to pray together, to struggle together, to go to jail together, to stand up for freedom together, knowing that we will be free one day.

This will be the day when all of God's children will be able to sing with a new meaning, "My country, 'tis of thee, sweet land of liberty, of thee I sing. Land where my fathers died, land of the pilgrim's pride, from every mountainside, let freedom ring." And if America is to be a great nation, this must become true. So let freedom ring from the prodigious hilltops of New Hampshire. Let freedom ring from the mighty mountains of New York. Let freedom ring from the heightening Alleghenies of Pennsylvania! Let freedom ring from the snowcapped Rockies of Colorado! Let freedom ring from the curvaceous peaks of California! But not only that; let freedom ring from Stone Mountain of Georgia! Let freedom ring from Lookout Mountain of Tennessee! Let freedom ring from every hill and every molehill of Mississippi. From every mountainside, let freedom ring.

When we let freedom ring, when we let it ring from every village and every hamlet, from every state and every city, we will be able to speed up that day when all of God's children, black men and white men, Jews and Gentiles, Protestants and Catholics, will be able to join hands and sing in the words of the old Negro spiritual, "Free at last! free at last! thank God Almighty, we are free at last!"

Works Cited

Albert, Michael and Stephen R. Shalom. "The War In Afghanistan." ZMag.org. 14 October 2001. Znet. <http://www.zmag.org/ 55qaframe.htm> (10 May 2003).

"American Cultural History The Twentieth Century." King College Library. June 2002. <http://www.nhmccd.edu/contracts/ lrc/kc/decade10.html> (4 March 2003).

"The Avalon Project at Yale Law School." Yale.edu. 11 June 2003. The Lilliam Goldman Law Library. Mar. 2003 <http://www.yale.edu/ lawweb/avalon/purpose.htm> (24 March 2003).

Axelrod, Alan. *The Complete Idiot's Guide to American History.* New York: Alpha Books, 2000.

Axelrod, Alan. *The Complete Idiot's Guide to the American Revolution.* New York: Alpha Books, 1999.

Bates, Eric. "Teeing Off on Terrorism." Mother Jones. 2003. <http://www.motherjones.com/news/outfront/2003/10/ma_289_01. html> (3 April 2003).

"Beyond the Cherry Tree: An Unlikely Leader." The Riverdeep Current. 2003. Riverdeep Interactive Learning Limited. <http://www.riverdeep.net/current/2000/02/ front.180200.washington.jhtml> (23 January 2003).

Boorstin, Daniel J., Brooks Mather Kelly, and Ruth Frankel Boorstin. *A History Of The United States.* Needham, Massachusetts: Prentice Hall, 1996.

Bos, Carole D. "Assassination of Abraham Lincoln." Click2History.com. 2003. <http://www.click2history.com/abraham_lincoln/ abraham_lincoln_ch1.htm> (28 February 2003).

Bowden, Mark. "Tales of the Tyrant." The Atlantic Monthly. May 2002. The Atlantic Monthly Group. Volume 289, No. 5; 35. <http://www.theatlantic.com/issues/2002/05/bowden.htm> (8 May 2003).

Brown, Dee. *Bury My Heart at Wounded Knee*. New York: Holt, Rinehart and Winston, 1970.

"The Cabildo: The Battle of New Orleans." Louisiana State Museum. 2002. <http://lsm.crt.state.la.us/cabildo/cab6.htm> (15 December 2002).

"Central Intelligence Agency". History Channel.com. June 2003. <http://www.historychannel.com/> (21 March 2003).

"Charles Babbage's Analytical Engine." Maxmon.com. A History of Computers. 1997. Maxfield & Montrose Interactive Inc. http://www.maxmon.com/1830ad.htm (24 March 2003).

Cialdini, Robert B. *Influence*. The Psychology of Persuasion. Quill. 1998.

"The Collected Quotations of "Baghdad Bob," Mohammed Saeed al-Sahaf: The Iraqi Minister of *Dis*Information." CFIF.org. 10 April 2003. Freedom Line.<http://www.cfif.org/htdocs/freedomline/ current/in_our_opinion/baghdad_bob.htm> (12 May 2003).

"Credit Mobilier and Union Pacific Railroad." Government Printing Office (1873) Central Pacific Railroad Photographic History Museum <http://www.cprr.com/Museum/Credit_Mobilier.html> (28 February 2003).

"Cu Chi Diadao (Cu Chi Tunnels)." Columbus Guides. 2003. Highbury Columbus Travel Publishing Ltd. <http://www.worldtouristattractions.travel-guides

"Cu Chi—Tunnels and Underground Warfare in Vietnam." Pilot Guides. 2000. Destination Vietnam < http://www.pilot.co.uk/destinations/ sites/cuchi.html> (21 March 2003).

Dan. "The Roaring Twenties." Schools History. July 2002. Schools History Organization. <http://www.schoolshistory.org.uk/america/ roaringtwenties.htm> (13 March 2003).

Davis, Ronald L.F. "Creating Jim Crow: In-Depth Essay." Jim Crow History.org. 2003. The History of Jim Crow. <http://www.jimcrowhistory.org/history/creating2.htm> (23 March 2003).

DeConde, Alexander. "Herbert Hoover Biography." The American Presidency. 2000. Grolier. March 13, 2003. <http://gi.grolier.com/presidents/ea/bios/31phoov.html> (13 March 2003).

Dinkins, David. "FDR and the New Deal." 2001. Pagewise, Inc. <http://va.essortment.com/fdrnewdealfra_rgst.htm> (13 March 2003).

Dirks, Tim. "The Great Films of the 1930's." Filmsite.org. 2002. <http://www.filmsite.org/30sintro.html> (13 March 2003).

"Dred Scott's Fight for Freedom." Africans in America. 1998. PBS. <http://www.pbs.org/wgbh/aia/part4/4p2932.html> (7 April 2003).

"Encyclopedia of the First World War: Trench Warfare." Spartacus Educational. June 8, 2003. <http://www.spartacus.schoolnet.co.uk/ FWWtrench.htm> (21 March 2003).

F & E RI. "FDR Biography." March, 2003. Franklin and Eleanor Roosevelt Institute. <http://www.feri.org/archives/fdrbio/ default.cfm> (13 March 2003).

"First Continental Congress." Kidport.com. 2003. Kidport Reference Library. <http://www.kidport.com/RefLib/UsaHistory/ AmericanRevolution/FirstCongress.htm#The%20First%20Contine ntal%20Congress%20Meeting> (14 December 2003).

"Greatest Engineering Achievements of the 20th Century." Greatest Achievements.org. 2000. National Academy of Engineering. <http://www.greatachievements.org/greatachievements/> (24 March 2003).

Gupta, Pranav and Jonathan Lee. "Problems of the Great Depression." The Great Depression and the New Deal. March 7, 1996. <http://www.bergen.org/AAST/Projects/depression/problems.html> (13 March 2003).

Harlow, Jennifer. "Compromise of 1877." United States of America Chronology. 1999. North Park University. <http://campus.northpark.edu/history/WebChron/USA/1877Comp.html> (28 February 2003).

Hartman, Gertrude. *America, Land of Freedom*. D.C Health and Company, 1959.

"The History of Rock n' Roll." History-of-rock.com. <http://www.history-of-rock.com/> (4 March 2003).

"The History of the Atomic Bomb." About.com. What You Need to Know About. <http://inventors.about.com/mbody.htm> (24 March 2003).

"Hitler, Adolf." Biography.com. 2000. Gale Group. <http://search.biography.com/print_record.pl?id=5537> (13 March 2003).

Hoogenboom, Ari. "Disputed Election." RBHayes.org. 1995. *Rutherford B. Hayes: Warrior and President.* <http://www.rbhayes.org/dispute.htm> (28 February 2003).

Kangas, Steve. "Timelines of the Great Depression." Hyperhistory.com. 2002. <http://www.hyperhistory.com/online_n2/connections_n2/great_depression.html> (21 March 2003).

Keegan, John. "Normandy: 1944." Brittanica Online. 1999. World War II Study Guide. <http://search.eb.com/normandy/week2/invasion.html> (13 March 2003).

Kindig, Thomas. "The Currency Act." USHistory.org. 2003.
<http://www.ushistory.org/declaration/related/currencyact.htm>
(24 November 2003).

"Korean War". History Channel.com June 2003.
<http://www.historychannel.com/> (21 March 2003).

Kornbluh, Peter and Malcolm Byrne. "The Iran-Contra Scandal in
Perspective." Digital National Security Archive. 1990.
<http://nsarchive.chadwyck.com/icessayx.htm> (18 March 2003).

Kraus, Michael. *The United States To 1865*. The University of Michigan
Press, 1959.

"Lee's Songbook." Washington Artillery of New Orleans Uniform
Standards. <http://www.washingtonartilleryuniformstandards.
bravepages.com/songbook_-_j.htm> (23 March 2003).

"Lewinsky Scandal." Encyclopedia.com. 2003.
<http://www.encyclopedia.com> (2 March 2003).

"Lewis and Clark in North Dakota. " Fort Mandan. The ND Lewis and
Clark Bicentennial Foundation. 2002.
<http://www.fortmandan.com/fortmandan.html> (5 Dec. 2002).

Loewen, James. *Lies My Teacher Told Me : Everything Your American
History Textbook Got Wrong*. New York: Touchstone Books,
1996.

Mangold, Tom and John Penycate. "The Tunnels of Cu Chi." 1988.
<www.oz.net/~vvawai/sw/sw31/pgs_03-14/tunnels.html>
(21 March 2003).

"The Media and the Vietnam War." About.com. 2003. Military History.
<http://militaryhistory.about.com/library/blmediainvietnam.htm?ia
m=eboom_SKD&terms=Vietnam+war+news> (18 Feb. 2003).

Miller, David. "To What Extent Did FDR's New Deal End the
Depression?" American History Class Page. September 2002.
<http://www.socialstudieshelp.com/Lesson_90_Notes.htm> (13
March 2003).

Mount, Steve. "The United States Constitution Online."
    USConstitution.net. 6 Jun. 2002. <http://www.usConstitution.net/
    consttime.html> (11 Dec. 2002).

"MSN Learning and Research." Encarta.msn.com. 2003.
    <http://encarta.msn.com/encnet/features/home.aspx> (7 December
    2002).

"Native Americans." NativeAmericans.com. 2003.
    <http://www.nativeamericans.com/> (24 October 2002).

Norrell, Robert J. ""Civil Rights Movement in the United States,"
    Microsoft® Encarta® Online Encyclopedia 2003
    <http://encarta.msn.com> (15 March 2003).

"The Olive Branch Petition." Rain.org. 2002. The Karpeles Manuscript
    Library Museums <http://www.rain.org/~karpeles/olivebdis.html>
    (14 December 2003).

O'Malley, Michael. "A Timeline Of Reconstruction: 1865-1870." History
    122 Syllabus. <http://chnm.gmu.edu/courses/122/
    recon/chron.html> (28 February 2003).

O'Sullivan, John L. "Annexation." United States Magazine and
    Democratic Review 17, No.1 (July-August 1845): 5-10.
    <http://web.grinnell.edu/courses/HIS/f01/HIS202-
    01/Documents/OSullivan.html> (22 March 2003).

Paine, Thomas. *Common Sense*. 1776. From Revolution to
    Reconstruction. March 2003. <http://odur.let.rug.nl/~usa/D/
    1776-1800/paine/CM/sense03.htm> (13 December 2003).

Parada, George. "The Concept of Blitzkrieg." Achtung Panzer. 2003.
    <http://www.achtungpanzer.com/blitz.htm> (13 March 2003).

Parada, George. "Erwin (Johannes Eugen) Rommel." Achtung Panzer.
    2003. <http://www.achtungpanzer.com/gen1.htm> (13 March
    2003).

Partos, Gabriel. *The World that Came in From the Cold*. London: Royal
    Institute of International Affairs, 1993.

"People & Events-Aaron Burr." PBS Online. 2000.The American
Experience <http://www.pbs.org/wgbh/amex/duel/peopleevents/
pande01.html> (5 Dec. 2002).

Phillips, Kevin. "The Great American Fortunes of 1900-1914." Wealth
and Democracy.com. 2000
<http://www.wealthanddemocracy.com/chart1.htm> (27 March
2003).

Polino, Valerie Ann. "Early Man in North America: The Known to the
Unknown." Yale-New Haven Teachers Institute. 2003.
<http://www.yale.edu/ynhti/curriculum/units/1980/2/
80.02.07.x.html> (24 October 2002).

"Pop Culture." FCCJ Deerwood Center Library. 2002.
<http://www.fccj.org/library/deerwood/reference/pop.htm>
(4 March 2003).

"Presidency in History." AmericanPresident.org. 2003.
<http://www.americanpresident.org/> (23 January 2003).

"Presidential Biographies." The Game Puppet. 2003.
<http://home.ptd.net/~larrysch/presidents/bios.htm> (23 January
2003).

Presley, Bruce, Beth Brown, Elaine Malfas, and Vickie Grassman. *A
Guide toMicrosoft Office 2000.* Lawrenceville Press, Inc., 2000.

"Reconstruction!! Confederate Military History, Volume 12: 2." Shotgun's
Home of the American Civil War. January 28, 2000
<http://www.civilwarhome.com/reconstruction.htm>
(28 February 2003).

Robinson, Susan. "The Plessy vs. Ferguson, 1892." Gibbs Magazine. June
2003. <http://www.gibbsmagazine.com/Plessy.htm> (15 March
2003).

"Samuel Adams Signer of Declaration of Independence." Virtualology.
2000. <http://www.samueladams.net/> (24 November 2003).

Shenkman, Richard. *One-Night Stands with American History*. New York: Quill, 1982.

"The South in 1814: Background to the Battle of New Orleans". Galafilm.com. 2002. War of 1812. <http://www.galafilm.com/1812/e/events/orleans.html> (15 December 2002).

"Tonkin Gulf Resolution." Encyclopedia.com. 2003. <http://www.encyclopedia.com/html/t/tonking1u.asp> (21 March 2003).

"Top Artists." RIAA.com. 2003. RIAA/Gold and Platinum. <http://www.riaa.com/Gold-Best-1.cfm> (18 Feb. 2003).

"Top Grossing Films Ever: Adjusted." The Movie Times. June 2003. <http://www.the-movie-times.com/thrsdir/alltime.mv?adjusted+ByAG> (18 Feb. 2003).

"The Treaty of Ghent of 1814." Indian Defense League of America. <http://tuscaroras.com/IDLA/pages/ghent.html> (15 December 2002).

"United States History American Revolution Chronology." United States History: American Revolution. 3 May. 2002. <http://carbon.cudenver.edu/~rpekarek/AmRev1767.html> (24 November 2003).

"Vietnam War." History Channel.com. June 2003 <http://www.historychannel.com/> (21 March 2003).

"The Vietnam War Index." Spartacus Educational. June 8, 2003. <http://www.spartacus.schoolnet.co.uk/vietnam.html> (21 March 2003).

"Washington Burned." HistoryCentral.com. 2003. War of 1812. <http://www.multied.com/1812/Washington.html> (15 December 2002).

Weems, Mason Locke. "The Fable of George Washington and the Cherry Tree." From *The Life of Washington*. 1809. The Papers of George

Washington. <http://gwpapers.virginia.edu/documents/weems/index.html> (23 January 2003).

"XYZ Correspondence." The American Presidency. 2003. Grolier. <http://gi.grolier.com/presidents/ea/side/xyzaffr.html> (21 January 2003).

Zinn, Howard. *A People's History of the United States:1492-Present.* New York: Perennial, 2001.

Zunes, Stephen. "United Nations Security Council Resolutions Currently Being Violated by Countries Other than Iraq." Foreign Policy in Focus. 2003. http://www.foreignpolicy-infocus.org/commentary/2002/0210unres.html (28 March 2003).

0-595-28479-5